BRITISH LITERATURE LIFEPAC 5
THE TWENTIETH CENTURY

CONTENTS

Author: **Krista L. White, B.S.**
Editor: Alan Christopherson, M.S.
Graphic Design: Alpha Omega Staff
     Lauren Durain, A.S.T.

D1560560

Alpha Omega Publications®

804 N. 2nd Ave. E., Rock Rapids, IA 51246-1759

BRITISH LITERATURE LIFEPAC 5
THE TWENTIETH CENTURY

OBJECTIVES:

When you have completed this LIFEPAC®, you should be able to:

1. Gain an understanding of the political, social and religious history of the first half of the twentieth century.
2. Discern the causes and the consequences of "the absence of God" from modern society.
3. Appreciate the influence of Christian writers in the twentieth century.
4. Discern the causes of modern literary trends.

VOCABULARY:

Archaic - outdated
Coalition - a temporary political alliance
Depravity - morally corrupt
Disintegration - a loss of unity
Fascism - a totalitarian form of government led by a dictator
Immanence - the indwelling of a god
Orthodoxy - traditional beliefs
Reparation - payments made by a defeated nation to the victor or victors
Transcendent - beyond the reach of human ability; superior

I. INTRODUCTION

The death of Queen Victoria in 1901 heralded the beginning of a New World. Advances in science and industry transformed societal values. In the name of "progress," moderns scoffed at their Victorian past, calling it **archaic*** and prudish. However, in their rush to embrace a way of life unencumbered by "worn out" traditions, moderns were left wanting. The basis of beauty, love, and humanity had disappeared from their lives.

The City–**Fernand Léger**

Many people felt the "absence of God." Writers especially chronicled their frustrations with a society that was left to grope for some kind of meaning and purpose in the midst of an ever-darkening world. In his book *Brave New World,* written in 1923, Aldous Huxley correctly predicted that the modern man would attempt to find peace in the pursuit of pleasures. However, God could never be fully replaced with the distractions offered by transportation, communication, and entertainment. Man was in desperate need of something beyond the material. Yet, modern society was unwilling to believe God's answers to the ultimate questions of life. Despair and disillusionment grew as science and technology moved God to the farther reaches of society.

World War I. The outbreak of the First World War in 1914 caused many people to doubt. They doubted not only God's goodness but also the goodness of technology. Since the Great War of 1815, many European nations had spent time and funds stockpiling arms. Advances in technology had also made possible the creation of weapons that were capable of causing mass destruction.

During the nineteenth century, the British Empire had increased its wealth and influence by establishing and maintaining colonies in India, Egypt, China, and Africa. Many of the lands teemed with natural resources; therefore, other nations coveted them. To protect itself and its possessions from German encroachment, Britain formed an alliance with France and Russia known as the Triple Entente. The Triple Alliance, formed by the Bismark in 1882, consisted of Germany, Austria, and Italy.

A series of diplomatic crises led up to the outbreak of the first world war. After Austria's annexation of Bosnia and Herzegovina, a Serbian nationalist assassinated the heir-apparent to the Austrian throne, Archduke Francis Ferdinand, on June 28, 1914. The murder, which was later proven to have been backed by the Serbian officials, led to Austria's declaration of war on Serbia. Russia supported the small country of Serbia. Germany supported Austria. The alliances of the two factions resulted in the bloodiest war in European history up until that time.

Britain suffered more than 2.5 million casualties during the fighting on land and at sea. Hundreds of thousands of British soldiers were killed or injured while fighting along the Western Front. Attempts by either side to advance their positions were almost impossible. The line of trenches that stretched from Switzerland to the English Channel was fortified with barbed wire. Whole brigades were often sent out across the divide only to be mown down by the enemy's machine guns. On the sea, Britain fought back German aggression and maintained control of trade routes. However, German U-boats (submarines) presented an unexpected challenge to merchant vessels and military ships alike.

In Britain, the threat of bombs being dropped by German zeppelins (gas-filled balloons, or dirigibles) and airplanes had a sobering effect on society. Political groups such as the woman's suffrage movement and the Labour advocates put their interests to rest during the war. Liberals and Conservatives in Parliament formed a **coalition*** government that was united in purpose. Both sides were determined to win the war. In 1916, Parliament signed a military draft. More than six million men between the ages of 18 and 41 were sent to fight. At home, thousands of people who could not be drafted were enlisted in the Home Guard, an organization the purpose of which was to warn of and prepare the ordinary citizen for bombing raids and the possibility of invasion.

On November 11, 1918, Germany agreed to the terms of an armistice, ending the war. The Treaty of Versailles dictated the terms of peace, providing limitations on Germany's military forces and imposing **reparation*** payments. In addition to attempts to prevent future wars among the European nations, the treaty also called for the establishment of the League of Nations. The League of Nations was intended in part to oversee the government of the former colonies of the Central Powers.

The aftermath of World War I caused economic difficulties for Britain similar to those caused by the war of 1815. The influx of soldiers caused an overabundance of labor, driving wages down. With more mouths to feed but less food with which to feed them, the cost of living went up. Strikes among lower class workers tore at the nation's stability.

However, the economic fallout of the war was not the greatest cause of instability. The influence of Sigmund Freud's *Interpretation of Dreams* (1901) and Albert Einstein's *Special Theory of Relativity* (1905) began to bear heavily upon the popular culture. Both works underscored the social implications of Darwin's theories, causing people to view reality through an increasingly materialistic lens. Man's actions were no more than the outworking of subconscious physical drives. Reality was simply a matter of one's point of view.

God's absence from the scene resulted in an attitude of pessimism among intellectuals. Many people hoped to solve the problems of modern society by effecting radical political changes. The worldwide economic depression of the 1930s caused many people to put their faith in socialism. The unemployment of more than three million workers proved to many people that capitalism had failed. The general public, weary of war and economic difficulties, approved of the government's increasing control over industry and utilities.

Irish Home Rule. Before the outbreak of World War I, Irish members of Parliament attempted to grant Ireland independence from British rule. However, the attempt failed. Not all of Ireland's citizens wanted to be independent. Those who favored British supervision were generally Protestants living in Northern Ireland. The Irish republicans were generally Roman Catholics from the south who demanded home rule.

From 1912–1922, the two groups engaged in violent conflict known as the Irish Revolution. To quell the rising tension, Parliament granted Ireland independence in 1914 but postponed its enactment until after the war. Frustrated by Parliament's decision, revolutionaries incited a rebellion in Dublin on Easter Sunday 1916. The uprising was met with brute military force. Many citizens were killed. The British military and a police force known as the "Black and Tans" occupied Ireland, maintaining a state of martial law.

In further rebellion against the British rule, Irish members of Parliament declared an independent Irish Free State in 1918. However, British Parliament did not recognize the governing power of the Irish Free State until 1922, and then only under the condition that separate governments would be granted to northern and southern Ireland, this in accord with the wishes of the Protestant north, which wanted to remain a part of the British Empire. Much of the south, however, rejected this agreement, wishing all of Ireland to be unified as one independent government. Seeing violence as the only recourse, militant independence groups formed the Irish Republican Army (IRA) to purge Ireland of British rule. The struggle for independence continues to this day.

World War II. In defiance of the Treaty of Versailles, Germany began to increase its military power and expand its borders during the 1930s. Adolf Hitler, Germany's new chancellor, wanted to increase the power and influence of the Arian race throughout Europe. He believed in Nietzsche's philosophy of will to power, advancing the idea that Germans were the superior race and were destined to rule the earth.

Initially, the English ignored the propaganda of the Nazi Party. In an attempt to maintain peace, Prime Minister Neville Chamberlain made concessions to Germany's blatant violations of the Treaty of Versailles. Not until Germany invaded Poland in 1939 did Britain take military measures to stop Hitler's expansionism. France joined Britain but soon fell to German and Italian aggression. Under the leadership of the **fascist*** dictator Benito Mussoulini, Italy had entered into an alliance with Germany.

After Germany gained military superiority over France, it began to drop bombs on England. The air raids weakened the British people, both emotionally and economically. Feelings of helplessness and despair were staved off only by the gallant efforts of the Royal Air Force (RAF) and the inspiring speeches of Winston Churchill, Britain's new prime minister.

In 1941 the United States joined the Allied Powers (Britain and the Union of Soviet Socialist Republics) to defeat the Axis Powers (Germany, Italy, and Japan). American funds and military supplies allowed for a British invasion of North Africa, which drove the Germans out of Egypt in 1942. English and American troops then invaded Italy, conquering the southern region. Mussoulini was later overthrown.

On the eastern front, the Soviet Union struggled to hold back German advancement. In 1943 German troops were stopped at the gates of Stalingrad. Russian soldiers drove the enemy back, forcing them to retreat into the targeted cities of British bombers. The RAF's bombardment of German supply stations in 1943 weakened the Axis Powers. After the D-Day invasion in June of 1944, British and American troops invaded Germany

3

from the west. Russia's invasion from the east and the capture of Berlin culminated in Germany's defeat in 1945.

Postwar Britain. After the war, Britain was faced with the task of reconstruction. The German Luftwaffe had destroyed millions of homes and other buildings. Food and gas shortages caused further difficulties for Britons. Desperate for change, Britain elected Labour party members to the House of Commons. Along with other conservative party members, Winston Churchill was removed from office. In 1946, the new prime minister put into motion a series of welfare programs that would eventually provide social security for Britons "from the cradle to the grave." The National Insurance Act passed in 1946 provided funds for periods of unemployment, sickness, maternity leave, retirement, and death. In 1948, the National Health Service was passed. It provided free medical care for all Britons. The Labour Party also sought to provide for British citizens by nationalizing industry. The coal and steel industries, the Bank of England, and essential utilities were eventually placed under government control.

The financial burden of socialism, however, proved to be too heavy for a nation still laden with war debts. The $3,750,000,000 loan that the United States had granted Great Britain was not enough to provide benefits for its citizens and revitalize England's flailing economy. In 1951, the Conservative Party was returned to power. Under the leadership of Churchill, the number of welfare benefits were cut. On June, 2, 1953, Elizabeth II was crowned queen of England.

In its struggle to defend the world from the expansion of Hitlerism, Britain lost an empire. In 1947 India was granted independence. Efforts to maintain peace among India's religious groups was too costly. Britain's withdrawal resulted in a civil war in which hundreds of thousands of people were killed. Regions of India, however, chose to remain a member of the Commonwealth of Nations.

Britain created the Commonwealth in 1931 to grant independence to former colonies while maintaining close economic and diplomatic ties. Canada, Australia, New Zealand, South Africa, Kenya, Uganda, Ireland, and India were at one time a part of the Commonwealth of Nations. During the 1960s, many dominions became independent nations. Although stripped of its former military and economic power, Britain nevertheless maintains a place of importance as a world leader.

Modern British Literature. In the wake of two world wars and the theories of Freud, Darwin, Neitzche and Marx, writers began to ask questions. If man is just an animal controlled by internal and external forces, then what should guide our actions and thoughts? What determines what is good and what is evil? How is man to think of himself? How is he to relate to other human beings? What is the meaning of life?

During the 1890s, the Aesthetic movement of "art for art's sake" anticipated these questions. Its answers revealed a rising disdain for traditional manners and beliefs. The abstract intellectualism of late Victorian life left many people wanting something more beyond the material world. Advocates of the "art for art's sake" movement believed that meaning resided in the experience of art. Art was the "supreme reality." The experience of it therefore could not be judged on moral grounds. Art, and the inner life that it affected, **transcended*** society's ideas of good or evil.

In the twentieth century, the search for meaning turned increasingly inward. Human reality, some people believed, existed not only in experience but also in the mind's interpretation of those experiences. The theories of Freud had cast doubt on man's ability to know truth. Three people could experience the same event yet come away with three distinct interpretations of what happened. The truth concerning the human condition was not sought in objective revelations, such as the Bible, but in memories, feelings, and desires. The inner man was the key to the true meaning of life.

Novelists such as Virginia Woolf and James Joyce developed techniques that allowed the reader to delve into the consciousness and examine the inner dimension of the human condition. In opposition to the Victorian upper-class society that surrounded her, Woolf emphasized personal morals and values by communicating the memories and intuitions of her characters through the use of the "stream of consciousness" technique, which attempts to tell a story through the natural flow of a character's thoughts. The focus on subjective experiences left out facts, such as historical and geographical settings, that might not enter the mind of the character. The only reality that existed was in the consciousness of the character. Joyce applied the "stream of consciousness" technique to convey multiple views of reality. In his novel *Ulysses*, Joyce departs from conventional forms of storytelling by focusing on the experiences of several different characters during a single day; each interpreting events differently.

Poetry more so than fiction was affected by the revolutions of the age. Before World War I, the Modernist movement in the visual arts gave birth to the Imagist movement in literature. Leaders of the movement stressed clear, precise images, avoiding all that was romantic. With the help of Ezra Pound, the leader of the Imagists, T. S. Eliot wrote *The Waste Land* (1922). The long poem was revolutionary, combining concrete images with metaphysical meanings. Eliot's use of the stream of consciousness technique effectively expressed the **disintegration*** of modern society.

Eliot's interest in meaning beyond the physical was not isolated. He was preceded by the Irish poet W. B. Yeats. Through the use of symbols and images from Irish culture, Yeats created a mystical belief system that replaced his dismay in Irish Roman Catholicism. Yeats's experimental use of Irish folk songs and legends also helped to fan the flames of nationalism. However, his interest and participation in politics was purely for the benefit of the arts, which he believed held the keys to life's deeper meanings.

Another important Irish writer during the twentieth century was George Bernard Shaw. As a member of the Fabian Society, Shaw was keenly interested in the ability of art to effect social and political change. Shaw's plays condemned the evils of capitalism and the oppression of women in a male-dominated society.

Other writers who were concerned about the human condition predicted society's dismal future. In his futuristic novel *Brave New World* (1932), Aldous Huxley conveyed his fears that the godless, immoral modern world was headed toward barbarism. Although he was an unbeliever, Huxley acknowledged a need for meaning and purpose beyond the material.

Although the theme of man's falleness runs through the literature of both the modern and the postmodern ages, few writers have been willing to embrace Christianity. Many of them have turned to mysticism and drugs to escape the reality of their sin. However, some of them have turned to Christ and found rest for their weary souls. Included among those writers who discovered the answers to modernity's questions of meaning and significance in the pages of Scripture were T. S. Eliot and C. S. Lewis.

After their conversions, both Lewis and Eliot strove to influence the culture through their writings. In his set of lyric poems, *Four Quartets*, Eliot asserted that mankind's only hope for salvation from the destructive powers of the modern age was in the sanctifying work of the Holy Spirit. Lewis wrote many books, both fiction and nonfiction, that presented the Christian faith to modern readers. Among his works, *The Chronicles of Narnia* have enjoyed lasting popularity among children and adults alike. The books are rich with Christian symbolism. In the following excerpt from *The Silver Chair*, Lewis confronts modern man's dilemma by telling him that his desire for God can be met only through Jesus Christ. (The Lion is a figure of Christ.)

"Are you not thirsty?" said the Lion.

"I'm dying of thirst," said Jill.

"Then drink," said the Lion.

"May I—could I—would you mind going away while I do?" said Jill.

The Lion answered this only by a look and a very low growl....

"I daren't come and drink," said Jill.

"Then you will die of thirst," said the Lion.

"Oh dear!" said Jill, coming another step nearer. "I suppose I must go, and look for another stream then."

"There is no other stream," said the Lion.

◆ **Answer *true* or *false* for each of the following statements.**

1.1 _true_ The First World War caused people to doubt the goodness of God and the goodness of technology.

1.2 _false_ Britain's alliance with France and Russia before World War I was known as the Triple Alliance.

1.3 _false_ During World War I, Britain lost few soldiers while fighting on the Western Front.

1.4 _false_ Liberals and Conservatives refused to put their differences aside during World War I, causing a divided British government.

1.5 _false_ The Treaty of Versailles imposed limitations on England's military forces after World War I.

1.6 _true_ The economic depression after World War I caused many Britons to put their faith in socialism.

1.7 _true_ The cultural influence of the theories of Sigmund Freud and Albert Einstein caused people to view reality through an increasingly materialistic lens.

1.8 _false_ "The absence of God" from society caused many people to adopt an optimistic outlook.

1.9 _true_ Britain refuses to grant Ireland total independence because many Protestants living in northern Ireland wish to remain under British rule.

1.10 _false_ Hitler's expansionist plans were based on his belief that Jews were a superior race destined to rule the earth.

1.11 _false_ During World War II, Britain entered an alliance with Italy to stop Hitler's advance across Europe.

1.12 _true_ Germany's defeat culminated in the invasion by Russian troops from the east and British and American troops from the west.

1.13 _false_ After World War II, members of the ruling Labour Party cut benefits for the poor and lower class to pay for war debts owed to the United States.

1.14 _false_ Before World War I, all of Britain's colonies became independent nations.

1.15 _false_ The influence of Freud's theories caused many writers to be more concerned about factual details of a story than about a character's feelings and thoughts.

1.16 _true_ The stream of consciousness technique attempts to tell a story through the natural flow of a character's thoughts.

1.17 _false_ T. S. Eliot and W. B. Yeats discovered the answers to modernity's questions of meaning and significance in the pages of Scripture.

6

1.18   _true_   Yeats's poetry helped to encourage the desire for Irish independence.

1.19   _false_   George Bernard Shaw believed that art should not be used to advance moral or political causes.

1.20   _true_   In his book *Brave New World*, Aldus Huxley predicted that the modern world was headed toward barbarism.

Thomas Hardy (1840–1928). Novelist, poet, and short-story writer Thomas Hardy was greatly affected by the "disappearance of God" from Victorian culture during the later part of the nineteenth century. Born the son of a stonemason with Protestant beliefs, Hardy hoped to take Holy Orders in the Anglican Church. He attended "local" school in Dorchester, studying Latin, French, and German. As a young man, he taught Sunday school and apprenticed himself to an architect so that he could earn enough money to enter Cambridge. However, after reading books on higher criticism, Hardy began to doubt the Bible's infallibility and its supreme authority in spiritual matters. By the time he was twenty-five, he had lost any interest in the ministry and in religion in general. Hardy's inability to believe in God's sovereign rule over humans led him to pen some of English literature's most pessimistic novels and poems. As one writer has noted, he understood quite clearly the implications of the materialist's worldview. If God did not exist, then life was without purpose or meaning. Man's fate was merely the consequence of uncontrollable desires and forces. Much of Hardy's work illustrates his belief that life is bitterly ironic.

In 1861 Hardy moved to London to work for a company that specialized in church architecture. He continued his education by reading poetry and fiction, attending the theater, and frequenting art galleries. After returning to Dorchester in 1867, Hardy began work on his first novel, *The Poor Man and the Lady*. Publishers rejected both it and his first attempts at poetry.

In 1868 while doing some architectural work in Cornwall, Hardy met and fell in love with Emma Gifford, the sister-in-law to the rector of St. Juliot. After three disappointing attempts to publish a critically acclaimed novel (*Desperate Memories* in 1871, *Under the Greenwood Tree* in 1873, and *A Pair of Blue Eyes* in 1872), Hardy found literary and financial success with *Far From the Madding Crowd*, published in 1874. The novel, which was published serially, allowed Hardy to marry Emma and pursue a career as a writer. Hardy followed his initial success with a steady stream of novels, including *The Return of the Native* (1878), *The Mayor of Casterbridge* (1886), *The Woodlanders* (1887), *Tess of the D'Urbervilles* (1891), *The Well-Beloved* (1892), and *Jude the Obscure* (1896). After receiving much condemnation for *Jude the Obscure* as an obscene and "pessimistic" work, Hardy gave up writing fiction and turned to poetry.

In 1898 Hardy published *Wessex Poems*. The collection was no less pessimistic than his novels. Despite further criticism, Hardy continued to write poetry during the twentieth century. He experimented with verse forms and used a language that was close to the people. In 1902 he published his second volume of poetry, *Poems of the Past and Present*. Six more collections followed, including *Time's Laughingstocks* (1909), *Satires of Circumstance* (1914), *Moments of Visions* (1917), *Late Lyrics* (1922), *Human Shows* (1925), and *Winter Words* (1928). From 1903–1908, Hardy periodically diverted his lyrical energies to publish an epic-drama about the wars with Napoleon that he titled *The Dynasts*.

Two years after Emma died in 1912, Hardy married Florence Dugdale. Admired by the public for his earlier work, Hardy received the gold medal of the Royal Society of Literature and was visited by the Prince of Wales. Hardy died in 1928. As one of England's literary elite, he is buried in Westminster Abbey.

Underline the correct answer in each of the following statements.

1.21   Thomas Hardy was raised in a(n) (<u>Protestant,</u> Roman Catholic, atheistic) home.

1.22   After reading works on (<u>higher criticism,</u> evolution, God's sovereignty), Hardy abandoned his desire become a(n) (<u>architect,</u> stonemason, minister).

1.23   The "disappearance of God" from Victorian culture caused Hardy to write poetry and novels that are considered (optimistic, hopeful, <u>pessimistic</u>).

1.24   Hardy's first literary success was achieved in 1874 with the serially published (*Under the Greenwood Tree*, *Far From the Madding Crowd*, *Jude the Obscure*).

1.25   After receiving much criticism for (*Far From the Madding Crowd*, <u>*Jude the Obscure*</u>, *Tess of the D'Urbervilles*), Hardy gave up his career as a(n) (<u>poet</u>, novelist, architect).

1.26   Hardy's first volume of poetry, titled (*Time's Laughingstocks*, *Far From the Madding Crowd*, <u>*Wessex Poems*</u>), was published in (1898, 1901, 1910).

1.27   In his poetry written during the twentieth century, Hardy experimented with (<u>verse forms</u>, prose forms, dramatic monologues), using a language of the (upper class, <u>common people</u>, clergy).

What to Look For:

Hardy was greatly affected by the "disappearance of God" caused by the new "scientific" mindset that dominated late Victorian culture. As you read, notice Hardy's reaction to God's "absence." How does he celebrate or lament the loss? What must Hardy conclude about life, love, and religion if the supernatural does not exist?

The Respectable Burgher
In this poem, Hardy outlines the effects of high criticism on his view of the Bible.

Since Reverend Doctors now declare
That clerks and people must prepare
To doubt if Adam ever were;
To hold the flood a local scare;
To argue, though the stolid stare,   5
That everything had happened ere
The prophets to its happening sware;
That David was no giant-slayer,
Nor one to call a God-obeyer
In certain details we could spare,   10
But rather was a debonair
Shrewd bandit, skilled as banjo-player;
That Solomon sang the fleshly Fair,
And gave the Church no thought whate'er;
That Esther with her royal wear,   15
And Mordecai, the son of Jair,
And Joshua's triumphs, Job's despair,
And Balaam's ass's bitter blare;
Nebuchadnezzar's furnace-flare,
And Daniel and the den affair,   20
And other stories rich and rare,
Were writ to make old doctrine wear
Something of a romantic air;
That the Nain widow's only heir,
And Lazarus with cadaverous glare   25
(As done in oils by Piombo's care)
Did not return from Sheol's lair,

That Jael set a fiendish snare,
That Pontius Pilate acted square,
That never a sword cut Malchus' ear;
And (but for shame I must forbear)   30
That—did not reappear!...
—Since thus they hint, nor turn a hair,
All churchgoing will I forswear,
And sit on Sundays in my chair,
And read that moderate man Voltaire.*   35

*Voltaire (1694–1778) - French philosopher and writer who called for the destruction of the Catholic Church.

Neutral Tones

We stood by a pond that winter day,
And the sun was white, as though chidden of God,
And a few leaves lay on the starving sod;
        —They had fallen from an ash, and were gray.

Your eyes on me were as eyes that rove
Over tedious riddle of years ago;
And some words played between us to and fro
        On which lost the more by our love.

The smile on your mouth was the deadest thing
Alive enough to have strength to die;
And a grin of bitterness swept thereby
        Like an ominous bird a-wing...

Since then, keen lessons that love deceives,
And wrings with wrong, have shaped to me
Your face, and the God-curst sun, and a tree,
        And a pond edged with grayish leaves.

Fill in each of the following blanks with the correct explanation or answer.

1.28   According to "The Respectable Burgher," what is the major cause for "God's disappearance" from religion?

The new "scientific" mindset present in the culture.

1.29   If the stories of Adam and David are not true, then why do the "Reverend Doctors" of higher criticism think that they were included in the Bible?

_____

1.30   Explain why the burgher decides to read Voltaire on Sundays instead of going to church.

Because he is a man of science and reason.

1.31   The sun is the universe's source of life and heat. In the poem "Neutral Tones," why do you think the sun is described as "white, as though chidden of God?"

Its drained of color.

1.32   Describe the relationship between the two lovers. Is it passionate? Is it meaningful?

No, its an apathetic love.

1.33   What is significant about the poet's conclusion that "love deceives?" What does this conclusion convey about a world without God?

A world without God is very devilish and cruel.

9

Joseph Conrad (1857–1924). Teodor Josef Konrad Korzeniowski was born in the Polish Ukraine. His father was a Polish aristocrat who was forced into exile in northern Russia for his support of Poland's independence. Conrad's mother died when he was seven while the family was still living in Russia. His father died not long after they returned to Poland when Conrad was eleven. Conrad was reared by his maternal uncle.

Sympathetic to his father's political ideas but not willing to suffer further under Russian rule, Conrad decided to become a merchant marine. In 1874, he traveled to Marseilles and became a sailor on a French ship. At the age of twenty-one, Conrad signed on with the English merchant navy, learning his third language, English, in just six short voyages aboard a small coasting ship. In 1886, Conrad earned his master mariner certificate and became a British citizen. He settled in England in 1894. A year later, he married an English woman, Jessie George, and published his first novel, *Almayer's Folly*.

As one writer has noted, many of Conrad's novels and short stories are set at sea and in foreign lands, supplying a world removed from British civilization and morality. His first major novels, *The Nigger of the Narcissus* (1897) and *Lord Jim* (1900), present crisis situations in which crew members are revealed for who they truly are and not as what civilization has made them to be.

Considered one of the leading Modernist writers, Conrad was pessimistic about man's situation. He acknowledged that the "disappearance of God" had created a hopeless situation for mankind. Left to ourselves, there would be nothing but darkness and horror. Conrad's most popular novella *Heart of Darkness* (1902), based on his 1890 steamboat trip up the Congo River, illustrates his view of man most vividly. In keeping with Conrad's typical narrative style, this story is told from several different viewpoints. The multiplicity of views, as one writer has noted, emphasizes Conrad's belief that individual understandings of reality do not always lead us to the truth.

Conrad's view of man is consistent with the biblical view of man. He acknowledged that man was prone to moral failure. However, as a Modernist, Conrad refused to see the hope that is provided for man in the life and death of Jesus Christ. Man was doomed. Conrad's other novels that explore man's moral corruptibility include *Typhoon* (1902), *Nostromo* (1904) (considered his masterpiece), *The Shadow Line* (1917), *The Secret Agent* (1907) and *Under Western Eyes* (1911).

Although Conrad was appreciated and encouraged by other writers such as Henry James and Ford Madox Ford, Conrad did not achieve financial success until the 1913 publication of his novel *Chance*. Since that time, however, the masterful prose style of the Pole-turned-Briton has "enlightened" modern readers with the reality: "The heart is deceitful above all things, and desperately wicked: who can know it?" (Jeremiah 17:9).

Circle the letter of the line that best answers each of the following questions.

1.34   Who was Joseph Conrad's father?

a.   Polish aristocrat who was exiled in Russia for his support of Poland's independence
b.   German diplomat who worked in Austria
c.   French philosopher who immigrated to America
d.   Polish stonemason who enjoyed writing poetry

1.35   From 1874 to 1894, how did Conrad make his living?

    a. writer
    (b.) seaman
    c. teacher
    d. diplomat

1.36   In 1895 Conrad married Jessie George and published his first novel. What was it titled?

    a. *The Nigger of the Narcissus*
    b. *Heart of Darkness*
    c. *Nostromo*
    (d.) *Almayer's Folly*

1.37   Why did Conrad set his novels and short stories at sea and in foreign lands?

    (a.) He wanted to supply a world removed from the influence of western civilization.
    b. He enjoyed writing in other languages.
    c. He believed that the heart of man was pure when removed from society.
    d. He wanted to supply a world that would enhance man's inner goodness.

1.38   What is typical of Conrad's narrative style?

    a. He tells the story from a single viewpoint.
    (b.) He tells the story from several different viewpoints.
    c. He emphasizes one viewpoint over another.
    d. He tells the story using an omniscient narrative.

1.39   What was Conrad's view of the human condition?

    a. optimistic
    b. hopeful
    (c.) pessimistic
    d. indifferent

1.40   Which of his novels is considered Conrad's masterpiece?

    a. *Heart of Darkness*
    (b.) *Nostromo*
    c. *Typhoon*
    d. *Almayer's Folly*

What to Look For:

Many critics have concluded that *Heart of Darkness* is a tale about one man's descent into hell. As you read, pay attention to the religious imagery that Marlow uses to describe his experiences. How does this emphasize the concept that his journey to the heart of Africa had spiritual significance? What is so revealing about Kurtz's final words? What does he finally realize about a world that revels in the deeds of darkness?

The Heart of Darkness
by Joseph Conrad

(Part One from *Blackwood's Edinburgh Magazine,* February 1899)

The *Nellie,* a cruising yawl, swung to her anchor without a flutter of the sails, and was at rest. The flood had made, the wind was nearly calm, and being bound down the river, the only thing for us was to come to and wait for the turn of the tide.

The sea-reach of the Thames stretched before us like the beginning of an interminable* waterway. In the offing the sea and the sky were welded together without a joint, and in the luminous space the tanned sails of the barges drifting up with the tide seemed to stand still in red clusters of canvas sharply peaked, with gleams of varnished sprits. A haze rested on the low shores that ran out to sea in vanishing flatness. The air was dark above Gravesend, and farther back still seemed condensed into a mournful gloom, brooding motionless over the biggest, and the greatest, town on earth.

The Director of Companies was our captain and our host. We four affectionately watched his back as he stood in the bows looking to seaward. On the whole river there was nothing that looked half so nautical. He resembled a pilot, which to a seaman is trustworthiness personified. It was difficult to realize his work was not out there in the luminous estuary,* but behind him, within the brooding gloom.

Between us there was, as I have already said somewhere, the bond of the sea. Besides holding our hearts together through long periods of separation, it had the effect of making us tolerant of each other's yarns—and even convictions. The Lawyer—the best of old fellows—had, because of his many years and many virtues, the only cushion on deck, and was lying on the only rug. The Accountant had brought out already a box of dominoes, and was toying architecturally with the bones. Marlow sat cross-legged right aft, leaning against the mizzen-mast. He had sunken cheeks, a yellow complexion, a straight back, an ascetic aspect, and, with his arms dropped, the palms of hands outwards, resembled an idol. The Director, satisfied the anchor had good hold, made his way aft and sat down amongst us. We exchanged a few words lazily. Afterwards there was silence on board the yacht. For some reason or other we did not begin that game of dominoes. We felt meditative, and fit for nothing but placid staring. The day was ending in a serenity that had a still and exquisite brilliance. The water shone pacifically; the sky, without a speck, was a benign immensity of unstained light; the very mist on the Essex marshes was like a gauzy and radiant fabric, hung from the wooded rises inland, and draping the low shores in diaphanous folds. Only the gloom to the west, brooding over the upper reaches, became more sombre every minute, as if angered by the approach of the sun.

And at last, in its curved and imperceptible fall, the sun sank low, and from glowing white changed to a dull red without rays and without heat, as if about to go out suddenly, stricken to death by the touch of that gloom brooding over a crowd of men.

Forthwith a change came over the waters, and the serenity became less brilliant but more profound. The old river in its broad reach rested unruffled at the decline of day, after ages of good service done to the race that peopled its banks, spread out in the tranquil dignity of a waterway leading to the uttermost ends of the earth. We looked at the venerable stream not in the vivid flush of a short day that comes and departs for ever, but in the pacific yet august light of abiding memories. And indeed nothing is easier for a man who has, as the phrase goes, "followed the sea" with reverence and affection, than to evoke the great spirit of the past upon the lower reaches of the Thames. The tidal current runs to and fro in its unceasing service, crowded with memories of men and ships it had borne to the rest of home or to the battles of the sea. It had known and served all the men of whom the nation is proud, from Sir Francis Drake to Sir John Franklin, knights all, titled and untitled—the great knights-errant of the sea. It had borne all the ships whose names are like jewels flashing in the night of time, from the *Golden Hind* returning with her round flanks full of treasure, to be visited by the Queen's Highness and thus pass out of the gigantic tale, to the *Erebus* and *Terror,* bound on other conquests—and that never returned. It had known the ships and the men. They had sailed from Deptford, from Greenwich, from Erith—the adventurers and the settlers; kings' ships and the ships of men on 'Change; captains, admirals, the dark "interlopers" of the Eastern trade, and the commissioned "generals" of East India fleets. Hunters for gold or pursuers of fame, they all had gone out on that stream, bearing the sword, and often the torch, messengers of the might within the land, bearers of a spark from the sacred fire. What greatness had not floated on the ebb of that river into the mystery of an unknown earth?—The dreams of men, the seed of commonwealths, the germs of empires.

The sun set; the dusk fell on the stream, and lights began to appear along the shore. The Chapman lighthouse, a three-legged thing erect on a mud-flat, shone strongly. Lights of ships moved in the fairway—a great stir of lights going up and going down. And farther west on the upper reaches the place of the monstrous town was still marked ominously on the sky, a brooding gloom in sunshine, a lurid glare under the stars.

"And this also," said Marlow suddenly, "has been one of the dark places of the earth."

He was the only man of us who still "followed the sea." The worst that could be said of him was that he did not represent his class. He was a seaman, but he was a wanderer too, while most seamen lead, if one may so express it, a sedentary life. Their minds are of the stay-at-home order, and their home is always with them—the ship; and so is their country—the sea. One ship is very much like another, and the sea is always the same. In the immutability* of their surroundings the foreign shores, the foreign faces, the changing immensity of life, glide past, veiled not by a sense of mystery but by a slightly disdainful ignorance; for there is nothing mysterious to a seaman unless it be the sea itself, which is the mistress of his existence and as inscrutable* as Destiny. For the rest, after his hours of work a casual stroll or a casual spree on shore suffices to unfold for him the secret of a whole continent, and generally he finds the secret not worth knowing. The yarns of seamen have a direct simplicity, the whole meaning of which lies within the shell of a cracked nut. But Marlow was not typical (if his propensity to spin yarns be excepted), and to him the meaning of an episode was not inside like a kernel but outside, enveloping the tale which brought it out only as a glow brings out a haze, in the likeness of one of these misty halos that sometimes are made visible by the spectral illumination of moonshine.

His uncalled-for remark did not seem at all surprising. It was just like Marlow. It was accepted in silence. No one took the trouble to grunt even; and presently he said, very slow,—

"I was thinking of very old times, when the Romans first came here, nineteen hundred years ago....Light came out of this river since—you say Knights? Yes; but it is like a running blaze on a plain, like a flash of lightning in the clouds. We live in the flicker—may it last as long as the old earth keeps rolling! But darkness was here yesterday. Imagine the feelings of a commander of a fine—what d'ye call 'em?—trireme in the Mediterranean, ordered suddenly to the north; run overland across the Gauls in a hurry; put in charge of one of these craft the legionaries,—a wonderful lot of handy men they must have been too—used to build, apparently by the hundred, in a month or two, if we may believe what we read. Imagine him here—the very end of the world, a sea the colour of lead, a sky the colour of smoke, a kind of ship about as rigid as a concertina—and going up this river with stores, or orders, or what you like. Sandbanks, marshes, forests, savages,—precious little to eat fit for a civilized man, nothing but Thames water to drink. No Falernian wine here, no going ashore. Here and there a military camp lost in a wilderness, like a needle in a bundle of hay—cold, fog, tempests, disease, exile, and death,—death skulking in the air, in the water, in the bush. They must have been dying like flies here. Oh yes—he did it. Did it very well, too, no doubt, and without thinking much about it either, except afterwards to brag of what he had gone through in his time, perhaps. They were men enough to face the darkness. And perhaps he was cheered by keeping his eye on a chance of promotion to the fleet at Ravenna by-and-by, if he had good friends in Rome and survived the awful climate. Or think of a decent young citizen in a toga—perhaps too much dice, you know—coming out here in the train of some prefect, or tax-gatherer, or trader, even, to mend his fortunes. Land in a swamp, march through the woods, and in some inland post feel the savagery, the utter savagery, had closed round him,—all that mysterious life of the wilderness that stirs in the forest, in the jungles, in the hearts of wild men. There's no initiation either into such mysteries. He has to live in the midst of the incomprehensible, which is also detestable. And it has a fascination, too, that goes to work upon him. The fascination of the abomination—you know. Imagine the growing regrets, the longing to escape, the powerless disgust, the surrender, the hate."

He paused.

"Mind," he began again, lifting one arm from the elbow, the palm of the hand outwards, so that, with his legs folded before him, he had the pose of a Buddha preaching in European clothes and without a lotus-flower— "Mind, none of us would feel exactly like this. What saves us is efficiency—the devotion to efficiency. But these chaps were not much account, really. They were no colonists; their administration was merely a squeeze, and nothing more, I suspect. They were conquerors, and for that, you want only brute force—nothing to boast of, when you have it, since your strength is just an accident arising from the weakness of others. They grabbed what they could get for the sake of what was to be got. It was just robbery with violence, aggravated murder on a great scale, and men going at it blind—as is very proper for those who tackle a darkness. The conquest of the earth, which mostly means the taking it away from those who have a different complexion or slightly flatter noses than ourselves, is not a pretty thing when you look into it too much. What redeems it is the idea only. An idea at the back of it; not a sentimental pretense but an idea; and an unselfish belief in the idea—something you can set up, and bow down before, and offer a sacrifice to...."

He broke off. Flames glided in the river, small green flames, red flames, white flames, pursuing, overtaking, joining, crossing each other—then separating slowly or hastily. The traffic of the great city went on in the deepening night upon the sleepless river. We looked on, waiting patiently—there was nothing else to do till the end of the flood; but it was only after a long silence, when he said, in a hesitating voice, "I suppose you fellows remember I did once turn fresh-water sailor for a bit," that we knew we were fated, before the ebb began to run, to hear about one of Marlow's inconclusive experiences.

"I don't want to bother you much with what happened to me personally," he began, showing in this remark the weakness of many tellers of tales who seem so often unaware of what their audience would best like to hear; "yet to understand the effect of it on me you ought to know how I got out there, what I saw, how I went up that river to the place where I first met the poor chap. It was the farthest point of navigation and the culminating point of my experience. It seemed somehow to throw a kind of light on everything about me—and into my thoughts. It was sombre enough too—and pitiful—not extraordinary in any way—not very clear either. No, not very clear. And yet it seemed to throw a kind of light.

"I had then, as you remember, just returned to London after a lot of Indian Ocean, Pacific, China Seas—a regular dose of the East—six years or so, and I was loafing about, hindering you fellows in your work and invading your homes, just as though I had got a heavenly mission to civilize you. It was very fine for a time, but after a bit I did get tired of resting. Then I began to look for a ship—I should think the hardest work on earth. But the ships wouldn't even look at me. And I got tired of that game too.

"Now when I was a little chap I had a passion for maps. I would look for hours at South America, or Africa, or Australia, and lose myself in all the glories of exploration. At that time there were many blank spaces on the earth, and when I saw one that looked particularly inviting on a map (but they all look that) I would put my finger on it and say, When I grow up I will go there. The North Pole was one of these places, I remember. Well, I haven't been there yet, and shall not try now. The glamour's off. Other places were scattered about the Equator, and in every sort of latitude all over

the two hemispheres. I have been in some of them, and...well, we won't talk about that. But there was one yet—the biggest, the most blank, so to speak—that I had a hankering after.

"True, by this time it was not a blank space any more. It had got filled since my boyhood with rivers and lakes and names. It had ceased to be a blank space of delightful mystery—a white patch for a boy to dream gloriously over. It had become a place of darkness. But there was in it one river especially, a mighty big river, that you could see on the map, resembling an immense snake uncoiled, with its head in the sea, its body at rest curving afar over a vast country, and its tail lost in the depths of the land. And as I looked at the map of it in a shop-window, it fascinated me as a snake would a bird—a silly little bird. Then I remembered there was a big concern, a Company for trade on that river. Dash it all! I thought to myself, they can't trade without using some kind of craft on that lot of fresh water—steam-boats! Why shouldn't I try to get charge of one? I went on along Fleet Street, but could not shake off the idea. The snake had charmed me.

"You understand it was a Continental concern, that Trading society; but I have a lot of relations living on the Continent, because it's cheap and not so nasty as it looks, they say.

"I am sorry to own I began to worry them. This was already a fresh departure for me. I was not used to get things that way, you know. I always went my own road and on my own legs where I had a mind to go. I wouldn't have believed it of myself; but, then—you see—I felt somehow I must get there by hook or by crook. So I worried them. The men said, 'My dear fellow,' and did nothing. Then—would you believe it?—I tried the women. I, Charlie Marlow, set the women to work—to get a job. Heavens! Well, you see, the notion drove me. I had an aunt, a dear enthusiastic soul. She wrote: 'It will be delightful. I am ready to do anything, anything for you. It is a glorious idea. I know the wife of a very high personage in the Administration, and also a man who has lots of influence with,' etc., etc. She was determined to make no end of fuss to get me appointed skipper of a river steam-boat, if such was my fancy.

"I got my appointment—of course; and I got it very quick. It appears the Company had received news that one of their captains had been killed in a scuffle with the natives. This was my chance, and it made me the more anxious to go. It was only months and months afterwards, when I made the attempt to recover what was left of the body, that I heard the original quarrel arose from a misunderstanding about some hens. Yes, two black hens. Fresleven—that was the fellows name, a Dane—thought himself wronged somehow in the bargain, so he went ashore and started to hammer the chief of the village with a stick. Oh, it didn't surprise me in the least to hear this, and at the same time to be told that Fresleven was the gentlest, quietest creature that ever walked on two legs. No doubt he was; but he had been a couple of years already out there engaged in the noble cause, you know, and he probably felt the need at last of asserting his self-respect in some way. Therefore he whacked the old nigger mercilessly, while a big crowd of his people watched him, thunderstruck, till some man—I was told the chief's son—in desperation at hearing the old chap yell, made a tentative jab with a spear at the white man—and of course it went quite easy between the shoulder-blades. Then the whole population cleared into the forest, expecting all kinds of calamities to happen, while, on the other hand, the steamer Fresleven commanded left also in a bad panic, in charge of the engineer, I believe. Afterwards nobody seemed to trouble much about Fresleven's remains, till I got out and stepped into his shoes. I couldn't let it rest, though; but when an opportunity offered at last to meet my predecessor, the grass growing through his ribs was tall enough to hide his bones. They were all there. The supernatural being had not been touched after he fell. And the village was deserted, the huts gaped black, rotting, all askew within the fallen enclosures. A calamity had come to it, sure enough. The people had vanished. Mad terror had scattered them, men, women, and children, through the bush, and they had never returned. What became of the hens I don't know either. I should think the cause of progress got them, anyhow. However, through this glorious affair I got my appointment, before I had fairly begun to hope for it.

"I flew around like mad to get ready, and before forty-eight hours I was crossing the Channel to show myself to my employers, and sign the contract. In a very few hours I arrived in a city that always makes me think of a whited sepulchre. Prejudice no doubt. I had no difficulty in finding the Company's offices. It was the biggest thing in the town, and everybody I met was full of it. They were going to run an over-sea empire, and make no end of coin by trade.

"A narrow and deserted street in deep shadow, high houses, innumerable windows with venetian blinds, a dead silence, grass sprouting between the stones, imposing carriage archways right and left, immense double doors standing ponderously ajar. I slipped through one of these cracks, went up a swept and ungarnished staircase, as arid as a desert, and opened the first door I came to. Two women, one fat and the other slim, sat on straw-bottomed chairs, knitting black wool. The slim one got up and walked straight at me—still knitting with downcast eyes—and only just as I began to think of getting out of her way, as you would for a somnambulist,* stood still, and looked up. Her dress was as plain as an umbrella-cover, and she turned round without a word and preceded me into a waiting-room. I gave my name, and looked about. Deal table in the middle, plain chairs all round the walls, on one end a large shining map, marked with all the colours of a rainbow. There was a vast amount of red—good to see at any time, because one knows that some real work is done in there, a deuce of a lot of blue, a little green, smears of orange, and, on the East Coast, a purple patch, to show where the jolly pioneers of progress drink the jolly lager-beer. However, I wasn't going into any of these. I was going into the yellow. Dead in the centre. And the river was there—fascinating—deadly—like a snake. Ough! A door opened, a white-haired secretarial head, but wearing a compassionate expression, appeared, and a skinny forefinger beckoned me into the sanctuary. Its light was dim, and a heavy writing-desk squatted in the middle. From behind that structure came out an impression of pale plumpness in a frock-coat. The great man himself. He was five feet six, I should judge, and had his grip on the handle-end of ever so many millions. He shook hands, I fancy, murmured vaguely, was satisfied with my French. Bon voyage.

"In about forty-five seconds I found myself again in the waiting-room with the compassionate secretary, who, full of desolation and sympathy, made me sign some document. I believe I undertook amongst other things not to disclose any trade secrets. Well, I am not going to.

"I began to feel slightly uneasy. You know I am not used to such ceremonies, and there was something ominous in the atmosphere. It was just as though I had been let into some conspiracy—I don't know—something not quite right; and I was glad to get out. In the outer room the two women knitted black wool feverishly. People were arriving, and the younger one was walking back and forth introducing them. The old one sat on her chair. Her flat cloth slippers were propped up on a foot-warmer, and a cat reposed on her lap. She wore a starched white affair on her head, had a wart on one cheek, and silver-rimmed spectacles hung on the tip of her nose. She glanced at me above the glasses. The swift and indifferent placidity of that look troubled me. Two youths with foolish and cheery countenances were being piloted over, and she threw at them the same quick glance of unconcerned wisdom. She seemed to know all about them and about me too. An eerie feeling came over me. She seemed uncanny and fateful. Often far away there I thought of these two, guarding the door of Darkness, knitting black wool as for a warm pall, one introducing, introducing, continuously to the unknown, the other scrutinizing the cheery and foolish faces with unconcerned old eyes. Ave! Old knitter of black wool. *Morituri te salutant.* Not many of those she looked at ever saw her again— not half, by a long way.

"There was yet a visit to the doctor. 'A simple formality,' assured me the secretary, with an air of taking an immense part in all my sorrows. Accordingly a young chap wearing his hat over the left eyebrow, some clerk I suppose,—there must have been clerks in the business, though the house was as still as a house in a city of the dead—came from somewhere up-stairs, and led me forth. He was shabby and careless, with ink-stains on the sleeves of his jacket, and his cravat was large and billowy, under a chin shaped like the toe of an old boot. It was a little too early for the doctor, so I proposed a drink, and thereupon he developed a vein of joviality. As we sat over our vermuths he glorified the Company's business, and by-and-by I expressed casually my surprise at him not going out there. He became very cool and collected all at once. 'I am not such a fool as I look, quoth Plato to his disciples,' he said sententiously,* emptied his glass with great resolution, and we rose.

"The old doctor felt my pulse, evidently think-ing of something else the while. 'Good, good for there,' he mumbled, and then with a certain eager-ness asked me whether I would let him measure my head. Rather surprised, I said Yes, when he produced a thing like calipers and got the dimen-sions back and front and every way, taking notes carefully. He was an unshaven little man in a threadbare coat like a gaberdine,* with his feet in slippers, and I thought him a harmless fool. 'I always ask leave, in the interests of science, to measure the crania of those going out there,' he said. 'And when they come back too?' I asked. 'Oh, I never see them,' he remarked; 'and, moreover, the changes take place inside, you know.' He smiled, as if at some quiet joke. 'So you are going out there. Famous. Interesting too.' He gave me a searching glance, and made another note. 'Ever any madness in your family?' he asked, in a mat-ter-of-fact tone. I felt very annoyed. 'Is that ques-tion in the interests of science too?' 'It would be,' he said, without taking notice of my irritation, 'interesting for science to watch the mental changes of individuals, on the spot, but...' 'Are you an alienist?' I interrupted. 'Every doctor should be—a little,' answered that original, imper-turbably. 'I have a little theory which you Messieurs who go out there must help me to prove. This is my share in the advantages my country shall reap from the possession of such a magnifi-

cent dependency. The mere wealth I leave to oth-ers. Pardon my questions, but you are the first Englishman coming under my observation....' I hastened to assure him I was not in the least typ-ical. 'If I were,' said I, 'I wouldn't be talking like this with you.' 'What you say is rather profound, and probably erroneous,' he said, with a laugh. 'Avoid irritation more than exposure to the sun. Adieu. How do you English say, eh? Good-bye. Ah! Good-bye. Adieu. In the tropics one must before everything keep calm.' ...He lifted a warning fore-finger.... *D'u calme, du calme. Adieu.'*

"One thing more remained to do—say good-bye to my excellent aunt. I found her triumphant. I had a cup of tea—the last decent cup of tea for many days; and in a room that most soothingly looked just as you would expect a lady's drawing-room to look, we had a long quiet chat by the fire-side. In the course of these confidences it became quite plain to me I had been represented to the wife of the high dignitary, and goodness knows to how many more people besides, as an exceptional and gifted creature—a piece of good fortune for the Company—a man you don't get hold of every day. Good Heavens! and I was going to take charge of a two-penny-halfpenny river-steam-boat with a penny whistle attached! It appeared, however, I was also one of the Workers, with a capital—you know. Something like an emissary of light, some-thing like a lower sort of apostle. There had been a lot of such rot let loose in print and talk just about that time, and the excellent woman, living right in the rush of all that humbug, got carried off her feet. She talked about 'weaning those ignorant millions from their horrid ways, 'till, upon my word, she made me quite uncomfortable. I ven-tured to hint that the Company was run for profit.

"'You forget, dear Charlie, that the labourer is worthy of his hire,' she said, brightly. It's queer how out of touch with truth women are. They live in a world of their own, and there had never been anything like it, and never can be. It is too beauti-ful altogether, and if they were to set it up it would go to pieces before the first sunset. Some confound-ed fact we men have been living contentedly with ever since the day of creation would start up and knock the whole thing over.

"After this I got embraced, told to wear flannel, be sure to write often, and so on—and I left. In the street—I don't know why—a queer feeling came to me that I was an impostor. Odd thing that I, who used to clear out for any part of the world at twen-ty-four hours' notice, with less thought than most men give to the crossing of a street, had a moment—I won't say of hesitation, but of startled pause, before this commonplace affair. The best way I can explain it to you is by saying that, for a second or two, I felt as though, instead of going to the centre of a continent, I were about to set off for the centre of the earth.

"I left in a French steamer, and she called in every blamed port they have out there, for, as far as I could see, the sole purpose of landing soldiers and custom-house officers. I watched the coast. Watching a coast as it slips by the ship is like thinking about an enigma. There it is before you—smiling, frowning, inviting, grand, mean, insipid, or savage, and always mute with an air of whispering, Come and find out. This one was almost featureless, as if still in the making, with an aspect of monotonous grimness. The edge of a colossal jungle, so dark green as to be almost black, fringed with white surf, ran straight, like a ruled line, far, far away along a blue sea whose glitter was blurred by a creeping mist. The sun was fierce, the land seemed to glisten and drip with steam. Here and there greyish-whitish specks showed up clustered inside the white surf, with a flag flying above them perhaps—settlements some centuries old, and still no bigger than pinheads on the untouched expanse of their background. We pounded along, stopped, landed soldiers; went on, landed custom-house clerks to levy toll in what looked like a God-forsaken wilderness, with a tin shed and a flag-pole lost in it; landed more soldiers—to take care of the custom-house clerks presumably. Some, I heard, got drowned in the surf; but whether they did or not, nobody seemed particularly to care. They were just flung out there, and on we went. Every day the coast looked the same, as though we had not moved; but we passed various places—trading places—with names like Gran' Bassam, Little Popo, names that seemed to belong to some sordid farce acted in front of a sinister backcloth. The idleness of a passenger, my isolation amongst all these men with whom I had no point of contact, the oily and languid sea, the uniform sombreness of the coast, seemed to keep me away from the truth of things within the toil of a mournful and senseless delusion. The voice of the surf heard now and then was a positive pleasure, like the speech of a brother. It was something natural, that had its reason, that had a meaning. Now and then a boat from the shore gave one a momentary contact with reality. It was paddled by black fellows. You could see from afar the white of their eyeballs glistening. They shouted, sang; their bodies streamed with perspiration; they had faces like grotesque masks—these chaps; but they had bone, muscle, a wild vitality, an intense energy of movement, that was as natural and true as the surf along their coast. They wanted no excuse for being there. They were a great comfort to look at. For a time I would feel I belonged still to a world of straightforward facts; but the feeling would not last long. Something would turn up to scare it away. Once, I remember, we came upon a man-of-war anchored off the coast. There wasn't even a shed there, and she was shelling the bush. It appears the French had one of their wars going on thereabouts. Her ensign dropped limp like a rag; the muzzles of the long eight-inch guns stuck out all over the low hull; the greasy, slimy swell swung her up lazily and let her down, swaying her thin masts. In the empty immensity of earth, sky, and water, there she was, incomprehensible, firing into a continent. Pop, would go one of the eight-inch guns; a small flame would dart and vanish, a little white smoke would disappear, a tiny projectile would give a feeble screech—and nothing happened. Nothing could happen. There was a touch of insanity in the proceeding, a sense of lugubrious drollery in the sight; and it was not dissipated by somebody on board assuring me earnestly there was a camp of natives—he called them enemies!—hidden out of sight somewhere.

"We gave her her letters (I heard the men in that lonely ship were dying of fever at the rate of three a-day) and went on. We called at some more places with farcical names, where the merry dance of death and trade goes on in a still and earthy atmosphere as of an overheated catacomb; all along the formless coast bordered by dangerous surf, as if Nature herself had tried to ward off intruders; in and out of rivers, streams of death in life, whose banks were rotting into mud, whose waters, thickened into slime, invaded the contorted mangroves, that seemed to writhe at us in the extremity of an impotent despair. Nowhere did we stop long enough to get a particularized impression, but the general sense of vague and oppressive wonder grew upon me. It was like a weary pilgrimage amongst hints for nightmares.

"It was upward of thirty days before I saw the mouth of the big river. We anchored off the seat of the government. But my work would not begin till some two hundred miles farther on. So as soon as I could I made a start for a place thirty miles higher up.

"I had my passage on a little sea-going steamer. Her captain was a Swede, and knowing me for a seaman, invited me on the bridge. He was a young man, lean, fair, and morose, with lanky hair and a shuffling gait. As we left the miserable little wharf, he tossed his head contemptuously at the shore. 'Been living there?' he asked. I said, 'Yes.' 'Fine lot these government chaps—are they not?' he went on, speaking English with great precision and considerable bitterness. 'It is funny what some people will do for a few francs a-month. I wonder what becomes of that kind when it goes up country?' I said to him I expected to see that soon. 'So-o-o!' he exclaimed. He shuffled athwart, keeping one eye ahead vigilantly. 'Don't be too sure,' he continued. 'The other day I took up a man who hanged himself on the road. He was a Swede, too.' 'Hanged himself! Why, in God's name?' I cried. He kept on looking out watchfully. 'Who knows? The sun too much for him, or the country perhaps.'

"At last we turned a bend. A rocky cliff appeared, mounds of turned-up earth by the shore, houses on a hill, others, with iron roofs, amongst a waste of excavations, or hanging to the declivity. A continuous noise of the rapids above hovered over this scene of inhabited devastation. A lot of people, mostly black and naked, moved about like ants. A jetty projected into the river. A blinding sunlight drowned all this at times in a sudden recrudescence* of glare. 'There's your Company's station,' said the Swede, pointing to three wooden barrack-like structures on the rocky slope. 'I will send your things up. Four boxes did you say? So. Farewell.'

"I came upon a boiler wallowing in the grass, then found a path leading up the hill. It turned aside for the boulders, and also for an undersized railway-truck lying there on its back with its wheels in the air. One was off. The thing looked as dead as the carcass of some animal. I came upon more pieces of decaying machinery, a stack of rusty rails. To the left a clump of trees made a shady spot, where dark things seemed to stir feebly. I blinked, the path was steep. A horn tooted to the right, and I saw the black people run. A heavy and dull detonation shook the ground, a puff of smoke came out of the cliff, and that was all. No change appeared on the face of the rock. They were building a railway. The cliff was not in the way or anything; but this objectless blasting was all the work going on.

"A slight clinking behind me made me turn my head. Six black men advanced in a file, toiling up the path. They walked erect and slow, balancing small baskets full of earth on their heads, and the clink kept time with their footsteps. Black rags were wound round their loins, and the short ends behind wagged to and fro like tails. I could see every rib, the joints of their limbs were like knots in a rope; each had an iron collar on his neck, and all were connected together with a chain whose bights swung between them, rhythmically clinking. Another report from the cliff made me think suddenly of that ship of war I had seen firing into a continent. It was the same kind of ominous voice; but these men could by no stretch of imagination be called enemies. They were called criminals, and the outraged law, like the bursting shells, had come to them, an insoluble mystery from over the sea. All their meagre breasts panted together, the violently dilated nostrils quivered, the eyes stared stonily uphill. They passed me within six inches, without a glance, with that complete, deathlike indifference of unhappy savages. Behind this raw matter one of the reclaimed, the product of the new forces at work, strolled despondently, carrying a rifle by its middle. He had a uniform jacket with one button off, and seeing a white man on the path, hoisted his weapon to his shoulder with alacrity. This was simple prudence, white men being so much alike at a distance that he could not tell who I might be. He was speedily reassured, and with a large, white, rascally grin, and a glance at his charge, seemed to take me into partnership in his exalted trust. After all, I also was a part of the great cause of these high and just proceedings.

"Instead of going up, I turned and descended to the left. My idea was to let that chain-gang get out of sight before I climbed the hill. You know I am not particularly tender; I've had to strike and to fend off. I've had to resist and to attack sometimes—that's only one way of resisting—without counting the exact cost, according to the demands of such sort of life as I had blundered into. I've seen the devil of violence, and the devil of greed, and the devil of hot desire; but, by all the stars! these were strong, lusty, red-eyed devils, that swayed and drove men—men, I tell you. But as I stood on this hillside, I foresaw that in the blinding sunshine of that land I would become acquainted with a flabby, pretending, weak-eyed devil of a rapacious* and pitiless folly. How insidious he could be, too, I was only to find out several months later and a thousand miles farther. For a moment I stood appalled, as though by a warning. Finally I descended the hill, obliquely, towards the trees I had seen.

"I avoided a vast artificial hole somebody had been digging on the slope, the purpose of which I found it impossible to divine. It wasn't a quarry or a sandpit, anyhow. It was just a hole. It might have been connected with the philanthropic desire of giving the criminals something to do. I don't know. Then I nearly fell into a very narrow ravine, almost no more than a scar in the hillside. I discovered that a lot of imported drainage-pipes for the settlement had been tumbled in there. There wasn't one that was not broken. It was a wanton smash-up. At last I got under the trees. My purpose was to stroll into the shade for a moment; but it seemed to me I had stepped into the gloomy circle of some Inferno. The river was near, and an uninterrupted, uniform, headlong, rushing noise filled the mournful stillness of the grove, where not a breath stirred, not a leaf moved with a mysterious sound, as though the tearing pace of the launched earth had suddenly become audible.

"Black shapes crouched, lay, sat between the trees, leaning against the trunks, clinging to the earth, half coming out, half effaced within the dim light, in all the attitudes of pain, abandonment, and despair. Another mine on the cliff went off, followed by a slight shudder of the soil under my feet. The work was going on. The work! And this was the place where some of the helpers had withdrawn to die.

"They were dying slowly—it was very clear. They were not enemies, they were not criminals, they were nothing earthly now,— nothing but black shadows of disease and starvation, lying confusedly in the greenish gloom. Brought from all the recesses of the coast in all the legality of time contracts, lost in uncongenial surroundings, fed on unfamiliar food, they sickened, became inefficient, and were then allowed to crawl away and rest. These moribund shapes were free as air—and nearly as thin. I began to distinguish the gleam of eyes under the trees. Then, glancing down, I saw a face near my hand. The black bones reclined at full length with one shoulder against the tree, and slowly the eyelids rose and the sunken eyes looked up at me, enormous and vacant, a kind of blind, white flicker in the depths of the orbs, which died out slowly. The man seemed young—almost a boy—but you know with them it's hard to tell. I found nothing else to do but to offer him one of my good Swede's ship's biscuits I had in my pocket. The fingers closed slowly on it and held—there was no other movement and no other glance. He had tied a bit of white worsted round his neck—Why? Where did he get it? Was it a badge—an ornament—a charm—a propitiatory act? Was there any idea at all connected with it? It looked startling round his black neck, this bit of white thread from beyond the seas.

"Near the same tree two more bundles of acute angles sat with their legs drawn up. One, with his chin propped on his knees, stared at nothing, in an intolerable and appalling manner. His brother phantom rested its forehead, as if overcome with a great weariness; and all about others were scattered in every pose of contorted collapse, as in some picture of a massacre or a pestilence. While I stood horror-struck, one of these creatures rose to his hands and knees, and went off on all-fours towards the river to drink. He lapped out of his hand, then sat up in the sunlight, crossing his shins in front of him, and after a time let his woolly head fall on his breastbone.

"I didn't want any more loitering in the shade, and I made haste towards the station. When near the buildings I met a white man, in such an unexpected elegance of get-up that in the first moment I took him for a sort of vision. I saw a high starched collar, white cuffs, a light alpaca jacket, snowy trousers, a clear necktie, and varnished boots. No hat. Hair parted, brushed, oiled, under a green-lined parasol held in a big white hand. He was amazing, and had a pen-holder behind his ear.

"I shook hands with this miracle, and I learned he was the Company's chief accountant, and that all the book-keeping was done at this station. He had come out for a moment, he said, 'to get a breath of fresh air.' The expression sounded wonderfully odd, with its suggestion of sedentary desk-life. I wouldn't have mentioned the fellow to you at all, only it was from his lips that I first heard the name of the man who is so indissolubly connected with the memories of that time. Moreover, I respected the fellow. Yes; I respected his collars, his vast cuffs, his brushed hair. His appearance was certainly that of a hairdresser's dummy; but in the great demoralization of the land he kept up his appearance. That's backbone. His starched collars and got-up shirt-fronts were achievements of character. He had been out nearly three years; and, later on, I could not help asking him how he managed to sport such linen. He had just the faintest blush, and said modestly, 'I've been teaching one of the native women about the station. It was difficult. She had a distaste for the work.' Thus this man had verily accomplished something. And he was devoted to his books.

"Everything in the station was in a muddle,— heads, things, buildings. Strings of dusty niggers with splay feet arrived and departed; and a stream of manufactured goods, rubbishy cottons, beads, and brass-wire set into the depths of darkness, and in return came a precious trickle of ivory.

"I had to wait in the station for ten days—an eternity. I lived in a hut in the yard, but to be out

19

of the chaos I would sometimes get into the accountant's office. It was built of horizontal planks, and so badly put together that, as he bent over his high desk, he was barred from neck to heels with narrow strips of sunlight. There was no need to open the big shutter to see. It was hot there too; big flies buzzed fiendishly, and did not sting, but stabbed. I sat generally on the floor, while, of faultless appearance (and even slightly scented), perching on a high stool, he wrote, he wrote. Sometimes he stood up for exercise. When a truckle-bed with a sick man (some invalided agent from up-country) was put in there, he exhibited a gentle annoyance. 'The groans of this sick person,' he said, 'distract my attention. And without that it is extremely difficult to guard against clerical errors in this climate.'

"One day he remarked, without lifting his head, 'In the interior you will no doubt meet Mr. Kurtz.' On my asking who Mr. Kurtz was, he said he was a first-class agent; and seeing my disappointment at this information, he added slowly, laying down his pen, 'He is a very remarkable person.' Further questions elicited from him that Mr. Kurtz was at present in charge of a trading post, a very important one, in the true ivory-country, at 'the very bottom of there. Sends in as much ivory as all the others put together....' He began to write again. The sick man was too ill to groan. The flies buzzed in a great peace.

"Suddenly there was a growing murmur of voices and a great tramping of feet. A caravan had come in. A violent babble of uncouth sounds burst out on the other side of the planks. All the carriers were speaking together, and in the midst of the uproar the lamentable voice of the chief agent was heard 'giving it up' tearfully for the twentieth time that day....He rose slowly. 'What a frightful row,' he said. He crossed the room gently to look at the sick man, and returning, said to me, 'He does not hear.' 'What! Dead?' I asked, startled. 'No, not yet,' he answered, with great composure. Then, alluding with a toss of the head to the tumult in the station-yard, 'When one has got to make correct entries, one comes to hate those savages—hate them to the death.' He remained thoughtful for a moment. 'When you see Mr. Kurtz,' he went on, 'tell him from me that everything here'—he glanced at the desk— 'is very satisfactory. I don't like to write to him—with those messengers of ours you never know who may get your letter—at that Central Station.' He stared at me for a moment with his mild, bulging eyes. 'Oh, he will go far, very far,' he began again. 'He will be a somebody in the Administration before long. They, above—the

Council in Europe, you know—mean him to be.'

"He turned to his work. The noise outside had ceased, and presently as I went out I stopped at the door. In the steady buzz of flies the homeward-bound agent was lying flushed and insensible; the other, bent over his books, was making correct entries of perfectly correct transactions; and fifty feet below the doorstep I could see the still tree-tops of the grove of death.

"Next day I left that station at last, with a caravan of sixty men, for a two-hundred-mile tramp.

"No use telling you much about that. Paths, paths, everywhere; a stamped-in network of paths spreading over the empty land, through long grass, through burnt grass, through thickets, down and up chilly ravines, up and down stony hills ablaze with heat; and a solitude, a solitude, nobody, not a hut. The population had cleared out a long time ago. Well, if a lot of mysterious niggers armed with all kinds of fearful weapons suddenly took to travelling on the road between Deal and Gravesend, catching the yokels right and left to carry heavy loads for them, I fancy every farm and cottage thereabouts would get empty very soon. Only here the dwellings were gone too. Still, I passed through several abandoned villages. There's something pathetically childish in the ruins of grass walls. Day after day, with the stamp and shuffle of sixty pair of bare feet behind me, each pair under a 60-lb. load. Camp, cook, sleep, strike camp, march. Now and then a carrier dead in harness, at rest in the long grass near the path, with an empty water-gourd and his long staff lying by his side. A great silence around and above. Perhaps on some quiet night the tremor of far-off drums, sinking, swelling, a tremor vast, faint; a sound weird, appealing, suggestive, and wild—and perhaps with as respectable a meaning as the sound of bells in a Christian country. Once a white man in an unbuttoned uniform, camping on the path with an armed escort of lank Zanzibaris, very hospitable and festive, not to say drunk. Was looking after the upkeep of the road, he declared. Can't say I saw any road or any upkeep, unless the body of a middle-aged negro, with a bullet-hole in the forehead, upon which I absolutely stumbled three miles farther on, may be considered as a permanent improvement. I had a white companion too, not a bad chap, but rather too fleshy and with the exasperating habit of fainting on the hot hillsides, miles away from the least bit of shade and water. Annoying, you know, to hold your own coat like a parasol over a man's head while he is coming-to. I couldn't help asking him once what he meant by coming there at all. 'To make money, of course. What do you think?' he said, scornfully. Then he got fever, and had to be carried in a hammock slung on a pole. As he weighed sixteen stone I had no end of rows with the carriers. They jibbed, ran away, sneaked off with their loads in the night—quite a mutiny. So, one evening, I made a speech in English with gestures, not one of which was lost to the sixty pairs of eyes before me, and the next morning I started the hammock off in front all right. An hour afterwards I came upon the whole concern wrecked in a bush—man, hammock, groans, blankets, horrors. The heavy pole had skinned his poor nose. He was very anxious for me to kill somebody, but there wasn't the shadow of a carrier near. I remembered the old doctor,— 'It would be interesting for science to watch the mental changes of individuals, on the spot.' I felt I was becoming scientifically interesting. However, all that is to no purpose. On the fifteenth day I came in sight of the big river again, and hobbled into the Central Station. It was on a back water surrounded by scrub and forest, with a pretty border of smelly mud on one side, and on the three others enclosed by a crazy fence of rushes. A neglected gap was all the gate it had, and the first glance at the place was enough to let you see the flabby devil was running that show. White men with long staves in their hands appeared languidly from amongst the buildings, strolling up to take a look at me, and then retired out of sight somewhere. One of them, a stout, excitable chap with black moustache's, informed me with great volubility* and many digressions, as soon as I told him who I was, that my steamer was at the bottom of the river. I was thunderstruck. What, how, why? Oh, it was 'all right.' The 'manager himself' was there. All quite correct. 'Everybody had behaved splendidly! splendidly!'— 'You must,' he said in agitation, 'go and see the general manager at once. He is waiting!'

"I did not see the real significance of that wreck at once. I fancy I see it now, but I am not sure—not at all. Certainly the affair was too stupid—when I think of it—to be altogether natural. Still...at the moment it presented itself simply as a confounded nuisance. The steamer was sunk. They had started two days before in a sudden hurry up the river with the manager on board, in charge of some volunteer skipper, and before they had been out three hours they tore the bottom out of her on stones, and she sank near the south bank. I asked myself what I was to do there, now my boat was lost. As a matter of fact, I had plenty to do in fishing my command out of the river. I had to set about it the very next day. That, and the repairs when I brought the pieces to the station, took some months.

"My first interview with the manager was curious. He did not ask me to sit down after my twenty-mile walk that morning. He was commonplace in complexion, in feature, in manners, and in voice. He was of middle size and of ordinary build. His eyes, of the usual blue, were perhaps remarkably cold, and he certainly could make his glance fall on one as trenchant* and heavy as an axe. But even at these times the rest of his person seemed to disclaim the intention. Otherwise there was only an indefinable faint expression of his lips, something stealthy—a smile—not a smile—I remember it, but I can't explain. It was unconscious, this smile was, though just after he had said something it got intensified for an instant. It came at the end of his speeches like a seal applied on the words to make the meaning of the commonest phrase appear absolutely inscrutable. He was a common trader, from his youth up, employed in these parts—nothing more. He was obeyed, yet he inspired neither love nor fear, nor even respect. He inspired uneasiness. That was it! Uneasiness. Not a definite mistrust—just uneasiness—nothing more. You have no idea how effective such a...a...faculty can be. He had no genius for organizing, for initiative, or for order even. That was evident in such things as the deplorable state of the station. He had no learning, no intelligence. His position had come to him— why? Perhaps because he was never ill...He had served three terms of three years out there ... Because triumphant health in the general rout of constitutions is a kind of power in itself. When he went home on leave he rioted on a large scale— pompously. Jack ashore—with a difference—in externals only. This one could gather from his casual talk. He originated nothing, he could keep the routine going—that's all. But he was great. He was great by this little thing that it was impossible to tell what could control such a man. He never gave that secret away. Perhaps there was nothing within him. Such a suspicion made one pause—for out there there were no external checks. Once when various tropical diseases had laid low almost every 'agent' in the station, he was heard to say, 'Men who come out here should have no entrails.' He sealed the utterance with that smile of his, as though it had been a door opening into a darkness he had in his keeping. You fancied you had seen things—but the seal was on. When annoyed at meal-times by the constant quarrels of the white men about precedence, he ordered an immense round table to be made, for which a special house had to be built. This was the station's mess-room. Where he sat was the first place—the rest were nowhere. One felt this to be his unalterable conviction. He was neither civil nor uncivil. He was quiet. He allowed his 'boy'—an overfed young negro from the coast—to treat the white men, under his very eyes, with provoking insolence.

"He began to speak as soon as he saw me. I had been very long on the road. He could not wait. Had to start without me. The up-river stations had to be relieved. There had been so many delays already that he did not know who was dead and who was alive, and how they got on—and so on, and so on. He paid no attention to my explanations, and, playing with a stick of sealing-wax, repeated several times that the situation was 'very grave, very grave.' There were rumors that a very important station was in jeopardy, and its chief, Mr. Kurtz, was ill. Hoped it was not true. Mr. Kurtz was...I felt weary and irritable. Hang Kurtz, I thought. I interrupted him by saying I had heard of Mr. Kurtz on the coast. 'Ah! So they talk of him down there,' he murmured to himself. Then he began again, assuring me Mr. Kurtz was the best agent he had, an exceptional man, of the greatest importance to the Company; therefore I could understand his anxiety. He was, he said, 'very, very uneasy.' Certainly he fidgeted on his chair a good deal, exclaimed, 'Ah, Mr. Kurtz!' broke the stick of sealing-wax and seemed dumbfounded by the accident. Next thing he wanted to know 'how long it would take to'...I interrupted him again. Being hungry, you know, and kept on my feet too, I was getting savage. 'How can I tell?' I said. 'I haven't even seen the wreck yet—some months, no doubt.' All this talk seemed to me so futile. 'Some months,' he said. 'Well, let us say three months before we can make a start. Yes. That ought to do the affair.' I flung out of his hut (he lived all alone in a clay hut with a sort of verandah) muttering to myself my opinion of him. He was a chattering idiot. Afterwards I took it back when it was borne in upon me startlingly with what extreme nicety he had estimated the time requisite for the 'affair.'

"I went to work the next day, turning, so to speak, my back on that station. In that way only it seemed to me I could keep my hold on the redeeming facts of life. Still, one must look about sometimes; and then I saw this station, these men strolling aimlessly about in the sunshine of the yard. I asked myself sometimes what it all meant? They wandered here and there with their absurd long staves in their hands, like a lot of faithless pilgrims bewitched inside a fence. The word ivory rang in the air, was whispered, was sighed. You would think they were praying to it. A taint of imbecile rapacity blew through it all, like a whiff from some corpse. By Jove! I've never seen anything so unreal in my life. And outside, the silent wilderness surrounding this cleared speck on the earth struck me as something great and invincible, like evil or truth, waiting patiently for the passing away of this fantastic invasion.

"Oh, these months! Well, never mind. Various things happened. One evening a grass shed full of calico,* cotton prints, beads, and I don't know what else, burst into a blaze so suddenly that you would have thought the earth had opened to let an avenging fire consume all that trash. I was smoking my pipe quietly by my dismantled steamer, and saw them all cutting capers in the light, with their arms lifted high, when the stout man with moustache's came tearing down to the river, a tin pail in his hand, assured me that everybody was 'behaving splendidly, splendidly,' dipped about a quart of water and tore back again. I noticed there was a hole in the bottom of his pail.

"I strolled up. There was no hurry. You see the thing had gone off like a box of matches. It had been hopeless from the very first. The flame had leaped high, driven everybody back, lighted up everything—and collapsed. The shed was already a heap of embers glowing fiercely. A nigger was being beaten near by. They said he had caused the fire in some way; be that as it may, he was screeching most horribly. I saw him, later on, for several days, sitting in a bit of shade looking very sick and trying to recover himself: afterwards he arose and went out—and the wilderness without a sound took him into its bosom again. As I approached the glow from the dark I found myself at the back of two men, talking. I heard the name of Kurtz pronounced, then the words 'take advantage of this unfortunate accident.' One of the men was the manager. I wished him a good evening. 'Did you ever see anything like it—eh?' he said; 'it is incredible,' and walked off. The other man remained. He was a first-class agent, young, gentlemanly, a bit reserved, with a forked little beard and a hooked nose. He was stand-offish with the other agents. They on their side said he was the manager's spy upon them. As to me, I had hardly ever spoken to him before. We got into talk, and by-and-by we strolled away from the hissing ruins. Then he asked me to his room, which was in the main building of the station. He struck a match, and I perceived that this young aristocrat had not only a silver-mounted dressing-case but also a whole candle all to himself. Just at that time the manager was the only man supposed to have any right to candles. Native mats covered the clay walls; a collection of spears, assegais, shields, knives was hung up in trophies. The business entrusted to this fellow was the making of bricks—so I had been informed; but there wasn't a fragment of a brick anywhere in the station, and he had been there more than a year—waiting. It seems he could not make bricks without something, I don't know what—straw maybe. Anyways, it could not be found there, and as it was not likely to be sent from Europe, it did not appear clear to me what he was waiting for. An act of special creation perhaps. However, they were all waiting—all the sixteen or twenty pilgrims of them—for something; and upon my word it did not seem an uncongenial occupation, from the way they took it, though the only thing that ever came to them was disease—as far as I could see. They beguiled the time by backbiting and intriguing against each other in a foolish kind of way. There was an air of plotting about that station, but nothing came of it, of course. It was as unreal as everything else—as the philanthropic pretense of the whole concern, as their talk, as their government, as their show of work. The only real feeling was a desire to get appointed to a trading-post where ivory was to be had, so that they could earn percentages. They intrigued and slandered and hated each other only on that account,—but as to effectually lifting a little finger—oh no. By heavens! there is something after all in the world allowing one man to steal a horse while another must not look at a halter. Steal a horse straight out. Very well. He has done it. Perhaps he can ride. But there is a way of looking at a halter that would provoke the most charitable of saints into a kick.

"I had no idea why he wanted to be sociable, but as we chatted in there it suddenly occurred to me the fellow was trying to get at something—in fact, pumping me. He alluded constantly to Europe, to the people I was supposed to know there—putting leading questions as to my acquaintances in the sepulchral city, and so on. His little eyes glittered like mica discs with curiosity, though he tried to keep up a bit of superciliousness.* At first I was astonished, but very soon I became awfully curious to see what he would find out from me. I couldn't possibly imagine what I had in me to make it worth his while. His allusions were Chinese to me. It was very pretty to see how he baffled himself, for in truth my body was full of chills, and my head had nothing in it but that wretched steamboat business. It was evident he took me for a perfectly shameless prevaricator.* At last he got angry, and, to conceal a movement of furious annoyance, he yawned. I rose. Then I noticed a small sketch in oils, on a panel, representing a woman, draped and blindfolded, carrying a lighted torch. The background was sombre—almost black. The movement of the woman was stately, and the effect of the torchlight on the face was sinister.

"It arrested me, and he stood by, civilly holding a half-pint bottle of champagne (medical comforts) with the candle stuck in it. To my question he said Mr. Kurtz had painted this—in this very station more than a year ago—while waiting for means to go to his trading-post. 'Tell me, pray,' said I, 'who is this Mr. Kurtz?'

"'The chief of the Inner Station,' he answered in a short tone, looking away. 'Much obliged,' I said, laughing. 'And you are the brickmaker of the Central Station. Every one knows that.' He was silent for a while. 'He is a prodigy,' he said at last. 'He is an emissary of pity, and science, and

progress, and devil knows what else. We want,' he began to declaim suddenly, 'for the guidance of the cause entrusted to us by Europe, so to speak, higher intelligence, wide sympathies, a singleness of purpose.' 'Who says that?' I asked. 'Lots of them,' he replied. 'Some even write that; and so he comes here, a special being, as you ought to know.' 'Why ought I to know?' I interrupted, really surprised. He paid no attention. 'Yes. To-day he is chief of the best station, next year he will be assistant-manager, two years more and...but I daresay you know what he will be in two years' time. You are of the new gang—the gang of virtue. The same people who sent him specially also recommended you. Oh, don't say no. I've my own eyes to trust.' Light dawned upon me. My dear aunt's influential acquaintances were producing an unexpected effect upon that young man. I nearly burst into a laugh. 'Do you read the Company's confidential correspondence?' I asked. He hadn't a word to say. It was great fun. 'When Mr. Kurtz,' I continued severely, 'is General Manager, you won't have the opportunity.'

"He blew the candle out suddenly, and we went outside. The moon had risen. Black figures strolled about listlessly, pouring water on the glow, whence proceeded a sound of hissing. Steam ascended in the moonlight; the beaten nigger groaned somewhere. 'What a row the brute makes!' said the indefatigable man with the moustache's, appearing near us. 'Serve him right. Transgression—punishment—bang! Pitiless, pitiless. That's the only way. This will prevent all future conflagrations.* I was just telling the manager'.... He noticed my companion, and became crestfallen all at once. 'Not in bed yet,' he said, with a kind of obsequious* heartiness; 'it's so natural. Ha! Danger—agitation.' He vanished. I went on to the river-side, and the other followed me. I heard a scathing murmur at my ear, 'Heaps of muffs—go to.' The pilgrims could be seen in knots gesticulating, discussing. Several had still their staves in their hands. I verily believe they took these sticks to bed with them. Beyond the fence the forest stood up spectrally in the moonlight, and through the dim stir, through the faint sounds of that lamentable courtyard, the silence of the land went home to one's very heart—its mystery, its greatness, the amazing reality of its concealed life. The hurt nigger moaned feebly somewhere near by, and then fetched a deep sigh that made me mend my pace away from there. I felt a hand introducing itself under my arm. 'My dear sir,' said the fellow, 'I don't want to be misunderstood, and especially by you, who will see Mr. Kurtz long before I can have that pleasure. I wouldn't like him to get a false idea of my disposition....'

"I let him run on, this papier-mache Mephistopheles, and it seemed to me that if I tried I could poke my forefinger through him, and find nothing inside but a little loose dirt, maybe. He, don't you see, had been planning to be assistant-manager by-and-by under the present man, and I could see that the coming of that Kurtz had upset them both not a little. He talked precipitately, and I did not try to stop him. I had my shoulders against the wreck of my steamer, hauled up on the slope like a carcass of some big river animal. The smell of mud, of primeval mud, by Jove! was in my nostrils, the high stillness of primeval forest was before my eyes; there were shiny patches on the black creek. The moon had spread over everything a thin layer of silver—over the rank grass, over the mud, upon the wall of matted vegetation standing higher than the wall of a temple, over the great river I could see through a sombre gap glittering, glittering, as it flowed broadly by without a murmur. All this was great, expectant, mute, while the man jabbered about himself. I wondered whether the stillness on the face of the immensity looking at us two were meant as an appeal or as a menace. What were we who had strayed in here? Could we handle that dumb thing, or would it handle us? I felt how big, how confoundedly big, was that thing that couldn't talk and perhaps was deaf as well. What was in there? I could see a little ivory coming out from there, and I had heard Mr. Kurtz was in there. I had heard enough about it too—God knows! Yet somehow it didn't bring any image with it—no more than if I had been told an angel or a fiend was in there. I believed it in the same way one of you might believe there are inhabitants in the planet Mars. I knew once a Scotch sailmaker who was certain, dead sure, there were people in Mars. If you asked him for some idea how they looked and behaved, he would get shy and mutter something about 'walking on all-fours.' If you as much as smiled, he would—though a man of sixty—offer to fight you. I would not have gone so far as to fight for Kurtz, but I went for him near enough to a lie. You know I hate, detest, and can't bear a lie, not because I am straighter than the rest of us, but simply because it appals me. There is a taint of death, a flavour of mortality in lies,— which is exactly what I hate and detest in the world—what I want to forget. It makes me miserable and sick, like biting something rotten would do. Temperament, I suppose. Well, I went near enough to it by letting the young fool there believe anything he liked to imagine as to my influence in Europe. I became in an instant as much of a pretense as the rest of the bewitched pilgrims. This simply because I had a notion it somehow would be of help to that Kurtz whom at the time I did not see—you understand. He was just a word for me. I did not see the man in the name any more than you

do. Do you see him? Do you see the story? Do you see anything? It seems to me I am trying to tell you a dream—making a vain attempt, because no relation of a dream can convey the dream-sensation, that commingling of absurdity, surprise, and bewilderment in a tremor of struggling revolt, that notion of being captured by the incredible which is of the very essence of dreams...."

He was silent for a while.

"...No, it is impossible; it is impossible to convey the life-sensation of any given epoch of one's existence—that which makes its truth, its meaning—its subtle and penetrating essence. It is impossible. We live, as we dream— alone...."

He paused again as if reflecting, then added—

"Of course in this you fellows see more than I could then. You see me, whom you know...."

It had become so pitch dark that we listeners could hardly see one another. For a long time already he, sitting apart, had been no more to us than a voice. There was not a word from anybody. The others might have been asleep, but I was awake. I listened, I listened on the watch for the sentence, for the word, that would give me the clue to the faint uneasiness inspired by this narrative that seemed to shape itself without human lips in the heavy night-air of the river.

"... Yes—I let him run on," Marlow began again, "and think what he pleased about the powers that were behind me. I did! And there was nothing behind me! There was nothing but that wretched, old, mangled steamboat I was leaning against, while he talked fluently about 'the necessity for every man to get on.' 'And when one comes out here, you conceive, it is not to gaze at the moon.' Mr. Kurtz was a 'universal genius,' but even a genius would find it easier to work with 'adequate tools—intelligent men.' He did not make bricks—why, there was a physical impossibility in the way—as I was well aware; and if he did secretarial work for the manager, it was because 'no sensible man rejects wantonly the confidence of his superiors.' Did I see it? I saw it. What more did I want? What I really wanted was rivets, by heaven! Rivets. To get on with the work—to stop the hole. Rivets I wanted. There were cases of them down at the coast—cases—piled up—burst—split! You kicked a loose rivet at every second step in that station yard on the hillside. Rivets had rolled into the grove of death. You could fill your pockets with rivets for the trouble of stooping down—and there wasn't one rivet to be found where it was wanted.

We had plates that would do, but nothing to fasten them with. And every week the messenger, a lone negro, letter-bag on shoulder and staff in hand, left our station for the coast. And several times a week a coast caravan came in with trade goods,—ghastly glazed calico that made you shudder only to look at it, glass beads value about a penny a quart, confounded spotted cotton handkerchiefs. And no rivets. Three carriers could have brought all that was wanted to set that steamboat afloat.

"He was becoming confidential now, but I fancy my unresponsive attitude must have exasperated him at last, for he judged it necessary to inform me he feared neither God nor devil, let alone any mere man. I said I could see that very well, but what I wanted was a certain quantity of rivets—and rivets were what really Mr. Kurtz wanted, if he had only known it. Now letters went to the coast every week....'My dear sir,' he cried, 'I write from dictation.' I demanded rivets. There was a way—for an intelligent man. He changed his manner; became very cold, and suddenly began to talk about a hippopotamus; wondered whether sleeping in the steamer (I stuck to my salvage night and day) I wasn't disturbed. There was an old hippo that had the bad habit of getting out on the bank and roaming at night over the station grounds. The pilgrims used to turn out in a body and empty every rifle they could lay hands on at him. Some even had sat up o' nights for him. All this energy was wasted, though. 'That animal has a charmed life,' he said; 'but you can say this only of brutes in this country. No man—you apprehend me?—no man here bears a charmed life.' He stood there for a moment in the moonlight with his delicate hooked nose set a little askew, and his mica eyes glittering without a wink. Then, with a curt goodnight, he strode off. I could see he was disturbed and considerably puzzled, which made me feel more hopeful than I had been for days. It was a great comfort to turn from that chap to my influential friend, the battered, twisted, ruined, tin-pot steamboat. I clambered on board. She rang under my feet like an empty Huntley and Palmer biscuit-tin kicked along a gutter; she was nothing so solid in make, and rather less pretty in shape, but I had expended enough hard work on her to make me love her. No influential friend would have served me better. She had given me a chance to come out a bit—to find out what I could do. No, I don't like work. I had rather laze about and think of all the fine things that can be done. I don't like work—no man does—but I like what is in the work—the chance to find yourself. Your own reality—for yourself, not for others—what no other man can ever know. They can only see the mere show, and never can tell what it really means.

"I was not surprised to see somebody sitting aft, on the deck, with his legs dangling over the mud. You see I rather chummed with the few mechanics there were in that station, whom the other pilgrims naturally despised—on account of their imperfect manners, I suppose. This was the foreman—a boiler-maker by trade—a good worker. He was a lank, bony, yellow-faced man, with big intense eyes. His aspect was worried, and his head was as bald as the palm of my hand; but his hair in falling seemed to have stuck to his chin, and had prospered in the new locality, for his beard hung down to his waist. He was a widower with six young children (he had left them in charge of a sister of his to come out there), and the passion of his life was pigeon-flying. He was an enthusiast and a connoisseur. He raved about pigeons. After work hours he used sometimes to come over from his hut for a talk about his children and his pigeons. At work, when he had to crawl in the mud under the bottom of the steamboat, he would tie up that beard of his in a kind of white serviette he brought for the purpose. It had loops to go over his ears. In the evening he could be seen squatted on the bank rinsing that wrapper in the creek with great care, then spreading it solemnly on a bush to dry.

"I slapped him on the back and shouted 'We shall have rivets!' He scrambled to his feet exclaiming 'No! Rivets!' as though he couldn't believe his ears. Then in a low voice, 'You...eh?' I don't know why we behaved like lunatics. I put my finger to the side of my nose and nodded mysteriously. 'Good for you!' he cried, snapped his fingers above his head, lifting one foot. I tried a jig. We capered on the iron deck. A frightful clatter came out of that hulk, and the virgin forest on the other bank of the creek sent it back in a thundering roll upon the sleeping station. It must have made some of the pilgrims sit up in their hovels. A dark figure obscured the lighted doorway of the manager's hut, vanished, then, a second or so after, the doorway itself vanished too. We stopped, and the silence driven away by the stamping of our feet flowed back again from the recesses of the land. The great wall of vegetation, an exuberant and entangled mass of trunks, branches, leaves, boughs, festoons, motionless in the moonlight, was like a rioting invasion of soundless life, a rolling wave of plants, piled up, crested, ready to topple over the creek, to sweep every little man of us out of his little existence. And it moved not. A deadened burst of mighty splashes and snorts reached us from afar, as though an ichthyosaurus had been taking a bath of glitter in the great river. 'After all,' said the boiler-maker in a reasonable tone, 'why shouldn't we get the rivets?' Why not, indeed! I did not know of any reason why we shouldn't. 'They'll come in three weeks,' I said confidently.

"But they didn't. Instead came an invasion, an infliction, a visitation. It came in sections during the next three weeks, each section headed by a donkey carrying a white man in new clothes and tan shoes, bowing from that elevation right and left to the impressed pilgrims. A quarrelsome band of footsore sulky niggers trod on the heels of the donkey. A lot of tents, camp-stools, tin boxes, white cases, brown bales would be shot down in the courtyard, and the air of mystery would deepen a little over the muddle of the station. Five such installments came, with their absurd air of disorderly flight with the loot of innumerable outfit shops and provision stores, that, one would think, they were lugging, after a raid, into the wilderness for equitable division. It was an inextricable mess of things decent in themselves but that human folly made look like the spoils of thieving.

"This devoted band called itself the Eldorado Expedition, and I believe they were sworn to secrecy. Their talk, however, was the talk of sordid buccaneers. It was reckless without hardihood,* greedy without audacity, and cruel without courage. There was not an atom of foresight or of serious intention in the whole batch of them, and they did not seem aware these things are wanted for the work of the world. Their desire was to tear treasure out of the bowels of the land with no more moral purpose at the back of it than there is in burglars breaking into a safe. Who paid the expenses of the noble enterprise I don't know; but the uncle of our manager was leader of that lot.

"In exterior he resembled a butcher in a poor neighbourhood, and his eyes had a look of sleepy cunning. He carried his fat paunch with ostentation on his short legs, and all the time his gang infested the station spoke to no one but his nephew. You could see these two roaming about all day long with their heads close together in an everlasting confab.

"I had given up worrying myself about the rivets. One's capacity for that kind of folly is more limited than you would suppose. I said Hang!—and let things slide. I had plenty of time for meditation, and now and then I would give some thought to Kurtz. I wasn't very curious about him. No. Still, I was curious to see whether this man, who had come out equipped with moral ideas of some sort, would climb to the top after all, and how he would set about his work when there."

(**Part Two** from *Blackwood's Edinburgh Magazine*, March 1899)

"One evening as I was lying flat on the deck of my steamboat, I heard voices approaching—and there were the nephew and the uncle strolling along the bank. I laid my head on my arm again, and had nearly lost myself in a doze, when somebody said in my ear, as it were: 'I am as harmless as a little child, but I don't like to be dictated to. Am I the manager—or am I not? I was ordered to send him there. It's incredible.'...I became aware that the two were standing on the shore alongside the forepart of the steamboat, just below my head. I did not move; it did not occur to me to move. I was sleepy. 'It is unpleasant,' grunted the uncle. 'He has asked the Administration to be sent there,' said the other, 'with the idea of showing what he could do; and I was instructed accordingly. Look at the influence that man must have. Is it not frightful?' They both agreed it was frightful, then made several bizarre remarks: 'Make rain and fine weather—one man—the Council—by the nose'—bits of absurd sentences that got the better of my drowsiness, so that I had pretty near the whole of my wits about me when the uncle said, 'The climate may do away with this difficulty for you. Is he alone there?' 'Yes,' answered the manager; 'he sent his assistant down the river with a note to me in these terms: "Clear this poor devil out of the country, and don't bother sending more of that sort. I had rather be alone than have the kind of men you can dispose of with me." It was more than a year ago. Can you imagine such impudence!' 'Anything since then?' asked the other, hoarsely. 'Ivory,' jerked the nephew; 'lots of it—prime sort—lots—most annoying, from him.' 'And with that?' questioned the heavy rumble. 'Invoice,' was the reply fired out, so to speak. Then silence. They had been talking about Kurtz.

"I was broad awake by this time, but, lying perfectly at ease, remained still, having no inducement to change my position. 'How did that ivory come all this way?' growled the elder man, who seemed very vexed. The other explained that it had come with a fleet of canoes in charge of an English half-caste clerk Kurtz had with him; that Kurtz had apparently intended to return himself, the station being by that time bare of goods and stores, but after coming three hundred miles, had suddenly decided to go back, which he started to do alone in a small dug-out with four paddlers, leaving the half-caste to continue down the river with the ivory. The two fellows there seemed astounded at anybody attempting such a thing. They were at a loss for an adequate motive. As to me, I seemed to see Kurtz for the first time. It was a distinct glimpse. The dug-out, four paddling savages, and the lone white man turning his back suddenly on the headquarters, on relief, on thoughts of home—

perhaps; setting his face towards the depths of the wilderness, towards his empty and desolate station. I did not know the motive. Perhaps he was just simply a fine fellow who stuck to his work for its own sake. His name, you understand, had not been pronounced once. He was 'that man.' The half-caste, who, as far as I could see, had conducted a difficult trip with great prudence and pluck, was invariably alluded to as 'that scoundrel.' The 'scoundrel' had said the 'man' had been ill—had recovered.... The two below me moved away then a few paces, and strolled back and forth at some little distance. I heard: 'Military post—doctor—two hundred miles—quite alone now—unavoidable delays— nine months—no news—strange rumors.' They approached again, just as the manager was saying, 'Nobody unless a species of wandering trader—a pestilential fellow, snapping ivory from the natives.' Who was it they were talking about now? I gathered in snatches that this was some man supposed to be in Kurtz's district, and of whom the manager did not approve. 'We will not be free from unfair competition till one of these fellows is hanged for an example,' he said. 'Certainly,' grunted the other; 'get him hanged! Why not? Anything—anything can be done in this country. That's what I say; nobody here, you understand, here can endanger your position. And why? You stand the climate—you outlast them all. The danger is in Europe; but there before I left I took care to—' They moved off and whispered, then their voices rose again. 'The extraordinary series of delays is not my fault. I did my possible.' The fat man sighed, 'Very sad.' 'And the pestiferous absurdity of his talk,' continued the other; 'he bothered me enough when he was here. "Each station should be like a beacon on the road towards better things, a centre for trade of course, but also for humanizing, improving, instructing." Conceive you—that ass! And he wants to be manager! No, it's—' Here he got choked by excessive indignation, and I lifted my head the least bit. I was surprised to see how near they were—right under me. I could have spat upon their hats. They were looking on the ground, absorbed in thought. The manager was switching his leg with a slender twig: his sagacious relative lifted his head. 'You have been well since you came out this time?' he asked. The other gave a start. 'Who? I? Oh! Like a charm—like a charm. But the rest—oh, my goodness! All sick. They die so quick, too, that I haven't the time to send them out of the country—it's incredible!' 'H'm. Just so,' grunted the uncle. 'Ah! my boy, trust to this—I say, trust to this.' I saw him extend his short flipper of an arm for a semi-

circular gesture that took in the forest, the creek, the mud, the river—seemed to beckon with a dishonouring flourish before the sunlit face of the land a treacherous appeal to the lurking death, to the hidden evil, to the profound darkness of its heart. It was so startling that I leaped to my feet and looked back at the edge of the forest, as though I had expected an answer of some sort to that black display of confidence. You know the foolish notions that come to one sometimes. The high stillness confronted these two figures with its ominous patience, waiting for the passing away of a fantastic invasion.

"They swore aloud together—out of sheer fright, I believe—then pretending not to know anything of my existence, turned back to the station. The sun was low; and leaning forward side by side, they seemed to be tugging painfully uphill their two ridiculous shadows of unequal length, that trailed behind them slowly over the tall grass without bending a single blade.

"In a few days the Eldorado Expedition went into the patient wilderness, that closed upon them as the sea closes over a diver. Long afterwards the news came that all the donkeys were dead. I know nothing as to the fate of the less valuable animals. They, no doubt, like the rest of us, found what they deserved. I did not inquire. I was then rather excited at the prospect of meeting Kurtz very soon. When I say very soon I mean comparatively. It was just two months from the day we left the creek when we came to the bank below Kurtz's station.

"Going up that river was like travelling back to the earliest beginnings of the world, when vegetation rioted on the earth and the big trees were kings. An empty stream, a great silence, an impenetrable forest. The air was warm, thick, heavy, sluggish. There was no joy in the brilliance of sunshine. The long stretches of the waterway ran on, deserted, into the gloom of overshadowed distances. On silvery sandbanks hippos and alligators sunned themselves side by side. The broadening waters flowed through a mob of wooded islands; you lost your way on that river as you would in a desert, and butted all day long against shoals, trying to find the channel, till you thought yourself bewitched and cut off for ever from everything you had known once—somewhere—far away—in another existence perhaps. There were moments when one's past came back to one, as it will sometimes when you have not a moment to spare to yourself; but it came in the shape of an unrestful and noisy dream, remembered with wonder amongst the overwhelming realities of this strange world of plants, and water, and silence. And this stillness of life did not in the least resemble a peace. It was the stillness of an implacable force brooding over an inscrutable intention. It looked at you with a vengeful aspect. I got used to it afterwards; I did not see it any more; I had no time. I had to keep guessing at the channel; I had to discern, mostly by inspiration, the signs of hidden banks; I watched for sunken stones; I was learning to clap my teeth smartly before my heart flew out, when I shaved by a fluke some infernal sly old snag that would have ripped the life out of the tin-pot steamboat and drowned all the pilgrims; I had to keep a look-out for the signs of dead wood we could cut up in the night for the next day's steaming. When you have to attend to things of that sort, to the mere incidents of the surface, the reality—the reality, I tell you—fades. The inner truth is hidden—luckily, luckily. But I felt it all the same; I felt often its mysterious stillness watching me at my monkey tricks, just as it watches you fellows performing on your respective tight-ropes for—what is it? half-a-crown a tumble—"

"Try to be civil, Marlow," growled a voice, and I knew there was at least one listener awake besides myself.

"I beg your pardon. I forgot the heartache which makes up the rest of the price. And indeed what does the price matter, if the trick be well done? You do your tricks very well. And I didn't do badly either, since I managed not to sink that steamboat on my first trip. It's a wonder to me yet. Imagine a blindfolded man set to drive a van over a bad road. I sweated and shivered over that business considerably, I can tell you. After all, for a seaman, to scrape the bottom of the thing that's supposed to float all the time under his care is the unpardonable sin. No one may know of it, but you never forget the thump—eh? A blow on the very heart. You remember it, you dream of it, you wake up at night and think of it—years after—and go hot and cold all over. I don't pretend to say that steamboat floated all the time. More than once she had to wade for a bit, with twenty cannibals splashing around and pushing. We had enlisted some of these chaps on the way for a crew. Fine fellows—cannibals—in their place. They were men one could work with, and I am grateful to them. And, after all, they did not eat each other before my face: they had brought along a provision of hippo-meat which went rotten, and made the mystery of the wilderness stink in my nostrils. Phoo! I can sniff it now. I had the manager on board and three or four pilgrims with their staves—all complete. Sometimes we came upon a station close by the bank, clinging to the skirts of the unknown, and the white men rushing out of a tumble-down hovel, with great gestures of joy and surprise and welcome, seemed very strange,—had the appearance of being held there captive by a spell. The word *ivory* would ring in the air for a while—and on we went again into the silence, along empty reaches, round the still bends, between the high walls of our winding way, reverberating in hollow claps the ponderous beat of the stern-wheel. Trees, trees, millions of trees, massive, immense, running up high; and at their foot, hugging the bank against the stream, crept the little begrimed steamboat, like a sluggish beetle crawling on the floor of a lofty portico. It made you feel very small, very lost, and yet it was not altogether depressing that feeling. After all, if you were small, the grimy beetle crawled on—which was just what you wanted it to do. Where the pilgrims imagined it crawled to I don't know. To some place where they expected to get something, I bet! For me it crawled towards Kurtz—exclusively; but when the steam-pipes started leaking we crawled very slow. The reaches opened before us and closed behind, as if the forest had stepped leisurely across the water to bar the way for our return. We penetrated deeper and deeper into the heart of darkness. It was very quiet there. At night sometimes the roll of drums behind the curtain of trees would run up the river and remain sustained faintly, as if hovering in the air high over our heads, till the first break of day. Whether it meant war, peace, or prayer we could not tell. The dawns were heralded by the descent of a chill stillness; the wood-cutters slept, their fires burned low; the snapping of a twig would make you start. We were wanderers on a prehistoric earth, on an earth that wore the aspect of an unknown planet. We could have fancied ourselves the first of men taking possession of an accursed inheritance, to be subdued at the cost of profound anguish and of excessive toil. But suddenly, as we struggled round a bend, there would be a glimpse of rush walls, of peaked grass-roofs, a burst of yells, a whirl of black limbs, a mass of hands clapping, of feet stamping, of bodies swaying, of eyes rolling, under the droop of heavy and motionless foliage. The steamer toiled along slowly on the edge of a black and incomprehensible frenzy. The prehistoric man was cursing us, praying to us, welcoming us—who could tell? We were cut off from the comprehension of our surroundings; we glided past like phantoms, wondering and secretly appalled, as sane men would be before an enthusiastic outbreak in a madhouse. We could not understand, because we were too far and could not remember, because we were travelling in the night of first ages, of those ages that are gone, leaving hardly a sign—and no memories.

"The earth seemed unearthly. We are accustomed to look upon the shackled form of a conquered monster, but there—there you could look at a thing monstrous and free. It was unearthly, and the men were—No, they were not inhuman. Well, you know, that was the worst of it—this suspicion of their not being inhuman. It would come slowly to one. They howled, and leaped, and spun, and made horrid faces; but what thrilled you was just the thought of their humanity—like yours—the thought of your remote kinship with this wild and passionate uproar. Ugly. Yes, it was ugly enough; but if you were man enough you would admit to yourself that there was in you just the faintest trace of a response to the terrible frankness of that noise, a dim suspicion of there being a meaning in it which you—you so remote from the night of first ages—could comprehend. And why not? The mind of man is capable of anything—because everything is in it, all the past as well as all the future. What was there after all? Joy, fear, sorrow, devotion, valour, rage—who can tell?—but truth—truth stripped of its cloak of time. Let the fool gape and shudder—the man knows, and can look on without a wink. But he must at least be as much of a man as these on the shore. He must meet that truth with his own true stuff—with his own inborn strength. Principles? Principles won't do. Acquisitions, clothes, pretty rags—rags that would fly off at the first good shake. No; you want a deliberate belief. An appeal to me in this fiendish row—is there? Very well; I hear; I admit, but I have a voice too, and for good or evil mine is the speech that cannot be silenced. Of course, a fool, what with sheer fright and fine sentiments, is always safe. Who's that grunting? You wonder I didn't go ashore for a howl and a dance? Well, no—I didn't. Fine sentiments, you say? Fine sentiments be hanged! I had no time. I had to mess about with white-lead and strips of woolen blanket helping to put bandages on those leaky steam-pipes—I tell you. I had to watch the steering, and circumvent those snags, and get the tin-pot along by hook or by crook. There was surface-truth enough in these things to save a wiser man. And between whiles I had to look after the savage who was fireman. He was an improved specimen; he could fire up a vertical boiler. He was there below me, and, upon my word, to look at him was as edifying as seeing a dog in a parody of breeches and a feather hat, walking on his hind-legs. A few months of training had done for that really fine chap. He squinted at the steam-gauge and at the water-gauge with an evident effort of intrepidity—and he had filed teeth too, the poor devil, and the wool of his pate shaved into queer patterns, and three ornamental scars on each of his cheeks. He ought to have been clapping his hands and stamping his feet on the bank, instead of which he was hard at work, a thrall to strange witchcraft, full of improving knowledge. He was useful because he had been instructed; and what he knew was this—

that should the water in that transparent thing disappear, the evil spirit inside the boiler would get angry through the greatness of his thirst, and take a terrible vengeance. So he sweated and fired up and watched the glass fearfully (with an impromptu charm, made of rags, tied to his arm, and a piece of polished bone, as big as a watch, stuck flatways through his lower lip), while the wooded banks slipped past us slowly, the short noise was left behind, the interminable miles of silence—and we crept on, towards Kurtz. But the snags were thick, the water was treacherous and shallow, the boiler seemed indeed to have a sulky devil in it, and thus neither that fireman nor I had any time to peer into our creepy thoughts.

"Some fifty miles below the Inner Station we came upon a hut of reeds, an inclined and melancholy pole, with the unrecognizable tatters of what had been a flag of some sort flying from it, and a neatly stacked wood-pile. This was unexpected. We came to the bank, and on the stack of firewood found a flat piece of board with some faded pencil-writing on it. When deciphered it said: 'Wood for you. Hurry up. Approach cautiously.' There was a signature, but it was illegible—not Kurtz—a much longer word. Hurry up. Where? Up the river? 'Approach cautiously.' We had not done so. But the warning could not have been meant for the place where it could be only found after approach. Something was wrong above. But what—and how much? That was the question. We commented adversely upon the imbecility of that telegraphic style. The bush around said nothing, and would not let us look very far, either. A torn curtain of red twill hung in the doorway of the hut, and flapped sadly in our faces. The dwelling was dismantled; but we could see a white man had lived there not very long ago. There remained a rude table—a plank on two posts; a heap of rubbish reposed in a dark corner, and by the door I picked up a book. It had lost its covers, and the pages had been thumbed into a state of extremely dirty softness; but the back had been lovingly stitched afresh with white cotton thread, which looked clean yet. It was an extraordinary find. Its title was, *An Inquiry into some Points of Seamanship*, by a man Tower, Towson—some such name—Master in His Majesty's Navy. The matter looked dreary reading enough, with illustrative diagrams and repulsive tables of figures, and the copy was sixty years old. I handled this amazing antiquity with the greatest possible tenderness, lest it should dissolve in my hands. Within, Towson or Towser was inquiring earnestly into the breaking strain of ships' chains and tackle, and other such matters. Not a very enthralling book; but at the first glance you could see there a singleness of intention, an honest concern for the right way of going to work, which made these humble pages, thought out so many years ago, luminous with another than a professional light. The simple old sailor, with his talk of chains and purchases, made me forget the jungle and the pilgrims in a delicious sensation of having come upon something unmistakably real. Such a book being there was wonderful enough; but still more astounding were the notes pencilled in the margin, and plainly referring to the text. I couldn't believe my eyes! They were in cipher!* Yes, it looked like cipher. Fancy a man lugging with him a book of that description into this nowhere and studying it—and making notes—in cipher at that! It was an extravagant mystery.

"I had been dimly aware for some time of a worrying noise, and when I lifted my eyes I saw the wood-pile was gone, and the manager, aided by all the pilgrims, was shouting at me from the riverside. I slipped the book into my pocket. I assure you to leave off reading was like tearing myself away from the shelter of an old and solid friendship.

"I started the lame engine ahead. 'It must be this miserable trader—this intruder,' exclaimed the manager, looking back malevolently at the place we had left. 'He must be English,' I said. 'It will not save him from getting into trouble if he is not careful,' muttered the manager darkly. I observed with assumed innocence that no man was safe from trouble in this world.

"The current was more rapid now, the steamer seemed at her last gasp, the stern-wheel flopped languidly,* and I caught myself listening on tiptoe for the next beat of the float, for in sober truth I expected the wretched thing to give up every moment. It was like watching the last flickers of a life. But still we crawled. Sometimes I would pick out a tree a little way ahead to measure our progress towards Kurtz by, but I lost it invariably before we got abreast. To keep the eyes so long on one thing was too much for human patience. The manager displayed a beautiful resignation. I fretted and fumed and took to arguing with myself whether or no I would talk openly with Kurtz; but before I could come to any conclusion it occurred to me that my speech or my silence, indeed any action of mine, would be a mere futility. What did it matter what any one knew or ignored? What did it matter who was manager? One gets sometimes such a flash of insight. The essentials of this affair lay deep under the surface, beyond my reach, and beyond my power of meddling.

"Towards the evening of the second day we judged ourselves about eight miles from Kurtz's station. I wanted to push on; but the manager looked grave, and told me the navigation up there was so dangerous that it would be advisable, the sun being very low already, to wait where we were till next morning. Moreover, he pointed out that if the warning to approach cautiously were to be followed, we must approach in daylight—not at dusk, or in the dark. This was sensible enough. Eight miles meant nearly three hours' steaming for us, and I could also see suspicious ripples at the upper end of the reach. Nevertheless, I was annoyed beyond expression at the delay, and most unreasonably too, since one more night could not matter much after so many months. As we had plenty of wood, and caution was the word, I brought up in the middle of the stream. The reach was narrow, straight, with high sides like a railway cutting. The dusk came gliding into it long before the sun had set. The current ran smooth and swift, but a dumb immobility sat on the banks. The living trees, lashed together by the creepers and every living bush of the undergrowth, might have been changed into stone, even to the slenderest twig, to the lightest leaf. It was not sleep—it seemed unnatural, like a state of trance. Not the faintest sound of any kind could be heard. You looked on amazed, and began to suspect yourself of being deaf—then the night came suddenly, and struck you blind as well. About three in the morning some large fish leaped, and the loud splash made me jump as though a gun had been fired. When the sun rose there was a white fog, very warm and clammy, and more blinding than the night. It did not shift or drive; it was just there, standing all round you like something solid. At eight or nine, perhaps, it lifted as a shutter lifts. We had a glimpse of the towering multitude of trees, of the immense matted jungle, with the blazing little ball of the sun hanging over it—all perfectly still—and then the white shutter came down again, smoothly, as if sliding in greased grooves. I ordered the chain, which we had begun to heave in, to be paid out again. Before it stopped running with a muffled rattle, a cry, a very loud cry, as of infinite desolation, soared slowly in the opaque air. It ceased. A complaining clamour, modulated in savage discords, filled our ears. The sheer unexpectedness of it made my hair stir under my cap. I don't know how it struck the others: to me it seemed as though the mist itself had screamed, so suddenly, and apparently from all sides at once, did this tumultuous and mournful uproar arise. It culminated in a hurried outbreak of almost intolerably excessive shrieking, which stopped short, leaving us stiffened in a variety of silly attitudes, and obstinately listening to the nearly as appalling and excessive silence. 'Good God! What is the meaning——?' stammered at my elbow one of the pilgrims—a little fat man, with sandy hair and red whiskers, who wore side-spring boots, and pink pyjamas tucked into his socks. Two others remained open-mouthed a whole minute, then dashed into the little cabin, to rush out incontinently* and stand darting scared glances, with Winchesters at 'ready' in their hands. What we could see was just the steamer we were on, her outlines blurred as though she had been on the point of dissolving, and a misty strip of water, perhaps two feet broad, around her—and that was all. The rest of the world was nowhere, as far as our eyes and ears were concerned. Just nowhere. Gone, disappeared; swept off without leaving a whisper or a shadow behind.

"I went forward, and ordered the chain to be hauled in short, so as to be ready to trip the anchor and move the steamboat at once if necessary. 'Will they attack?' whispered an awed voice. 'We will all be butchered in this fog,' murmured another. The faces twitched with the strain, the hands trembled slightly, the eyes forgot to wink. It was very curious to see the contrast of expressions of the white men and of the black fellows of our crew, who were as much strangers to that part of the river as we, though their homes were only eight hundred miles away. The whites, of course greatly discomposed, had besides a curious look of being painfully shocked by such an outrageous row. The others had an alert, naturally interested expression; but their faces were essentially quiet, even those of the one or two who grinned as they hauled at the chain. Several exchanged short, grunting phrases, which seemed to settle the matter to their satisfaction. Their headman, a young, broad-chested black, severely draped in dark-blue fringed cloths, with fierce nostrils and his hair all done up artfully in oily ringlets, stood near me. 'Aha!' I said, just for good fellowship's sake. 'Catch 'im,' he snapped, with a bloodshot widening of his eyes and a flash of sharp teeth— 'catch 'im. Give 'im to us.' 'To you, eh?' I asked; 'what would you do with them?' 'Eat 'im!' he said, curtly, and, leaning his elbow on the rail, looked out into the fog in a dignified and profoundly pensive attitude. I would no doubt have been properly horrified, had it not occurred to me that he and his chaps must be very hungry: that they must have been growing increasingly hungry for at least this month past. They had been engaged for six months (I don't think a single one of them had any clear idea of time, as we at the end of countless ages have. They still belonged to the beginnings of time—had no inherited experience to teach them, as it were), and of course, as long as there was a piece of paper written over in accordance with some farcical law or other made down the river, it didn't enter anybody's head to trouble how they would live. Certainly they had brought with them some rotten hippo-meat, which couldn't have lasted very long, anyway, even if the pilgrims hadn't, in the midst of a shocking hullabaloo, thrown a considerable quantity of it overboard. It looked like a high-handed proceeding; but it was really a case of legitimate self-defence. You can't

breathe dead hippo waking, sleeping, and eating, and at the same time keep your precarious grip on existence. Besides that, they had given them every week three pieces of brass wire, each about nine inches long; and the theory was they were to buy their provisions with that currency in river-side villages. You can see how that worked. There were either no villages, or the people were hostile, or the director, who like the rest of us fed out of tins, with an occasional old he-goat thrown in, didn't want to stop the steamer for some more or less recondite reason. So, unless they swallowed the wire itself, or made loops of it to snare the fishes with, I don't see what good their extravagant salary could be to them. I must say it was paid with a regularity worthy of a large and honourable trading company. For the rest, the only thing to eat—though it didn't look eatable in the least—I saw in their possession was a few lumps of some stuff like half-cooked dough, of a dirty lavender colour, they kept wrapped in leaves, and now and then swallowed a piece of, but so small that it seemed done more for the look of the thing than for any serious purpose of sustenance. Why in the name of all the gnawing devils of hunger they didn't go for us—they were thirty to five—and have a good tuck in for once, amazes me now when I think of it. They were big powerful men, with not much capacity to weigh the consequences, with courage, with strength, even yet, though their skins were no longer glossy and their muscles no longer hard. And I saw that something restraining, one of those human secrets that baffle probability, had come into play there. I looked at them with a swift quickening of interest—not because it occurred to me I might be eaten by them before very long, though I own to you that just then I perceived—in a new light, as it were—how unwholesome the pilgrims looked, and I hoped, yes, I positively hoped, that my aspect was not so— what shall I say?—so—unappetising: a touch of fantastic vanity which fitted well with the dream-sensation that pervaded all my days at that time. Perhaps I had a little fever too. One can't live with one's finger everlastingly on one's pulse. I had often 'a little fever,' or a little touch of other things—the playful paw-strokes of the wilderness, the preliminary trifling before the more serious onslaught which came in due course. Yes; I looked at them as you would on any human being, with a curiosity of their impulses, motives, capacities, weaknesses, when brought to the test of an inexorable physical necessity. Restraint! What possible restraint? Was it superstition, disgust, patience, fear—or some kind of primitive honour? No fear can stand up to hunger, no patience can wear it out, disgust simply does not exist where hunger is; and as to superstition, beliefs, and what you may call principles, they are less than chaff in a breeze. Don't you know the devilry of lingering starvation, its exasperating torment, its black thoughts, its sombre and brooding ferocity? Well, I do. It takes a man all his inborn strength to fight hunger properly. It's really easier to face bereavement, dishonour, and the perdition of one's soul—than this kind of prolonged hunger. Sad, but true. And these chaps too had no earthly reason for any kind of scruple. Restraint! I would just as soon have expected restraint from a hyena prowling amongst the corpses of a battlefield. But there was the fact facing me—the fact dazzling, to be seen, like the foam on the depths of the sea, like a ripple on an unfathomable enigma, a mystery greater—when I thought of it—than the curious, inexplicable note of desperate grief in this savage clamour that had swept by us on the river-bank, behind the blind whiteness of the fog.

"Two pilgrims were quarrelling in hurried whispers as to which bank. 'Left.' 'No, no; how can you? Right, right, of course.' 'It is very serious,' said the manager's voice behind me; 'I would be desolated if anything should happen to Mr. Kurtz before we came up.' I looked at him, and had not the slightest doubt he was sincere. He was just the kind of man who would wish to preserve appearances. That was his restraint. But when he muttered something about going on at once, I did not even take the trouble to answer him. I knew, and he knew, that it was impossible. Were we to let go our hold of the bottom, we would be absolutely in the air—in space. We wouldn't be able to tell where we were going to—whether up or down stream, or across—till we fetched against one bank or the other,—and then we wouldn't know at first which it was. Of course I made no move. I had no mind for a smash-up. You couldn't imagine a more deadly place for a shipwreck. Whether drowned at once or not, we were sure to perish speedily in one way or another. 'I authorise you to take all the risks,' he said, after a short silence. 'I refuse to take any,' I said shortly; which was just the answer he expected, though its tone might have surprised him. 'Well, I must defer to your judgment. You are captain,' he said, with marked civility. I turned my shoulder to him in sign of my appreciation, and looked into the fog. How long would it last? It was the most hopeless look-out. The approach to this Kurtz grubbing for ivory in the wretched bush was beset by as many dangers as though he had been an enchanted princess sleeping in a fabulous castle. 'Will they attack, do you think?' asked the manager, in a confidential tone.

"I did not think they would attack, for several obvious reasons. The thick fog was one. If they left the bank in their canoes they would get lost in it, as we would be if we attempted to move. Still, I had also judged the jungle of both banks quite impenetrable—and yet eyes were in it, eyes that had seen us. The river-side bushes were certainly very thick; but the undergrowth behind was evidently penetrable. However, during the short lift I had seen no canoes anywhere in the reach—certainly not abreast of the steamer. But what made the idea of attack inconceivable to me was the nature of the noise—of the cries we had heard. They had not the fierce character boding of immediate hostile intention. Unexpected, wild, and violent as they had been, they had given me an irresistible impression of sorrow. The glimpse of the steamboat had for some reason filled those savages with unrestrained grief. The danger, if any, I expounded, was from our proximity to a great human passion let loose. Even extreme grief may ultimately vent itself in violence—but more generally takes the form of apathy....

"You should have seen the pilgrims stare! They had no heart to grin, or even to revile me; but I believe they thought me gone mad—with fright, maybe. I delivered a regular lecture. My dear boys, it was no good bothering. Keep a look-out? Well, you may guess I watched the fog for the signs of lifting as a cat watches a mouse; but for anything else our eyes were of no more use to us than if we had been buried miles deep in a heap of cotton-wool. It felt like it too—choking, warm, stifling. Besides, all I said, though it sounded extravagant, was absolutely true to fact. What we afterwards alluded to as an attack was really an attempt at repulse. The action was very far from being aggressive—it was not even defensive, in the usual sense: it was undertaken under the stress of desperation, and in its essence was purely protective.

"It developed itself, I should say, two hours after the fog lifted, and its commencement was at a spot, roughly speaking, about a mile and a half below Kurtz's station. We had just floundered and flopped round a bend, when I saw an islet, a mere grassy hummock of bright green, in the middle of the stream. It was the only thing of the kind; but as we opened the reach more, I perceived it was the head of a long sandbank, or rather of a chain of shallow patches stretching down the middle of the river. They were discoloured, just awash, and the whole lot was seen just under the water, exactly as a man's backbone is seen running down the middle of his back under the skin. Now, as far as I did see, I could go to the right or to the left of this. I didn't know either channel, of course. The banks looked pretty well alike, the depth appeared the same; but as I had been informed the station was on the west side, I naturally headed for the western passage.

"No sooner had we fairly entered it than I became aware it was much narrower than I had supposed. To the left of us there was the long uninterrupted shoal, and to the right a high steep bank heavily overgrown with bushes. Above the bush the trees stood in serried ranks. The twigs overhung the current thickly, and from distance to distance a large limb of some tree projected rigidly over the stream. It was then well on in the afternoon, the face of the forest was gloomy, and a broad strip of shadow had already fallen on the water. In this shadow we steamed up—very slowly, as you may imagine. I sheered her well inshore—the water being deepest near the bank, as the sounding-pole informed me.

"One of my hungry and forbearing friends was sounding in the bows just below me. This steamboat was exactly like a decked scow. On the deck there were two little teak-wood houses, with doors and windows. The boiler was in the fore-end, and the machinery right astern. Over the whole there was a light roof, supported on stanchions.* The funnel projected through that roof, and in front of the funnel a small cabin built of light planks served for a pilot-house. It contained a couch, two camp-stools, a loaded Martini-Henry leaning in one corner, a tiny table, and the steering-wheel. It had a wide door in front and a broad shutter at each side. All these were always thrown open, of course. I spent my days perched up there on the extreme fore-end of that roof, before the door. At night I slept, or tried to, on the couch. An athletic black belonging to some coast tribe, and educated by my poor predecessor, was the helmsman. He sported a pair of brass earrings, wore a blue cloth wrapper from the waist to the ankles, and thought all the world of himself. He was the most unstable kind of fool I had ever seen. He steered with no end of a swagger while you were by; but if he lost sight of you, he became instantly the prey of an abject funk, and would let that cripple of a steamboat get the upper hand of him in a minute.

"I was looking down at the sounding-pole, and feeling much annoyed to see at each try a little more of it stick out of that river, when I saw my poleman give up the business suddenly, and stretch himself flat on the deck, without even taking the trouble to haul his pole in. He kept hold on it though, and it trailed in the water. At the same time the fireman, whom I could also see below me, sat down abruptly before his furnace and ducked his head. I was amazed. Then I had to look at the river mighty quick, because there was a snag in the fairway. Sticks, little sticks, were flying about—thick: they were whizzing before my nose, dropping below me, striking behind me against my pilot-house. All this time the river, the shore, the woods, were very quiet—perfectly quiet. I could only hear the heavy splashing thump of the stern-wheel and the patter of these things. We cleared the snag clumsily. Arrows, by Jove! We were being shot at! I stepped in quickly to close the shutter on the land-side. That fool-helmsman, his hands on the spokes, was lifting his knees high, stamping his feet, champing his mouth, like a reined-in horse. Confound him! And we were staggering within ten feet of the bank. I had to lean right out to swing the heavy shutter, and I saw a face amongst the leaves on the level with my own, looking at me very fierce and steady; and then suddenly, as though a veil had been removed from my eyes, I made out, deep in the tangled gloom, naked breasts, arms, legs, glaring eyes—the bush was swarming with human limbs in movement, glistening, of bronze colour. The twigs shook, swayed, and rustled, the arrows flew out of them, and then the shutter came to. 'Steer her straight,' I said to the helmsman. He held his head rigid, face forward; but his eyes rolled, he kept on lifting and setting down his feet gently, his mouth foamed a little. 'Keep quiet!' I said in a fury. I might just as well have ordered a tree not to sway in the wind. I darted out. Below me there was a great scuffle of feet on the iron deck; confused exclamations; a voice screamed, 'Can you turn back?' I caught sight of a V-shaped ripple on the water ahead. What? Another snag! A fusillade burst out under my feet. The pilgrims had opened with their Winchesters, and were simply squirting lead into that bush. A deuce of a lot of smoke came up and drove slowly forward. I swore at it. Now I couldn't see the ripple or the snag either. I stood in the doorway, peering, and the arrows came in swarms. They might have been poisoned, but they looked as though they wouldn't kill a cat. The bush began to howl. Our wood-cutters raised a warlike whoop; the report of a rifle just at my back deafened me. I glanced over my shoulder, and the pilot-house was yet full of noise and smoke when I made a dash at the wheel. The fool-nigger had dropped everything, to throw the shutter open and let off that Martini-Henry. He stood before the wide opening, glaring, and I yelled at him to come back, while I straightened the sudden twist out of that steamboat. There was no room to turn even if I had wanted to, the snag was somewhere very near ahead in that confounded smoke, there was no time to lose, so I just crowded her into the bank—right into the bank, where I knew the water was deep.

"We tore slowly along the overhanging bushes in a whirl of broken twigs and flying leaves. The fusillade below stopped short, as I had foreseen it would when the squirts got empty. I threw my head back to a glinting whizz that traversed the pilot-house, in at one shutter-hole and out at the other. Looking past that mad helmsman, who was shaking the empty rifle and yelling at the shore, I saw vague forms of men running bent double, leaping, gliding, distinct, incomplete, evanescent.* Something big appeared in the air before the shutter, the rifle went overboard, and the man stepped back swiftly, looked at me over his shoulder in an

33

extraordinary, profound, familiar manner, and fell upon my feet. The side of his head hit the wheel twice, and the end of what appeared a long cane clattered round and knocked over a little camp-stool. It looked as though after wrenching that thing from somebody ashore he had lost his balance in the effort. The thin smoke had blown away, we were clear of the snag, and looking ahead I could see that in another hundred yards or so I would be free to sheer off, away from the bank; but my feet felt so very warm and wet that I had to look down. The man had rolled on his back and stared straight up at me; both his hands clutched that cane. It was the shaft of a spear that, either thrown or lunged through the opening, had caught him in the side just below the ribs; the blade had gone in out of sight, after making a frightful gash; my shoes were full; a pool of blood lay very still, gleaming dark-red under the wheel; his eyes shone with an amazing lustre. The fusillade burst out again. He looked at me anxiously, gripping the spear like something precious, with an air of being afraid I would try to take it away from him. I had to make an effort to free my eyes from his gaze and attend to the steering. With one hand I felt above my head for the line of the steam-whistle, and jerked out screech after screech hurriedly. The tumult of angry and warlike yells was checked instantly, and then from the depths of the woods went out such a tremulous* and prolonged wail of mournful fear and utter despair as may be imagined to follow the flight of the last hope from the earth. There was a great commotion in the bush; the shower of arrows stopped, a few dropping shots rang out sharply—then silence, in which the languid beat of the stern-wheel came plainly to my ears. I put the helm hard a-starboard at the moment when the pilgrim in pink pyjamas, very hot and agitated, appeared in the doorway. 'The manager sends me—' he began in an official tone, and stopped short. 'Good God!' he said, glaring at the wounded man.

"We two whites stood over him, and his lustrous and inquiring glance enveloped us both. I declare it looked as though he would presently put to us some question in an understandable language; but he died without uttering a sound, without moving a limb, without twitching a muscle. Only in the very last moment, as though in response to some sign we could not see, to some whisper we could not hear, he frowned heavily, and that frown gave to his black death-mask an inconceivably sombre, brooding, and menacing expression. The lustre of inquiring glance faded swiftly into vacant glassiness. 'Can you steer?' I asked the agent eagerly. He looked very dubious; but I made a grab at his arm, and he understood at once I meant him to steer whether or no. To tell you the truth, I was morbidly anxious to change my

shoes and socks. 'He is dead,' murmured the fellow, immensely impressed. 'No doubt about it,' said I, tugging like mad at the shoe-laces. 'And, by the way, I suppose Mr. Kurtz is dead as well by this time.'

"For the moment that was the dominant thought. There was a sense of extreme disappointment, as though I had found out I had been striving after something altogether without a substance. I couldn't have been more disgusted if I had travelled all this way for the sole purpose of talking with Mr. Kurtz. Talking with....I flung one shoe overboard, and became aware that that was exactly what I had been looking forward to—a talk with Kurtz. I made the strange discovery that I had never imagined him as doing, you know, but as discoursing. I didn't say to myself, 'Now I will never see him,' or 'Now I will never shake him by the hand,' but, 'Now I will never hear him.' The man presented himself as a voice. Not of course that I did not connect him with some sort of action. Hadn't I been told in all the tones of jealousy and admiration that he had collected, bartered, swindled, or stolen more ivory than all the other agents together. That was not the point. The point was in his being a gifted creature, and that of all his gifts the one that stood out pre-eminently, that carried with it a sense of real presence, was his ability to talk, his words—the gift of expression, the bewildering, the illuminating, the most exalted and the most contemptible, the pulsating stream of light, or the deceitful flow from the heart of an impenetrable darkness.

"The other shoe went flying unto the devil-god of that river. I thought, By Jove! it's all over. We are too late; he has vanished—the gift has vanished, by means of some spear, arrow, or club. I will never hear that chap speak after all,—and my sorrow had a startling extravagance of emotion, even such as I had noticed in the howling sorrow of these savages in the bush. I couldn't have felt more of lonely desolation somehow, had I been robbed of a belief or had missed my destiny in life.... Why do you sigh in this beastly way, somebody? Absurd? Well, absurd. Good Lord! mustn't a man ever—Here, give me some tobacco...."

...There was a pause of profound stillness, then a match flared, and Marlow's lean face appeared, worn, hollow, with downward folds and dropped eyelids, with an aspect of concentrated attention; and as he took vigorous draws at his pipe, it seemed to retreat and advance out of the night in the regular flicker of the tiny flame. The match went out.

"Absurd!" he cried. "This is the worst of trying to tell.... Here you all are, each moored with two good addresses, like a hulk with two anchors, a butcher round one corner, a policeman round another, excellent appetites, and temperature normal—you hear—normal from year's end to year's end. And you say, Absurd! Absurd be—exploded! Absurd! My dear boys, what can you expect from a man who out of sheer nervousness had just flung overboard a pair of new shoes. Now I think of it, it is amazing I did not shed tears. I am, upon the whole, proud of my fortitude. I was cut up to the quick at the idea of having lost the inestimable privilege of listening to the gifted Kurtz. Of course I was wrong. The privilege was waiting for me. Oh yes, I heard more than enough. And I was right, too. A voice. He was very little more than a voice. And I heard—him—it— this voice—other voices— all of them were so little more than voices—and the memory of that time itself lingers around me, impalpable, like a dying vibration of one immense jabber, silly, atrocious, sordid, savage, or simply mean, without any kind of sense. Voices, voices— even the girl herself—now—"

...He was silent for a long time.

"...I laid the ghost of his gifts at last with a lie," he began suddenly. "Girl! What? Did I mention a girl? Oh, she is out of it—completely. They—the women I mean—are out of it—should be out of it. We must help them to stay in that beautiful world of their own, lest ours gets worse. Oh, she had to be out of it. You should have heard the disinterred body of Mr. Kurtz saying, 'My Intended.' You would have perceived directly then how completely she was out of it. And the lofty frontal bone of Mr. Kurtz! They say the hair goes on growing sometimes, but this—ah—specimen, was impressively bald. The wilderness had patted him on the head, and, behold, it was like a ball—an ivory ball; it had caressed him, and—lo!—he had withered; it had taken him, loved him, embraced him, got into his veins, consumed his flesh, and sealed his soul to its own by the inconceivable ceremonies of some devilish initiation. He was its spoiled and pampered favourite. Ivory? I should think so. Heaps of it, stacks of it. The old mud shanty was bursting with it. You would think there was not a single tusk left either above or below the ground in the whole country. 'Mostly fossil,' the manager had remarked disparagingly. It was no more fossil than I am; but they call it fossil when it is dug up. It appears these niggers do bury the tusks sometimes—but evidently they couldn't bury this parcel deep enough to save the gifted Mr. Kurtz from his fate. We filled the steamboat with it, and had to pile a lot on the deck. Thus he could see and enjoy as long as he could see, because the appreciation of this favour had remained with him to the last. You should have heard him say, 'My ivory.' Oh yes, I heard him. 'My Intended, my ivory, my station, my river, my—' everything belonged to him. It made me hold my breath in expectation of hearing the wilderness burst into a prodigious peal of laughter that would shake the fixed stars in their places. Everything belonged to him—but that was a trifle. The thing was to know what he belonged to, how many powers of darkness claimed him for their own. That was the reflection that made you creepy all over. It was impossible—it was not good for one either—to try and imagine. He had taken a high seat amongst the devils of the land—I mean literally. You can't understand. How could you?—with solid pavement under your feet, surrounded by kind neighbours ready to cheer you or to fall on you, stepping delicately between the butcher and the policeman, in the holy terror of scandal and gallows and lunatic asylums—how can you imagine what particular region of the first ages a man's untrammelled* feet may take him into by the way of solitude— utter solitude without a policeman— by the way of silence—utter silence, where no warning voice of a kind neighbour can be heard whispering of public opinion. These little things make all the great difference. When they are gone you must fall back upon your own innate strength, upon your own capacity for faithfulness. Of course you may be too much of a fool to go wrong—too dull even to know you are being assaulted by the powers of darkness. I take it, no fool ever made a bargain for his soul with the devil: the fool is too much of a fool, or the devil too much of a devil—I don't know which. Or you may be such a thunderingly exalted creature as to be altogether deaf and blind to anything but heavenly sights and sounds. Then the earth for you is only a standing place—and whether to be like this is your loss or your gain I won't pretend to say. But most of us are neither one nor the other. The earth for us is a place to live in, where we must put up with sights, with sounds, with smells, too, by Jove!—breathe dead hippo, so to speak, and not be contaminated. And there, don't you see? your strength comes in, the faith in your ability for the digging of unostentatious* holes to bury the stuff in—your power of devotion, not to yourself, but to an obscure, back-breaking business. And that's difficult enough. Mind, I am not trying to excuse or even explain—I am trying to account to myself for—for—Mr. Kurtz—for the shade of Mr. Kurtz. This initiated wraith from the back of Nowhere honoured me with its amazing confidence before it vanished altogether. This was because it could speak English to me. The original Kurtz had been educated partly in England, and— as he was good enough to say himself—his sympathies were in the right place. His mother was half-English, his father was half-French. All Europe contributed to the making of Kurtz; and by-and-by I learned that, most appropriately, the International Society for the Suppression of Savage Customs had intrusted him with the making of a report, for its future guidance. And he had written it too. I've seen it. I've read it. It was eloquent, vibrating with eloquence, but too high-strung, I think. Seventeen pages of close writing he had found time for! But this must have been before his—let us say—nerves, went wrong, and caused him to preside at certain midnight dances ending with unspeakable rites, which—as far as I reluctantly gathered from what I heard at various times—were offered up to him—do you understand?—to Mr. Kurtz himself. But it was a beautiful piece of writing. The opening paragraph, however, in the light of later information, strikes me now as ominous. He began with the argument that we whites, from the point of development we had arrived at, 'must necessarily appear to them [savages] in the nature of supernatural beings—we approach them with the might as of deity,' and so on, and so on. 'By the simple exercise of our will we can exert a power for good practically unbounded,' etc. etc. From that point he soared and took me with him. The peroration* was magnificent, though difficult to remember, you know. It gave me the notion of an exotic Immensity ruled by an august Benevolence. It made me tingle with enthusiasm. This was the unbounded power of eloquence—of words—of burning noble words. There were no practical hints to interrupt the magic current of phrases, unless a kind of note at the foot of the last page, scrawled evidently much later, in an unsteady hand, may be regarded as the exposition of a method. It was very simple, and at the end of that moving appeal to every altruistic sentiment it blazed at you, luminous and terrifying, like a flash of lightning in a serene sky: 'Exterminate all the brutes!' The curious part was that he had apparently forgotten all about that valuable postscriptum,* because, later on, when he in a sense came to himself, he repeatedly entreated me to take good care of 'my pamphlet' (he called it), as it was sure to have in the future a good influence upon his career. I had full information about all these things, and, besides, as it turned out, I was to have the care of his memory. I've done enough for it to give me the indisputable right to lay it, if I choose, for an everlasting rest in the dust-bin of progress, amongst all the sweepings and, figuratively speaking, all the dead cats of civilisation. But then, you see, I can't choose. He won't be forgotten. Whatever he was, he was not common. He had the power to charm or frighten rudimentary souls into an aggravated witch-dance in his honour; he could also fill the small souls of the pilgrims with bitter misgivings: he had one devoted friend at least, and he had conquered one soul in the world that was neither rudimentary nor tainted with self-seeking. No; I can't forget him, though I am not prepared to affirm the fellow was exactly worth the life we lost in getting to him. I missed my late helmsman awfully—I missed him even while his body was still lying in the pilot-house. Perhaps you will think it passing strange this regret for a savage who was no more account than a grain of sand in a black Sahara. Well, don't you see, he had done something, he had steered; for months I had him at my back—a help—an instrument. It was a kind of partnership. He steered for me—I had to look after him, I worried about his deficiencies, and thus a subtle bond had been created, of which I only became aware when it was suddenly broken. And the intimate profundity of that look he gave me when he received his hurt remains to this day in my memory—like a claim of distant kinship affirmed in a supreme moment.

"Poor fool! If he had only left that shutter alone. He had no restraint, no restraint—just like Kurtz—a tree swayed by the wind. As soon as I had put on a dry pair of slippers, I dragged him out, after first jerking the spear out of his side, which operation I confess I performed with my eyes shut tight. His heels leaped together over the little doorstep; his shoulders were pressed to my breast; I hugged him from behind desperately. Oh! he was heavy, heavy; heavier than any man on earth, I should imagine. Then without more ado I tipped him overboard. The current snatched him as though he had been a wisp of grass, and I saw the body roll over twice before I lost sight of it for ever. All the pilgrims and the manager were then congregated on the awning-deck about the pilot-house, chattering at each other like a flock of excited magpies, and there was a scandalised murmur at my heartless promptitude.* What they wanted to keep that body hanging about for I can't guess. Embalm it, maybe. But I had also heard another, and a very ominous, murmur on the deck below. My friends the wood-cutters were likewise scandalised, and with a better show of reason—though I admit that the reason itself was quite inadmissible. Oh, quite! I had made up my mind that if my late helmsman was to be eaten, the fishes alone should have him. He had been a very second-rate helmsman while alive, but now he was dead he might have become a first-class temptation, and possibly cause some startling trouble. Besides, I was anxious to take the wheel, the man in pink pyjamas showing himself a hopeless duffer at the business.

"This I did directly the simple funeral was over. We were going half-speed, keeping right in the middle of the stream, and I listened to the talk about me. They had given up Kurtz, they had given up the station; Kurtz was dead, and the station had been burnt—and so on— and so on. The red-haired pilgrim was beside himself with the thought that at least this poor Kurtz had been properly revenged. 'Say! We must have made a glorious slaughter of them in the bush. Eh? What do you think? Say?' He positively danced, the bloodthirsty little gingery beggar. And he had nearly fainted when he saw the wounded man! I could not help saying, 'You made a glorious lot of smoke, anyhow.' I had seen, from the way the tops of the bushes rustled and flew, that almost all the shots had gone too high. You can't hit anything unless you take aim and fire from the shoulder; but these chaps fired from the hip with their eyes shut. The retreat, I maintained—and I was right—was caused by the screeching of the steam-whistle. Upon this they forgot Kurtz, and began to howl at me with indignant protests.

"The manager stood by the wheel murmuring confidentially about the necessity of getting well away down the river before dark at all events, when I saw in the distance a clearing on the river-side and the outlines of some sort of building. 'What's this?' I asked. He clapped his hands in wonder. 'The station!' he cried. I edged in at once, still going half-speed.

"Through my glasses I saw the slope of a hill interspersed with rare trees and perfectly free from undergrowth. A long decaying building on the summit was half buried in the high grass; the large holes in the peaked roof gaped black from afar; the jungle and the woods made a background. There was no enclosure or fence of any kind; but there had been one apparently, for near the house half a dozen slim posts remained in a row, roughly trimmed, and with their upper ends ornamented with round carved balls. The rails, or whatever there had been between, had disappeared. Of course the forest surrounded all that. The river-bank was clear, and on the water-side I saw a white man under a hat like a cart-wheel beckoning persistently with his whole arm. Examining the edge of the forest above and below, I was almost certain I could see movements—human forms gliding here and there. I steamed past prudently, then stopped the engines and let her drift down. The man on the shore began to shout, urging us to land. 'We have been attacked,' screamed the manager. 'I know—I know. It's all right,' yelled back the other, as cheerful as you please. 'Come along. It's all right. I am glad.'

"His aspect reminded me of something I had seen—something funny I had seen somewhere. As I manoeuvred to get alongside, I was asking myself, 'What does this fellow look like?' Suddenly I got it. He looked like a harlequin. His clothes had been made of some stuff that was brown holland probably, but it was covered with patches all over, with bright patches, blue, red, and yellow,—patches on the back, patches on the front, patches on elbows, on knees; coloured binding round his jacket, scarlet edging at the bottom of his trousers; and the sunshine made him look extremely gay and wonderfully neat withal, because you could see how beautifully all this patching had been done. A beardless, boyish face, very fair, no features to speak of, nose peeling, little blue eyes, smiles and

frowns chasing each other over that open countenance like sunshine and shadow on a wind-swept plain. 'Look out, captain!' he cried; 'there's a snag lodged in here last night.' What! Another snag? I confess I swore shamefully. I had nearly holed my cripple, to finish off that charming trip. The harlequin on the bank turned his little pug nose up to me. 'You English?' he asked, all smiles. 'Are you?' I shouted from the wheel. The smiles vanished, and he shook his head as if sorry for my disappointment. Then he brightened up. 'Never mind!' he cried encouragingly. 'Are we in time?' I asked. 'He is up there,' he replied, with a toss of the head up the hill, and becoming gloomy all of a sudden. His face was like the autumn sky, overcast one moment and bright the next.

"When the manager, escorted by the pilgrims, all of them armed to the teeth, had gone to the house, this chap came on board. 'I say, I don't like this. These natives are in the bush,' I said. He assured me earnestly it was all right. 'They are simple people,' he added; 'well, I am glad you came. It took me all my time to keep them off.' 'But you said it was all right,' I cried. 'Oh, they meant no harm,' he said; and as I stared he corrected himself, 'Not exactly.' Then vivaciously, 'My faith, your pilot-house wants a clean-up!' In the next breath he advised me to keep enough steam on the boiler to blow the whistle in case of any trouble. 'One good screech will do more for you than all your rifles. They are simple people,' he repeated. He rattled away at such a rate he quite overwhelmed me. He seemed to be trying to make up for lots of silence, and actually hinted, laughing, that such was the case. 'Don't you talk with Mr. Kurtz?' I said. 'You don't talk with that man—you listen to him,' he exclaimed with severe exaltation. 'But now—' He waved his arm, and in the twinkling of an eye was in the uttermost depths of despondency.* In a moment he came up again with a jump, possessed himself of both my hands, shook them continuously, while he gabbled: 'Brother sailor... honour... pleasure... delight... introduce myself... Russian... son of an arch-priest... Government of Tambov.... What? Tobacco! English tobacco; the excellent English tobacco! Now, that's brotherly. Smoke? Where's a sailor that does not smoke?'

"The pipe soothed him, and gradually I made out he had run away from school, had gone to sea in a Russian ship; ran away again; served some time in English ships; was now reconciled with the arch-priest. He made a point of that. 'But when one is young one must see things, gather experience, ideas; enlarge the mind.' 'Here!' I interrupted. 'You can never tell! Here I have met Mr. Kurtz,' he said, youthfully solemn and reproachful. I held my tongue after that. It appears he had persuaded a Dutch trading-house on the coast to fit him out with stores and goods, and had started for the interior with a light heart, and no more idea of what would happen to him than a baby. He had been wandering about that river for nearly two years alone, cut off from everybody and everything. 'I am not so young as I look. I am twenty-five,' he said. 'At first old Van Shuyten would tell me to go to the devil,' he narrated with keen enjoyment; 'but I stuck to him, and talked and talked, till at last he got afraid I would talk the hind-leg off his favourite dog, so he gave me some cheap things and a few guns, and told me he hoped he would never see my face again. Good old Dutchman, Van Shuyten. I've sent him one small lot of ivory a year ago, so that he can't call me a little thief when I get back. I hope he got it. And for the rest I don't care. I had some wood stacked for you. That was my old house. Did you see?'

"I gave him Towson's book. He made as though he would kiss me, but restrained himself. 'The only book I had left, and I thought I had lost it,' he said, looking at it ecstatically. 'So many accidents happen to a man going about alone, you know. Canoes get upset sometimes—and sometimes you've got to clear out so quick when the people get angry.' He thumbed the pages. 'You made notes in Russian?' I asked. He nodded. 'I thought they were written in cipher,' I said. He laughed, then became serious. 'I had lots of trouble to keep these people off,' he said. 'Did they want to kill you?' I asked. 'Oh no!' he cried, and checked himself. 'Why did they attack us?' I pursued. He hesitated, then said shamefacedly, 'They don't want him to go.' 'Don't they?' I said, curiously. He nodded a nod full of mystery and wisdom. 'I tell you,' he cried, 'this man has enlarged my mind.' He opened his arms wide, staring at me with his little blue eyes that were perfectly round.

(Part Three from *Blackwood's Edinburgh Magazine*, April 1899)

"I looked at him, lost in astonishment. There he was before me, in motley, as though he had absconded* from a troupe of mimes enthusiastic, fabulous. His very existence was improbable, inexplicable, and altogether bewildering. He was an insoluble problem. It was inconceivable how he had existed, how he had succeeded in getting so far, how he had managed to remain—why he did not instantly disappear. 'I went a little farther,' he said, 'then still a little farther—till I had gone so far that I don't know how I'll ever get back. Never mind. Plenty time. I can manage. You take Kurtz away quick—quick—I tell you.' The glamour of youth enveloped his particoloured* rags, his destitution, his loneliness, the essential desolation of his futile wanderings. For months—for years—his life hadn't been worth a day's purchase; and there

he was gallantly, thoughtlessly alive, to all appearance indestructible solely by the virtue of his few years and of his unreflecting audacity. I was seduced into something like admiration—like envy. Glamour urged him on, glamour kept him unscathed. He surely wanted nothing from the wilderness but space to breathe in and to push on through. His need was to exist, and to move onwards at the greatest possible risk, and with a maximum of privation. If the absolutely pure, uncalculating, unpractical spirit of adventure had ever ruled a human being, it ruled this be-patched youth. I almost envied him the possession of this modest and clear flame. It seemed to have consumed all thought of self so completely, that, even while he was talking to you, you forgot that it was he—the man before your eyes—who had gone through these things. I did not envy him his devotion to Kurtz, though. He had not meditated over it. It came to him, and he accepted it with a sort of eager fatalism. I must say that to me it appeared about the most dangerous thing in every way he had come upon so far.

"They had come together unavoidably, like two ships becalmed near each other, and lay rubbing sides at last. I suppose Kurtz wanted an audience, because on a certain occasion, when encamped in the forest, they had talked all night, or more probably Kurtz had talked. 'We talked of everything,' he said, quite transported at the recollection. 'I forgot there was such a thing as sleep. The night did not seem to last an hour. Everything! Everything!...Of love too.' 'Ah, he talked to you of love!' I said, much amused. 'It isn't what you think,' he cried, almost passionately. 'It was in general. He made me see things—things.'

"He threw his arms up. We were on deck at the time, and the head-man of my wood-cutters, lounging near by, turned upon him his heavy and glittering eyes. I looked around, and I don't know why, but I assure you that never, never before, did this land, this river, this jungle, the very arch of this blazing sky, appear to me so hopeless and so dark, so impenetrable to human thought, so pitiless to human weakness. 'And, ever since, you have been with him, of course?' I said.

"On the contrary. It appears their intercourse* was very much broken by various causes. He had, as he informed me proudly, managed to nurse Kurtz through two illnesses (he alluded to it as you would to some risky feat), but as a rule Kurtz wandered alone, far in the depths of the forest. 'Very often coming to this station, I had to wait days and days for him to turn up,' he said. 'Ah, it was worth waiting for!—sometimes.' 'What was he doing? exploring or what?' I asked. 'Oh yes, of course he had discovered lots of villages, a lake too—he did not know exactly in what direction; it was dangerous to inquire too much—but mostly his expeditions had been for ivory.' 'But he had no goods to trade with by that time,' I objected. 'There's a good lot of cartridges left even yet,' he answered, looking away. 'To speak plainly, he raided the country,' I said. He nodded. 'Not alone, surely!' He muttered something about the villages round that lake. 'Kurtz got the tribe to follow him, did he?' I suggested. He fidgeted a little. 'They adored him,' he said. The tone of these words was so extraordinary that I looked at him searchingly. It was curious to see his mingled eagerness and reluctance to speak of Kurtz. The man filled his life, occupied his thoughts, swayed his emotions. 'What can you expect?' he burst out; 'he came to them with thunder and lightning, you know—and they had never seen anything like it—and very terrible. He could be very terrible. You can't judge Mr. Kurtz as you would an ordinary man. No, no, no! Now—just to give you an idea—I don't mind telling you, he wanted to shoot me too one day—but I don't judge him.' 'Shoot you!' I cried. 'What for?' 'Well, I had a small lot of ivory the chief of that village near my house gave me. You see I used to shoot game for them. Well, he wanted it, and wouldn't hear reason. He said he would shoot me unless I gave him the ivory and cleared out of the country, because he could do so, and had a fancy for it, and there was nothing on earth to prevent him killing whom he jolly well pleased. And it was true too. I gave him the ivory. What did I care! But I didn't clear out. No, no. I couldn't leave him. I had to be careful, though, for a time. Then we got friendly, as before. He had his second illness then. Afterwards I had to keep out of the way again. But he was mostly living in those villages on the lake. When he came down to the river, sometimes he would take to me, and sometimes I had to keep out of his way. This man suffered too much. He hated all this, and somehow he couldn't get away. When I had a chance I begged him to try and leave while there was time. I offered to go back with him. And he would say yes, and then he would remain; go off on another ivory hunt; disappear for weeks; forget himself amongst these people—forget himself—you know.' 'Why! he's mad,' I said. He protested indignantly. Mr. Kurtz couldn't be mad. If I had heard him talk, only two days ago, I wouldn't dare hint at such a thing. I had taken up my binoculars while we talked, and was looking at the shore, sweeping the limit of the forest at each side and at the back of the house. The consciousness of there being people in that bush, so silent, so quiet—as silent and quiet as the ruined house on the hill—made me uneasy. There was no sign on the face of nature of this amazing tale of cruelty and greed that was not so much told as suggested

to me in desolate exclamations, completed by shrugs, in interrupted phrases, in hints ending in deep sighs. The woods were unmoved, like a mask—heavy, like the closed door of a prison—they looked with their air of hidden knowledge, of patient expectation, of unapproachable silence. The Russian was telling me that it was only lately that Mr. Kurtz had come down to the river, bringing along with him that lake tribe. He had been absent for several months—getting himself adored, I suppose—and had come down purposing a raid either across the river or down stream. Evidently the appetite for more ivory had got the better of the—what shall I say?—less material aspirations. However he had got much worse suddenly. 'I heard he was lying helpless, and so I came up—took my chance,' said the Russian. 'Oh, he is bad, very bad.' I kept my glass steadily on the house. There were no signs of life, but there was the ruined roof, the long mud wall peeping above the grass, with three little square window-holes, no two of the same size; all this brought within reach of my hand, as it were. And then I made a brusque movement, and one of the remaining posts of that vanished fence leaped up in the field of my glass. You remember I told you I had been struck at the distance by certain attempts at ornamentation, rather remarkable in the ruinous neglect of the place. Now I had suddenly a nearer view, and its first result was to make me throw my head back as if before a blow. Then I went carefully from post to post with my glass, and I saw my mistake. These round knobs were not ornamental but symbolic of some cruel and forbidding knowledge. They were expressive and puzzling, striking and disturbing, food for thought and also for the vultures if there had been any looking down from the sky; but at all events for such ants as were industrious enough to ascend the pole. They would have been even more impressive, those heads on the stakes, if their faces had not been turned to the house. Only one, the first I had made out, was facing my way. I was not so shocked as you may think. The start back I had given was really nothing but a movement of surprise. I had expected to see a knob of wood there, you know. I returned deliberately to the first I had seen—and there it was, black, dried, sunken, with closed eyelids—a head that seemed to sleep at the top of that pole, and, with the shrunken dry lips showing a narrow white line of the teeth, was smiling too, smiling continuously at some endless and jocose* dream of that eternal slumber.

"I am not disclosing any trade secrets. In fact the manager said afterwards that Mr. Kurtz had ruined that district. I have no opinion as to that, but I want you clearly to understand that there was nothing profitable in these heads being there.

They only showed that Mr. Kurtz lacked restraint in the gratification of his various lusts, that there was something wanting in him—some small matter which, when the pressing need arose, could not be found under his magnificent eloquence. Whether he knew of this deficiency himself I can't say. I think the knowledge came to him at last—only at the very last. But the wilderness had found him out early, and had taken on him a terrible vengeance for the fantastic invasion. It had tempted him with all the sinister suggestions of its loneliness. I think it had whispered to him things about himself which he did not know, things of which he had no conception till he took counsel with this great solitude—and the whisper had proved irresistibly fascinating. It echoed loudly within him because he was hollow at the core. I put down the glass, and the head that had appeared near enough to be spoken to seemed at once to have leaped away from me into the illusion of an inaccessible distance.

"The admirer of Mr. Kurtz hung his head. With a hurried, indistinct voice he began to tell me he had not dared to take these—say, symbols—down. He was not afraid of the natives; they would not move till Mr. Kurtz gave the word. His ascendancy was extraordinary. The camps of these people surrounded the place, and the chiefs came every day to see him. They crawled. 'I don't want to know anything of the ceremonies used when approaching Mr. Kurtz,' I shouted. Curious, this feeling that came over me that those details would be more intolerable to hear than those heads drying on the stakes under Mr. Kurtz's windows were to see. After all, that was only a savage sight, while I seemed at one bound to have been transported into some lightless region of subtle horrors, where pure, uncomplicated savagery was a positive relief, being something that had a right to exist, obviously in the sunshine. The young man looked at me with surprise. I suppose it did not occur to him Mr. Kurtz was no idol of mine. He forgot I hadn't heard any of these splendid monologues on, what was it? on love, justice, conduct of life—or what not. If it had come to crawling before Mr. Kurtz, he crawled as much as the veriest savage of them all. I had no idea of the conditions, he said: these heads were the heads of rebels. I shocked him excessively by laughing. Rebels! What would be the next definition I was to hear? There had been enemies, criminals, workers—and these were rebels. Those rebellious heads looked very pacific to me on their sticks. 'You don't know how such a life tries a man like Kurtz,' cried Kurtz's last disciple. 'Well, and you?' I said. 'I! I! I am a simple man. I have no great thoughts. I want nothing from anybody. How can you compare me to...?' His feelings were too much for speech, and suddenly he broke down. 'I don't understand,' he groaned. 'I've been doing my best to keep him alive, and that's enough. I had no hand in all this. I have no abilities. There hasn't been a drop of medicine or a mouthful of invalid food for months here. He was shamefully abandoned. A man like this, with such ideas. Shamefully! Shamefully! I—I—haven't slept for the last ten nights....'

"His voice lost itself in the calm of the evening. The long shadows of the forest had slipped down hill while we talked, had gone far beyond the ruined hovel, beyond the symbolic row of stakes. All this was in the gloom, while we down there were yet in the sunshine, and the stretch of the river abreast of the clearing glittered in a still and dazzling splendour, with a murky and overshadowed band above and below. Not a living soul was seen on the shore. The bushes did not rustle.

"Suddenly round the corner of the house a group of men appeared. It was as though they had come up from the ground. They waded waist-deep in the grass, in a compact body, bearing an improvised stretcher in their midst. Instantly, in the emptiness of the landscape, a cry arose whose shrillness pierced the still air like a sharp arrow flying straight to the very heart of the land; and, as if by enchantment, streams of human beings—of naked human beings—with spears in their hands, with bows, with shields, with wild glances and savage movements, were poured into the clearing by the dark-faced and pensive forest. The bushes shook, the grass swayed for a time, and then everything stood still in attentive immobility.

"'Now, if he does not speak to them we are all done for,' said the Russian at my elbow. The knot of men with the stretcher had stopped too, half-way to the steamer, as if petrified. I saw the man on the stretcher sit up, lank and with an uplifted arm, above the shoulders of the bearers. 'Let us hope that the man who can talk so well of love in general will find some particular reason to spare us this time,' I said. I resented bitterly the absurd danger of our situation, as if to be at the mercy of the atrocious phantom who ruled this land had been a dishonouring necessity. I could not hear anything, but through my glasses I saw the thin arm extended commandingly, the lower jaw moving, the eyes of that apparition shining darkly far in his bony head that nodded with grotesque jerks. Kurtz—Kurtz— that means short in German—don't it? Well, the name was as true as everything else in his life—and death. He looked at least seven feet long. His covering had fallen off, and his body emerged from it pitiful and appalling as from a winding-sheet. I could see the cage of his ribs all astir, the bones of his arm waving. It was as though an animated image of death carved out of old ivory had been shaking its hand with menaces at a motionless crowd of men made of dark and glittering bronze. I saw him open his mouth wide—it gave him a weirdly voracious aspect, as though he had wanted to swallow all the air, all the earth, all the men before him. A deep sound reached me faintly. He must have been shouting. He fell back suddenly. The stretcher shook as the bearers staggered forward again, and almost at the same time I noticed that the crowd of savages had already diminished, was vanishing without any perceptible movement of retreat, as if the forest that had ejected these beings so suddenly had drawn them in again as the breath is drawn in a long aspiration.

"Some of the pilgrims behind the stretcher carried his arms—two shot-guns, a heavy rifle, and a light revolver-carbine—the thunderbolts of that pitiful Jupiter. The manager bent over him murmuring as he walked beside his head. They laid him down in one of the little cabins, just a room for a bed-place and a camp-stool or two, you know. We had brought his belated correspondence, and a lot of torn envelopes and open letters littered his bed. His hand roamed feebly amongst these papers. I was struck by the fire of his eyes and the composed languor* of his expression. It was not so much the exhaustion of disease. He did not seem in pain. This shadow looked satiated and calm, as though for the moment it had had its fill of all the emotions.

"He rustled one of the letters, and looking in my face said, 'I am glad.' Somebody had been writing to him about me. These special recommendations again. The volume of tone he emitted without effort, almost without the trouble of moving his lips, amazed me. A voice! a voice! It was grave, profound, vibrating, while the man did not seem capable of a whisper. However, he had enough strength in him—factitious no doubt—to very nearly make an end of us, as you shall hear directly.

"The manager appeared in the doorway, so I stepped out at once and he drew the curtain after me. The Russian, eyed curiously by the pilgrims, was staring at the shore. I followed the direction of his glance.

"Several bronze figures could be made out in the distance, moving indistinctly against the gloomy border of the forest, and near the river two were standing, leaning on spears in the sunlight, under fantastic head-dresses of spotted skins, warlike, and still in statuesque repose. And from right to left along the lighted shore moved a wild and gorgeous apparition of a woman.

"She walked with measured steps, draped in striped and fringed cloths, treading the earth proudly, with a slight jingle and flash of barbarous ornaments. She carried her head high; her hair was done in the shape of a helmet; she had brass leggings to the knee, brass wire gauntlets to the elbow, a crimson spot on her tawny cheek, innumerable necklaces of glass beads on her neck; bizarre things, charms, gifts of witch-men, that hung about her, glittered and trembled at every step. She must have had the value of several elephant tusks upon her. She was savage and superb, wild-eyed and magnificent; there was something ominous and stately in her deliberate progress. And in the hush that had fallen suddenly upon the whole sorrowful land, the immense wilderness, the colossal body of the fecund and mysterious life seemed to look at her as though it had been looking at the image of its own tenebrous* and passionate soul.

"And we men also looked at her—at any rate I looked at her. She came abreast of the steamer, stood still, and faced us. Her long shadow fell to the water's edge. Her face had a tragic and fierce aspect of wild sorrow and of dumb fear mingled with the pain of a struggling, half-shaped emotion. She stood looking at us without a stir, and like the wilderness itself with an air of brooding over an inscrutable purpose. A whole minute passed, and then she made a step forward. There was a low jingle, a glint of yellow metal, a sway of fringed draperies, and she stopped. Had her heart failed her, or had her eyes, veiled with that mournfulness that lies over all the wild things of the earth, seen the hopelessness of longing that will find out sometimes even a savage soul in the lonely darkness of its being? Who can tell. Perhaps she did not know herself. The young fellow by my side growled. The pilgrims murmured at my back. She looked at us all as if her life had depended upon the unswerving steadiness of her glance. Suddenly she opened her bared arms and threw them up rigid above her head, as though in an uncontrollable desire to touch the sky, and at the same time the shadows of her arms darted out on the earth, swept around on the river, gathering the steamer into a shadowy embrace. Her sudden gesture seemed to demand a cry, but the unbroken silence that hung over the scene was more formidable than any sound could be.

"She turned, walked on, following the bank, and passed into the bushes to the left. Once only her eyes gleamed back at us in the dusk of the thickets and she disappeared.

"'If she had offered to come aboard I think I would have tried to shoot her,' said the man of

41

patches, nervously. 'I had been risking my life every day for the last fortnight to keep her out of the house. She got in once and kicked up a row about those miserable rags I picked up in the storeroom to mend my clothes with. I was not decent. At least it must have been that, for she talked to Kurtz for an hour, pointing at me now and then. I don't understand the dialect of this tribe. Luckily for me, I fancy Kurtz felt too ill that day to care, or there would have been mischief. I don't understand.... No—it's too much for me. Ah, well, it's all over now.'

"At this moment I heard Kurtz's deep voice behind the curtain, 'Save me!—save the ivory, you mean. Don't tell me. Save me! Why, I've had to save you. You are interrupting my plans now. Sick! Sick! Not so sick as you would like to believe. Never mind. I'll carry my ideas out yet—I will return. I'll show you what can be done. You with your little peddling notions—you are interfering with me. I will return. I....'

"The manager came out. He did me the honour to take me under the arm and lead me aside. 'He is very low, very low,' he said. He considered it necessary to sigh, but forgot to be consistently sorrowful. 'We have done all we could for him—haven't we? But there is no disguising the fact, Mr. Kurtz has done more harm than good to the Company. He did not see the time was not ripe for vigorous action. Cautiously, cautiously, that's my principle. We must be cautious yet. The district is closed to us for a time. Deplorable! Upon the whole, the trade will suffer. I don't deny there is a remarkable quantity of ivory—mostly fossil. We must save it, at all events—but look how precarious the position is— and why? Because the method is unsound.' 'Do you,' said I, looking at the shore, 'call it "unsound method"?' 'Without doubt,' he exclaimed, hotly. 'Don't you?' 'No method at all,' I murmured. 'Exactly,' he exulted. 'I anticipated this. A complete want of judgment. It is my duty to point it out in the proper quarter.' 'Oh,' said I, 'that fellow— what's his name?—the brickmaker, will make a readable report for you.' He appeared confounded for a moment. It seemed to me I had never breathed an atmosphere so vile, and I turned mentally to Kurtz for relief—positively for relief. 'Nevertheless, I think Mr. Kurtz is a remarkable man,' I said with emphasis. He started, dropped on me a cold heavy glance, said very quietly, 'He was,' and turned his back on me. My hour of favour was over. I found myself lumped along with Kurtz as a partisan of methods for which the time was not ripe. I was unsound. Ah! but it was something to have at least a choice of nightmares.

"I had turned to the wilderness really, not to Mr. Kurtz, who, I was ready to admit, was as good

as buried. And for a moment it seemed to me as if I also were buried in a vast grave full of unspeakable secrets. I felt an intolerable weight oppressing my breast, the smell of the damp earth, the unseen presence of victorious corruption, the darkness of an impenetrable night. The Russian tapped me on the shoulder. I heard him mumbling and stammering something about 'brother seaman—couldn't conceal—knowledge of matters that would affect Mr. Kurtz's reputation.' I waited. For him evidently Mr. Kurtz was not in his grave; I suspect that for him Mr. Kurtz was one of the immortals. 'Well!' said I at last, 'speak out. As it happens, I am Mr. Kurtz's friend—in a way.'

"He stated with a good deal of formality that had we not been 'of the same profession,' he would have kept the matter to himself without regard to consequences. He suspected 'there was an active ill-will towards him on the part of these white men that—' 'You are right,' I said, remembering a certain conversation I had overheard. 'The manager thinks you ought to be hanged.' He showed a concern at this intelligence which astonished me at first. 'I had better get out of the way quietly,' he said, earnestly. 'I can do no more for Kurtz now, and they would soon find a pretext....What's to stop them? There's a military post three hundred miles from here.' 'Well, upon my word,' said I, 'perhaps you had better go if you have any friends amongst the savages near by.' 'Plenty,' he said. 'They are simple people—and I want nothing, you know.' He stood biting his lip, then: 'I don't want any harm to happen to these whites here, but of course I was thinking of Mr. Kurtz's reputation— but you are a brother seaman and—' 'All right,' said I, after a time. 'Mr. Kurtz's reputation is safe with me.' I did not know how truly I spoke.

"He informed me, lowering his voice, that it was Kurtz who had ordered the attack to be made on the steamer. 'He hated sometimes the idea of being taken away—and then again...But I don't understand these matters. I am a simple man. He thought it would scare you away—that you would give it up, thinking him dead. I could not stop him. Oh, I had an awful time of it this last month.' 'Very well,' I said. 'He is all right now.' 'Ye-e-es,' he muttered, not very convinced apparently. 'Thanks,' said I; 'I shall keep my eyes open.' 'But quiet—eh?' he urged, anxiously. 'It would be awful for his reputation if anybody here....' I promised a complete discretion with great gravity. 'I have a canoe and three black fellows not very far. I am off. Could you give me a few Martini-Henry cartridges?' I could, and did, with proper secrecy. He helped himself, with a wink at me, to a handful of my tobacco. 'Between sailors—you know—good English tobacco.' At the door of the pilot-house he turned round—'I say, haven't you a pair of shoes you could spare?' He raised one leg. 'Look.' The soles were tied with knotted strings sandal-wise under his bare feet. I rooted out an old pair, at which he looked with admiration before tucking them under his left arm. One of his pockets (bright red) was bulging with cartridges, from the other (dark blue) peeped *Towson's Inquiry,* etc., etc. He seemed to think himself excellently well equipped for a renewed encounter with the wilderness. 'Ah! I'll never, never meet such a man again. You ought to have heard him recite poetry—his own too it was, he told me. Poetry!' He rolled his eyes at the recollection of these delights. 'Oh, he enlarged my mind!' 'Good-bye,' said I. He shook hands and vanished in the night. I ask myself whether I had ever really seen him—whether it was possible to meet such a phenomenon.

"When I woke up shortly after midnight his warning came to my mind with its hint of danger that seemed, in the starred darkness, real enough to make me get up for the purpose of having a look round. On the hill a big fire burned, illuminating fitfully a crooked corner of the station-house One of the agents with a picket of a few of our blacks, armed for the purpose, was keeping guard. But deep within the forest, red gleams that wavered, that seemed to sink and rise from the ground amongst confused columnar shapes of intense blackness, showed the exact position of the camp where Mr. Kurtz's adorers were keeping their uneasy vigil. The monotonous beating of a big drum filled the air with muffled shocks and a lingering vibration. A steady droning sound of many men chanting each to himself some weird incantation came out from the black, flat wall of the woods as the humming of bees comes out of a hive, and had a strange narcotic effect upon my half-awake senses. I believe I dozed off leaning over the rail, till an abrupt burst of yells, an overwhelming outbreak of a pent-up and mysterious frenzy, woke me up in a bewildered wonder. It was cut short all at once, and the low droning went on with an effect of audible and soothing silence. I glanced casually into the little cabin. A light was burning. Kurtz was not there.

"I think I would have raised an outcry if I had believed my eyes. But I didn't believe them at first, the thing seemed so impossible. The fact is I was completely unnerved. Sheer blank fright, pure abstract terror, unconnected with any distinct shape of physical danger. What made this emotion so overpowering was—how shall I define it?—the moral shock I received, as if something altogether monstrous, intolerable to thought and odious to the soul, had been thrust upon me unexpectedly. This lasted of course the merest fraction of a second, and then the usual sense of commonplace, deadly danger, the possibility of a sudden onslaught and massacre, or something of the kind, which I saw impending, was positively welcome and composing. It pacified me, in fact, and I did not raise an alarm.

"There was an agent buttoned up inside an ulster sleeping on a chair on deck within three feet of me. The yells had not awakened him, and he snored very slightly. I left him to his slumbers and leaped ashore. I did not betray Mr. Kurtz—it was ordered I should never betray him—it was written I should be loyal to the nightmare of my choice. I was anxious to deal with this shadow by myself alone,—and to this day I don't know why I was so jealous of sharing with any one the dismal blackness of this experience.

"As soon as I got on the bank I saw a trail—a broad trail through the grass. I remember the exultation with which I said to myself, 'He can't walk—he is crawling—I've got him.' The grass was wet with dew. I strode rapidly with clenched fists. I fancy I had some vague notion of falling upon him and giving him a drubbing.* I don't know. I had some imbecile thoughts. The knitting old woman with the cat obtruded herself upon me as a most improper person to be sitting at the other end of such an affair. I saw a row of pilgrims squirting lead in the air out of Winchesters held to the hip. I thought I would never get back to the steamer, and saw myself living alone and unarmed in the woods to an advanced age. Such silly things—you know. And I remember I confounded the beat of the drum with the beating of my heart, and was pleased at its calm regularity.

"I kept to the track though—then stopped to listen. The night was very clear: a dark blue space, sparkling with dew and starlight, where black things stood very still. I thought I saw a kind of motion ahead of me. I was strangely cocksure of everything that night. I actually left the track and ran in a wide semicircle, I verily believe chuckling to myself, so as to get in front of that stir, of that motion I had seen—if indeed I had seen anything. I was circumventing Kurtz as if it had been a boyish game for fun.

"I came upon him, and, if he had not heard me coming, I would have fallen over him too; but he got up in time in front of me. He rose, unsteady, long, pale, indistinct, like a vapour exhaled by the earth, and swayed slightly, misty and silent before me; while at my back the fires loomed between the trees, and the murmur of many voices issued from the forest. I had cut him off cleverly; but when actually confronting him I seemed to come to my senses, I saw the danger in its right proportion. It was by no means over yet. Suppose he began to shout. Though he could hardly stand, there was still plenty of vigour in his voice. 'Go away—hide yourself,' he said, in that profound tone. It was very awful. I glanced back. We were within thirty yards

43

from the nearest fire. A black figure stood up, strode on long black legs, waving long black arms, across the glow. It had horns—antelope horns, I think—on its head. Some sorcerer, some witchman, no doubt: it looked fiend-like enough. 'Do you know what you are doing?' I whispered. 'Perfectly,' he answered, raising his voice for that single word: it sounded to me far off and yet loud, like a hail through a speaking-trumpet. If he makes a row we are lost, I thought to myself. This clearly was not a case for fisticuffs, even apart from the very natural aversion I had to beat that Shadow—this wandering and tormented thing, that seemed released from one grave only to sink for ever into another. 'You will be lost,' I said—'utterly lost.' One gets sometimes such a flash of inspiration, you know. I did say the right thing, though indeed he could not have been more irretrievably lost than he was at this very moment, when the foundations of our intimacy were being laid—to endure—to endure—even to the end—even beyond.

"'I had immense plans,' he muttered irresolutely. 'Yes,' said I; 'but if you try to shout I'll smash your head with—' there was not a stick or a stone near. 'I will throttle you for good,' I corrected myself. 'I was on the threshold of great things,' he pleaded, in a voice of longing, with a wistfulness of tone that made my blood run cold. 'And now for this stupid scoundrel—' 'Your success in Europe is assured in any case,' I affirmed, steadily. I did not want to have the throttling of him, you understand—and indeed it would have been very little use for any practical purpose. I tried to break the spell—the heavy, mute spell of the wilderness—that seemed to draw him to its pitiless breast by the awakening of forgotten and brutal instincts, by the memory of gratified and monstrous passions. This alone, I was convinced, had driven him out to the edge of the forest, to the bush, towards the gleam of fires, the throb of drums, the drone of weird incantations; this alone had beguiled his unlawful soul beyond the bounds of permitted aspirations. And, don't you see, the terror of the position was not in being knocked on the head—though I had a very lively sense of that danger too—but in this, that I had to deal with a being to whom I could not appeal in the name of anything high or low. I had, even like the niggers, to invoke him—himself—his own exalted and incredible degradation. There was nothing either above or below him, and I knew it. He had kicked himself loose of the earth. Confound the man! he had kicked the very earth to pieces. He was alone, and I before him did not know whether I stood on the ground or floated in the air. I've been telling you what we said—repeating the phrases we pronounced,—but what's the good? They were common everyday words,—the familiar, vague sounds

exchanged on every waking day of life. But what of that? They had behind them, to my mind, the terrific suggestiveness of words heard in dreams, of phrases spoken in nightmares. Soul! If anybody had ever struggled with a soul, I am the man. And I wasn't arguing with a mad man either. Believe me or not, his intelligence was perfectly clear—concentrated, it is true, upon himself with horrible intensity, yet clear; and therein was my only chance—barring, of course, the killing him there and then, which wasn't so good, on account of unavoidable noise. But his soul was mad. Being alone in the wilderness, it had looked within itself, and, by heavens! I tell you, it had gone mad. I had—for my sins, I suppose, to go through the ordeal of looking into it myself. No eloquence could have been so withering as his final burst of sincerity. He struggled with himself, too. I saw it,—I heard it. I saw the inconceivable mystery of a soul that knew no restraint, no faith, and no fear, yet struggling blindly with itself. I kept my head pretty well; but when I had him at last stretched on the couch, I wiped my forehead, while my legs shook under me as though I had carried half a ton on my back down that hill. And yet I had only supported him, his bony arm clasped round my neck, and he was not much heavier than a child.

"And when next day we left at noon, the crowd, of whose presence behind the curtain of trees I had been acutely conscious all the time, flowed out of the woods again, filled the clearing, covered the slope with a mass of naked, breathing, quivering, bronze bodies. I steamed up a bit, then swung down-stream, and two thousand eyes followed the evolutions of the splashing, thumping, fierce river-demon beating the water with its terrible tail and breathing black smoke into the air. In front of the first rank, along the river, three men, plastered with bright red earth from head to foot, strutted to and fro restlessly. When we came abreast again, they faced the river, stamped their feet, nodded their horned heads, swayed their scarlet bodies; they shook towards the same river-demon a bunch of black feathers, a spotted skin with a pendent tail—something that looked like a dried gourd; they shouted periodically together strings of amazing words that resembled no sounds of human language; and the deep murmurs of the crowd, interrupted suddenly, were like the responses of some satanic litany.

"We had carried Kurtz into the pilot-house: there was more air there. Lying on the couch, he stared through the open shutter. There was an eddy in the mass of black heads, and the woman with helmeted head and tawny cheeks rushed out to the very brink of the stream. She put out her hands, shouted something, and all that wild mob took up the shout in an amazing chorus of articulated, rapid, breathless utterance.

"'Do you understand this?' I asked.

"He kept on looking out with fiery, longing eyes, with a mingle expression of wistfulness and hate. He did not answer me, but at my question I saw a smile, a smile of indefinable meaning, appear on his colourless lips that a moment after twitched convulsively with pain or rage. 'I will return,' he said, slowly, gasping as if the words of promise and menace had been torn out of him by a supernatural power.

"I pulled the string of the whistle, and I did this because I saw the pilgrims on deck getting out their rifles with an air of anticipating a jolly lark. At the sudden screech there was a movement of abject terror through that wedged mass of bodies. 'Don't! don't! you frighten them away,' cried someone on deck disconsolately. I pulled the string again and again. They broke and ran, they leaped, they crouched, they swerved, as if dodging the terrible sound. The three red chaps had fallen flat, face down on the shore, as though they had been shot dead. Only the barbarous and superb woman did not so much as flinch, and stretched tragically her bare arms after us over the brown and glittering river.

"And then that imbecile crowd down on the deck started their little fun, and I could see nothing more for smoke.

"The brown current ran swiftly out of the heart of darkness, bearing us down towards the sea with twice the speed of our upward progress; and Kurtz's life was running swiftly too, ebbing, ebbing out of his heart into the sea of inexorable time. The manager was very placid. He had no vital anxieties now. He took in both of us in a comprehensive and satisfied glance. The 'affair' had come off as well as could be wished. I saw the time approaching when I would be left alone of the party of 'unsound method.' The pilgrims looked upon me with disfavour. I was, so to speak, numbered with the dead. It is strange how I accepted this unforeseen partnership, this choice of nightmares forced upon me in the tenebrous land invaded by these mean and greedy phantoms.

"Kurtz discoursed. A voice! a voice! It rang deep to the very last. It survived his strength to hide in the magnificent folds of eloquence the barren darkness of his heart. Oh, he struggled! he struggled! The wastes of his weary brain were haunted by shadowy images now—images of wealth and fame revolving obsequiously round his unextinguishable gift of noble and lofty expression. My Intended, my station, my career, my ideas—these were the subjects for the occasional utterances of elevated sentiments. The shade of the original Kurtz frequented the bedside of the hollow sham, whose fate it was to be buried presently in the mould of primeval earth. But both the diabolic love and the unearthly hate of the mysteries it had penetrated fought for the possession of that soul satiated with primitive emotions, avid of lying fame, of sham distinction, of all the appearances of success and power.

"Sometimes he was contemptibly childish. He desired to have kings meet him at railway stations on his return from some ghastly Nowhere, where he intended to accomplish great things. 'You show them you have in you something that is really profitable, and then there will be no limits to the recognition of your ability,' he would say. 'Of course you must take care of the motives—right motives—always.' The long reaches that were like one and the same reach, monotonous bends that were exactly alike, slipped past the steamer with their multitude of secular trees looking patiently after this grimy fragment of another world, the forerunner of change, of conquest, of trade, of massacres, of blessings. I looked ahead—piloting. 'Close the shutter,' said Kurtz suddenly one day; 'I can't bear to look at this.' I did so. There was a silence. 'Oh, but I will wring your heart yet!' he cried at the invisible wilderness.

"We broke down—as I had expected—and had to lie up for repairs at the head of an island. This delay was the first thing that shook Kurtz's confidence. One morning he gave me a packet of papers and a photograph,—the lot tied together with a shoe-string. 'Keep this for me,' he said. 'This noxious fool' (meaning the manager) 'is capable of prying into my boxes when I am not looking.' In the afternoon I saw him. He was lying on his back with closed eyes, and I withdrew quietly, but I heard him mutter, 'Live rightly, die, die....' I listened. There was nothing more. Was he rehearsing some speech in his sleep, or was it a fragment of a phrase from some newspaper article? He had been writing for the papers and meant to do so again, 'for the furthering of my ideas. It's a duty.'

"His was an impenetrable darkness. I looked at him as you peer down at a man who is lying at the bottom of a precipice where the sun never shines. But I had not much time to give him, because I was helping the engine-driver to take to pieces the leaky cylinders, to straighten a bent connecting-rod, and in other such matters. I lived in a repulsive mess of nuts, bolts, spanners, hammers, ratchets—things I abominate, because I don't get on with them. I tended the little forge we fortunately had aboard; I toiled wearily in a wretched scrap-heap, unless I had the shakes too bad to stand.

"One evening coming in with a candle I was startled to hear him say a little querulously, 'I am lying here in the dark waiting for death.' The light was within a foot of his eyes. I managed to murmur, 'Oh, nonsense!' and stood over him as if transfixed.

"Anything approaching the expression that came over his face I have never seen before, and hope never to see again. Oh, I wasn't touched. I was fascinated. It was as though a veil had been rent. I saw on that ivory face the expression of strange pride, of mental power, of avarice, of blood-thirstiness, of cunning, of excessive terror, of an intense and hopeless despair. Did he live his life through in every detail of desire, temptation, and surrender during that supreme moment of complete knowledge? He cried whisperingly at some image, at some vision—he cried twice, with a cry that was no more than a breath—

"'The horror! The horror!'

"I blew the candle out and left the cabin. The pilgrims were dining in the mess-cabin. I took my place opposite the manager, who lifted his eyes to give me a questioning glance, which I successfully ignored. He leaned back, serene, with that peculiar smile of his sealing the unexpressed depths of his meanness. A continuous shower of small flies streamed upon the lamp, upon the cloth, upon our hands and faces. Suddenly the manager's boy put his insolent black face in the doorway, and said in a tone of scathing contempt—

"'Mistah Kurtz—he dead.'

"All the pilgrims rushed out to see. I remained, and went on with my dinner. I believe I was considered brutally callous. However, I did not eat much. There was a lamp in there—light, don't you know—and outside it was so beastly, beastly dark. I went no more near the remarkable man who had so unhesitatingly pronounced a judgment upon the adventures of his soul on this earth. The voice was gone. What else had been there? But I am of course aware that next day the pilgrims buried something in a muddy hole.

"And then they very nearly buried me.

"However, as you see, I did not go to join Kurtz there and then. I did not. I remained to dream the nightmare out to the end, and to show my loyalty to Kurtz once more. Destiny. My destiny! Droll thing life is—that mysterious arrangement of merciless logic for a futile purpose. The most you can hope from it is some knowledge of yourself—that comes too late—a crop of unextinguishable regrets. I have wrestled with death. It is the most unexciting contest you can imagine. It takes place in an impalpable greyness, with nothing underfoot, with nothing around, without spectators, without clamour, without glory, without the great desire of victory, without the great fear of defeat, in a sickly atmosphere of tepid scepticism, without much

belief in your own right, and still less in that of your adversary. If such is the form of ultimate wisdom, then life is a greater riddle than some of us think it to be. I was within a hair's-breadth of the last opportunity for pronouncement, and I found with humiliation that probably I would have nothing to say. That is the reason why I affirm that Kurtz was a remarkable man. He had something to say. He said it. Since I had peeped over the edge myself, I understand better the meaning of his stare, that could not see the flame of the candle, but was wide enough to embrace the whole universe, piercing enough to penetrate all the hearts that beat in the darkness. He had summed up—he had judged. 'The horror!' He was a remarkable man. After all, this was the expression of some sort of belief. It had candour, it had conviction, it had a vibrating note of revolt in its whisper, it had the appalling face of a glimpsed truth—the strange commingling of desire and hate. And it is not my own extremity I remember best—a vision of greyness without form filled with physical pain, and a careless contempt for the evanescence of all things—even of this pain itself. No! It is his extremity that I seem to have lived through. True, he had made that last stride, he had stepped over the edge, while I had been permitted to draw back my hesitating foot. And perhaps in this is the whole difference; perhaps all the wisdom, and all truth, and all sincerity, are just compressed into that inappreciable moment of time in which we step over the threshold of the invisible. Perhaps! I like to think my summing-up would not have been a word of careless contempt. Better his cry—much better. It was an affirmation, a moral victory paid for by innumerable defeats, by abominable terrors, by abominable satisfactions. But it was a victory. That is why I have remained loyal to Kurtz to the last, and even beyond, when long time after I heard once more, not his own voice, but the echo of his magnificent eloquence thrown to me from a soul as translucently pure as a cliff of crystal.

"No, they did not bury me, though there is a period of time which I remember mistily, with a shuddering wonder, like a passage through some inconceivable world that had no hope in it and no desire. I found myself in the sepulchral city resenting the sight of people hurrying through the streets to filch a little money from each other or to devour their infamous cookery, to gulp their unwholesome beer, to dream their insignificant and silly dreams. They trespassed upon my thoughts. They were intruders whose knowledge of life was to me an irritating pretense, because I felt so sure they could not possibly know the things I knew; and their bearing, which was simply the bearing of commonplace individuals going about their business in the assurance of perfect safety, was offensive to me like the outrageous flauntings of folly in the face of a danger it is unable to comprehend. I had no particular desire to enlighten them, but I had some difficulty in restraining myself from laughing in their faces, so full of stupid importance. I daresay I was not very well at that time. I tottered about the streets—there were various affairs to settle—grinning bitterly at perfectly respectable persons. I admit my behaviour was inexcusable, but then my temperature was seldom normal in these days. My dear aunt's endeavours to 'nurse up my strength' seemed altogether beside the mark. It was not my strength that wanted nursing, it was my imagination that wanted soothing. I kept the bundle of papers given me by Kurtz, not knowing exactly what to do with it. His mother had died lately, watched over, as I was told, by his Intended. A clean-shaved man, with an official manner and wearing gold-rimmed spectacles, called on me one day and made inquiries, at first circuitous, afterwards suavely pressing, about what he was pleased to denominate certain 'documents.' I was not surprised, because I had two rows with the manager on the subject out there. I had refused to give up the smallest scrap out of that package to him, and I took the same attitude with the spectacled man. He became darkly menacing at last, and with much heat argued that the Company had the right to every bit of information about their 'territories.' And, said he, 'Mr. Kurtz's knowledge of unexplored regions must have been necessarily extensive and peculiar—owing to his great abilities and to the deplorable circumstances in which he had been placed: therefore——' I assured him Mr. Kurtz's knowledge, however extensive, did not bear upon the problems of commerce or administration. He invoked then the name of science. 'It would be an incalculable loss if,' etc., etc. I offered him the report on the 'Suppression of Savage Customs,' with the postscriptum torn off. He took it up eagerly, but ended by sniffing at it with an air of contempt. 'This is not what we had a right to expect,' he remarked. 'Expect nothing else,' I said. 'There are only private letters.' He withdrew upon some threat of legal proceedings, and I saw him no more; but another fellow, calling himself Kurtz's cousin, appeared two days later, and was anxious to hear all the details about his dear relative's last moments. Incidentally he gave me to understand that Kurtz had been essentially a great musician. 'There was the making of an immense success,' said the man, who was an organist, I believe, with lank grey hair flowing over a greasy coat-collar. I had no reason to doubt his statement; and to this day I am unable to say what was Kurtz's profession, whether he ever had any—which was the greatest of his talents. I had thought him a painter who wrote for the papers, or a journalist who could paint—but even the cousin (who took snuff during the interview) could not tell me what he had been—exactly. He was a universal genius—on that point I agreed with the old chap, who thereupon blew his nose noisily into a large cotton handkerchief and withdrew in senile agitation, bearing off some family letters and memoranda without importance. Ultimately a journalist anxious to know something of the fate of his 'dear colleague' turned up. This visitor informed me Kurtz's real sphere ought to have been politics 'on the popular side.' He had furry straight eyebrows, bristly hair cropped short, an eye-glass on a broad ribbon, and, becoming expansive, confessed his opinion that Kurtz couldn't write a bit—'but heavens! how that man could talk! He electrified large meetings. He had faith—don't you see?—he had the faith. He could believe anything—anything. He would have been a splendid leader of an extreme party.' 'What party?' I asked. 'Any party,' answered the other. 'He was an—an—extremist.' Did I not think so? I assented. Did I know, he asked, with a sudden flash of curiosity, 'what induced him to go out there?' 'Yes,' said I, and forthwith handed him the famous Report for publication, if he thought fit. He glanced through it hurriedly, mumbling all the time, judged 'it would do,' and took himself off with this plunder.

"'I was left at last with a slim packet of letters and the girl's portrait. She struck me as beautiful— I mean she had a beautiful expression. I know that the sunlight can be made to lie too, yet that face on paper seemed to be a reflection of truth itself. One felt that no manipulation of light and pose could have conveyed the delicate shade of truthfulness upon those features. She looked out truthfully. She seemed ready to listen without mental reservation, without suspicion, without a thought for herself. I concluded I would go and give her back her portrait and those letters myself. Curiosity? Yes; and also some other feeling perhaps. All that had been Kurtz's had passed out of my hands: his soul, his body, his station, his plans, his ivory, his career. There remained only his memory and his Intended—and I wanted to give that up too to the past, in a way,—to surrender personally all that remained of him with me to that oblivion which is the last word of our common fate. I don't defend myself. I had no clear perception of what it was I really wanted. Perhaps it was an impulse of unconscious loyalty, or the fulfilment of one of those ironic necessities that lurk in the facts of human existence. I don't know. I can't tell. But I went.

"I thought his memory was like other memories of the dead that accumulate in every man's life,—a vague impress on the brain of shadows that had fallen on it in their swift and final passage; but before the high and ponderous door, between the tall houses of a street as still and decorous as a well-kept sepulchre, I had a vision of him on the stretcher, opening his mouth voraciously, as if to devour all the earth with all its mankind. He lived then before me; he lived as much as he had ever lived—a shadow insatiable of splendid appearances, of frightful realities; a shadow darker than the shadow of the night, and draped nobly in the folds of a gorgeous eloquence. The vision seemed to enter the house with me—the stretcher, the phantom-bearers, the wild crowd of obedient worshippers; the gloom of the forests; the glitter of the reach between the murky bends; the beat of the drum, regular and muffled like the beating of a heart—the heart of a conquering darkness. It was a moment of triumph for the wilderness, an invading and vengeful rush which, it seemed to me, I would have to keep back alone for the salvation of another soul. And the memory of what I had heard him say afar there, with the horned shapes stirring at my back, in the glow of fires, within the patient woods, those broken phrases came back to me, were heard again in their ominous and terrifying simplicity: 'I have lived—supremely!' 'What do you want here? I have been dead—and damned.' 'Let me go—I want more of it.' More of what? More blood, more heads on stakes, more adoration, rapine, and murder. I remembered his abject pleading, his abject threats, the colossal scale of his vile desires, the meanness, the torment, the tempestuous anguish of his soul. And later on his collected languid manner, when he said one day, 'This lot of ivory now is really mine. The Company did not pay for it. I collected it myself at my personal risk. I am afraid they will claim it as theirs. It is a difficult case. What do you think I ought to do—resist? Eh? I want no more than justice.' He wanted no more than justice. No more than justice. I rang the bell before a mahogany door on the first floor, and while I waited he seemed to stare at me out of the gleaming panel—stare with that wide and immense stare embracing, condemning, loathing all the universe. I seemed to hear the whispered cry, 'The horror! The horror!'

"The dusk was falling. I had to wait in a lofty drawing-room with three long windows from floor to ceiling that were like three luminous and bedraped columns. The bent gilt legs and backs of the furniture shone in indistinct curves. The tall marble fireplace had a cold and heavy whiteness. A grand piano stood massively in a corner, with dark gleams on the flat surfaces like a sombre and polished sarcophagus. A high door opened—closed. I rose.

"She came forward, all in black, with a pale head, floating towards me in the dusk. She was in mourning. It was more than a year since his death, more than a year since the news came; she seemed as though she would remember and mourn for ever. She took both my hands in hers and murmured, 'I had heard you were coming.' I noticed she was not very young—I mean not girlish. She had a mature capacity for fidelity, for belief, for suffering. The room seemed to have grown darker, as if all the sad light of the cloudy evening had taken refuge on her forehead. This fair hair, this pale visage, this pure brow, seemed surrounded by an ashy halo from which the dark eyes looked out at me. Their glance was guileless, profound, confident, and trustful. She carried her sorrowful head as though she were proud of that sorrow, as though she would say, I—I alone know how to mourn for him as he deserves. But while we were still shaking hands, such a look of awful desolation came upon her face that I perceived she was one of those creatures that are not the playthings of Time. For her he had died only yesterday. And, by Jove! the impression was so powerful that for me too he seemed to have died only yesterday—nay, this very minute. I saw her and him in the same instant of time—his death and her sorrow. I saw her sorrow in the very moment of his death. It was too terrible. Do you understand? I saw them together— I heard them together. She had said, with a deep catch of the breath, 'I have survived'; while my strained ears seemed to hear distinctly, mingled with her tone of despairing regret, the summing-up whisper of his eternal condemnation. I asked myself what I was doing there, with a sensation of panic in my heart as though I had blundered into a place of cruel and absurd mysteries not fit for a human being to behold. I wanted to get out. She motioned me to a chair. We sat down. I laid the packet gently on the little table, and she put her hand over it. 'You knew him well,' she murmured, after a moment of mourning silence.

"'Intimacy grows quickly out there,' I said. 'I knew him as well as it is possible for one man to know another.'

"'And you admired him,' she said. 'It was impossible to know him and not to admire him. Was it?'

"'He was a remarkable man,' I said, unsteadily. Then before the appealing fixity of her gaze, that seemed to watch for more words on my lips, I went on, 'It was impossible not to—'

"'Love him,' she finished eagerly, silencing me into an appalled dumbness. 'How true! how true! But when you think that no one knew him so well as I! I had all his noble confidence. I knew him best.'

"'You knew him best,' I repeated. And perhaps she did. But I fancied that with every word spoken the room was growing darker, and only her forehead, smooth and white, remained illumined by the unextinguishable light of belief and love.

"'You were his friend,' she went on. 'His friend,' she repeated, a little louder. 'You must have been, if he had given this to you, and sent you to me. I feel I can speak to you—oh! I must speak. I want you—you who have heard his last words—to know I have been worthy of him.... It is not pride.... Yes! I am proud to know I understood him better than anyone on earth—he said so himself. And since his mother died I have had no one—no one—to—to—'

"I listened. The darkness deepened. I was not even sure whether he had given me the right bundle. I rather suspect he wanted me to take care of another batch of his papers which, after his death, I saw the manager examining under the lamp. But in the box I had brought to his bedside there were several packages pretty well all alike, all tied with shoe-strings, and probably he had made a mistake. And the girl talked, easing her pain in the certitude of my sympathy; she talked as thirsty men drink. I had heard that her engagement with Kurtz had been disapproved generally. He wasn't rich enough or something. And indeed I don't know whether he had not been a pauper all his life. He had given me some reason to infer that it was his impatience of comparative poverty that drove him out there.

"'...Who was not his friend who had heard him speak once?' she was saying. 'He drew men towards him by what was best in them.' She looked at me with intensity. 'It is the gift of the great,' she went on, and the sound of her low voice seemed to have the accompaniment of all the other sounds, full of mystery, desolation, and sorrow, I had ever heard—the ripple of the river, the soughing* of the trees swayed by the wind, the murmurs of wild crowds, the faint ring of incomprehensible words cried from afar, the whisper of a voice speaking from beyond the threshold of an eternal darkness. 'But you have heard him! You know!' she cried.

"'Yes, I know,' I said with something like despair in my heart, but bowing my head before the faith that was in her, before that great and saving illusion that shone with an unearthly glow in the darkness, in the triumphant darkness from which I could not have defended her—from which I could not even defend myself.

"'What a loss to me—to us!'—she corrected herself with beautiful generosity; then added in a murmur, 'To the world.' By the last gleams of twilight I could see the glitter of her eyes, full of tears—of tears that would not fall.

"'I have been very happy—very fortunate—very proud,' she went on. 'Too fortunate. Too happy for a little while. And now I am unhappy for—for life.'

"She stood up; her fair hair seemed to catch all the remaining light in a glimmer of gold. I rose too.

"'And of all this,' she went on mournfully, 'of all his promise, and of all his greatness, of his gen-erous mind, of his noble heart, nothing remains—nothing but a memory. You and I—'

"'We shall always remember him,' I said, hastily.

"'No!' she cried. 'It is impossible that all this should be lost—that such a life should be sacrificed to leave nothing—but sorrow. You know he had vast plans. I knew them too—I could not perhaps understand,—but others knew of them. Something must remain. His words, at least, have not died.'

"'His words will remain,' I said.

"'And his example,' she whispered to herself. 'Wherever he went men looked up to him,—his goodness shone in every act. His example—'

"'True,' I said; 'his example too. Yes, his example. I forgot that.'

"'But I do not. I cannot—I cannot believe—not yet. I cannot believe that I shall never see him again, that nobody will see him again, never, never, never.'

"She put out her arms as if after a retreating figure, stretching them black and with clasped pale hands across the fading and narrow sheen of the window. Never see him. I saw him clearly enough then. I shall see this eloquent phantom as long as I live, and I shall see her too, a tragic and familiar Shade, resembling in this gesture another one, tragic also, and bedecked with powerless charms, stretching bare brown arms over the glitter of the infernal stream, the stream of darkness. She said suddenly very low, 'He died as he lived.'

"'His end,' said I, with dull anger stirring in me, 'was in every way worthy of his life.'

"'And I was not with him,' she murmured. My anger subsided before a feeling of infinite pity.

"'Everything that could be done—' I mumbled.

"'Ah, but I believed in him more than any one on earth—more than his own mother, more than—himself. He needed me! Me! I would have treasured every sigh, every murmur, every word, every sign, every glance.'

"I felt like a chill grip on my chest. 'Don't,' I said, in a muffled voice.

"'Forgive me. I—I—have mourned so long in silence—in silence.... You were with him—to the last? I think of his loneliness. Nobody near to understand him as I would have understood. Perhaps no one to hear....'

"'To the very end,' I said shakily. 'I heard his very last words....' I stopped in a fright.

"'Repeat them,' she said in a heart-broken tone. 'I want—I want—something—something—to—to live with.'

"I was on the point of crying at her, 'Don't you hear them?' The dusk was repeating them in a persistent whisper all around us, in a whisper that seemed to swell menacingly like the first whisper of a rising wind. 'The horror! The horror!'

"'His last word—to live with,' she murmured. 'Don't you understand I loved him—I loved him—I loved him!'

"I pulled myself together and spoke slowly.

"'The last word he pronounced was—your name.'

"I heard a light sigh, and then my heart stood still, stopped dead short by an exulting and terrible cry, by the cry of inconceivable triumph and of unspeakable pain. 'I knew it—I was sure!' She knew. She was sure. I heard her weeping, her face in her hands. It seemed to me that the house would collapse before I could escape, that the heavens would fall upon my head. But nothing happened. The heavens do not fall for such a trifle. Would they have fallen, I wonder, if I had rendered Kurtz that justice which was his due? Hadn't he said he wanted only justice? But I couldn't. I could not tell her. It would have been too dark—too dark altogether...."

Marlow ceased, and sat apart, indistinct and silent, in the pose of a meditating Buddha. Nobody moved for a time.

"We have lost the first of the ebb," said the Director, suddenly. I looked around. The offing was barred by a black bank of clouds, and the tranquil waterway leading to the uttermost ends of the earth flowed sombre under an overcast sky—seemed to lead also into the heart of an immense darkness.

(The end.)

absconded - to have gone away hurriedly and secretly, often to avoid punishment; hide

calico - printed white cotton cloth or any cotton cloth from the East, especially India

cipher - secret writing or code

conflagrations - big and destructive fires

despondency - loss of heart, courage or hope; discouragement; dejection

drubbing - beating, thrashing

estuary - a broad mouth of a river into which the tide flows

evanescent - gradually disappearring, soon passing away; vanishing

gaberdine - a man's long, loose outer garment or cloak, worn in the Middle Ages

hardihood - boldness; daring

immutability - not changeable; unable to change

incontinently - without self-control or restraint

inscrutable - cannot be understood; so mysterious or obscure that one cannot make out its meaning; incomprehensible

interminable - never stopping, unceasing, endless

intercourse - dealings between people, communication

jocose - full of jokes and humor

languidly - weakly, without energy, drooping

languor - lack of energy, weakness

obseqious - polite and obedient from hope of gain or fear

particoloured - colored differently in different parts, diversified

peroration - the end of an oration, summing up what was said, delivered with considerable force

postscriptum - a supplementary part added to a literary work

prevaricator - a person who turns aside from the truth in speech or action

promptitude - readiness in acting or deciding; promptness

rapacious - grasping, greedy

recrudescence - a breaking out afresh; renewed activity

sententously - full of meaning; saying much in a few words

somnambulist - sleepwalker

stanchions - upright bars or posts used as support for the deck of a ship

soughing - to make a rustling, rushing, or murmuring sound

stenebrous - dark, gloomy, dim

superciliousness - showing scorn or indifference because of a feeling of superiority; haughty proud and contemptious; disdainful

tremulous - trembling; quivering; quavering

trenchant - sharp, keen, cutting

unostentatious - not showy or pretentious; inconspicuous; modest

untrammelled - not hindered or restrained

venerable - worthy of reverence; deserving respect because of age, character, or importance

volubility - the tendency to talk too much; fondness for talking

 Fill in each of the following blanks with the correct explanation or answer.

1.41   On what real life adventure of Conrad's is the novella based?

_____

1.42   To whom is Captain Marlow telling his story? And where is he telling it?

_____

1.43   Why do you think Marlow refers to the Roman conquest of England before he begins his tale?

_____

1.44   List some significant details in Marlow's description of the Company headquarters and the city in which it is located.

_____

1.45   Describe the condition of the natives in the Company Station.

_____

1.46   How does the "brick maker" at the Central Station describe Mr. Kurtz?

_____

1.47   What aspects of the jungle lead Marlow to describe the heart of Africa as the "heart of darkness?"

_____

1.48   Why do the natives aboard Marlow's ship want to fight the natives in the jungle?

_____

1.49   After the natives attack the steamboat, what do the "pilgrims" think has happened to Kurtz?

_____

1.50   What is significant about Marlow's statement concerning Kurtz's baldness: "They say the hair goes on growing sometimes?"

_____

1.51   What reason does the Russian give for his admiration of Kurtz?

_____

1.52   Describe the appearance of the native woman who is devoted to Kurtz.

_____

1.53   After realizing that Kurtz has participated in barbaric ceremonies to win the admiration of the natives, why does Marlow describe him as "hollow at the core?"

_____

1.54   When he is pursuing Kurtz into the jungle, who does Marlow imagine is at the end of the path in the heart of the jungle?

_____

1.55   What are Kurtz's last words?

_____

1.56   When Marlow is visiting Kurtz's grieving "Intended," what does he say were Kurtz's last words, and why?

_____

Gilbert Keith Chesterton (1874–1936). Born in London, Gilbert Keith Chesterton was educated at St. Paul's School and later at Slade Art School. After giving up the prospect of becoming an artist, Chesterton turned to journalism and began writing articles for newspapers and magazines on a wide variety of subjects, including history, politics, economics, literature, and religion. In 1900, Chesterton published his first book, a collection of poetry titled *The Wild Knight*. As one critic has observed, most of Chesterton's poetry tends to "celebrate the Englishness of England, the nation of Beef and Beer." The first in his popular Father Brown mystery stories, *The Innocence of Father Brown*, appeared in 1911. In addition to his works of poetry and fiction, Chesterton also published several biographies and plays. His body of work totals more than a hundred books.

In 1911 Chesterton began contributing regularly to the *Eye Witness*, a weekly journal founded by his brother Cecil Chesterton (1879–1918) and his friend Hilaire Belloc (1870–1953). After he became the journal's editor in 1925, he renamed it *G. K.'s Weekly*. Chesterton used the publication to address the effects of capitalism and socialism on society. As one writer noted, Chesterton's keen historical insight allowed him to warn Britons of the "cultural chaos wrought by modernism."

By the time the First World War broke out, Chesterton was a well-loved and respected essayist. The War Propaganda Bureau asked him to write pamphlets in support of England's efforts. His war time essays were effective in helping the English people cope with feelings of hopelessness brought about by the threat of a German invasion.

Equally profound in his religious essays, Chesterton has been described as "the ablest and most exuberant proponent of orthodox Christianity of his time." Chesterton published important works, including *Heretics* (1905), *Orthodoxy* (1909), and *The Everlasting Man* (1925), that have had lasting appeal with Protestants and Catholics. (He converted to Roman Catholicism in 1922, but, as one critic has noted, his worldview contains elements of latent Protestantism. In particular, his faith in democracy stands in stark contrast to the hierarchical system of the Roman Catholic Church.) As an able and witty apologist, Chesterton commanded the respect of many of Christianity's most ardent critics, including George Bernard Shaw, who referred to him as the "colossal genius." T. S. Eliot once said of Chesterton, "He did more, I think, than any man of his time…to maintain the existence of the important minority in the modern world."

Underline the correct answer in each of the following statements.

1.57   G. K. Chesterton's poetry celebrates traditional (England, Germany, America).

1.58   Chesterton first achieved literary notoriety as a (novelist, politician, journalist).

1.59   During the (Second World War, First World War, Vietnam War), Chesterton was asked to write pamphlets in support of England's efforts to stave off (French, American, German) aggression.

1.60   Chesterton used (*G. K.'s Weekly*, *Orthodoxy*, *The Wild Knight*) to address publicly the effects of capitalism and socialism on society.

1.61   An able proponent of (conservative politics, capitalism, orthodox Christianity), Chesterton wrote religious essays that have commanded the respect of some of the most ardent skeptics.

1.62   Chesterton's religious essays have been (appreciated, condemned, banned) by both Catholics and Protestants.

What to Look For:

Before coming to Christ, C. S. Lewis was greatly affected by the apologetic writings of Chesterton. He once remarked that Chesterton's writings allowed him to see for the first time "the whole Christian outline of history set out in a form that seemed to me to make sense." As you read, notice Chesterton's answers to the skepticism of modern intellectuals. Why does he insist that an active belief in the existence of the Triune God is western civilization's only hope for "humanity and liberty and love?"

From: *Orthodoxy*—Chapter 8:

The Romance of Orthodoxy

It is customary to complain of the bustle and strenuousness of our epoch.* But in truth the chief mark of our epoch is a profound laziness and fatigue; and the fact is that the real laziness is the cause of the apparent bustle. Take one quite external case; the streets are noisy with taxicabs and motorcars; but this is not due to human activity but to human repose. There would be less bustle if there were more activity, if people were simply walking about. Our world would be more silent if it were more strenuous. And this which is true of the apparent physical bustle is true also of the apparent bustle of the intellect. Most of the machinery of modern language is labour-saving machinery; and it saves mental labour very much more than it ought. Scientific phrases are used like scientific wheels and piston-rods to make swifter and smoother yet the path of the comfortable. Long words go rattling by us like long railway trains. We know they are carrying thousands who are too tired or too indolent* to walk and think for themselves. It is a good exercise to try for once in a way to express any opinion one holds in words of one syllable. If you say

"The social utility of the indeterminate sentence is recognized by all criminologists as a part of our sociological evolution towards a more humane and scientific view of punishment," you can go on talking like that for hours with hardly a movement of the gray matter inside your skull. But if you begin "I wish Jones to go to gaol* and Brown to say when Jones shall come out," you will discover, with a thrill of horror, that you are obliged to think. The long words are not the hard words, it is the short words that are hard. There is much more metaphysical subtlety in the word *damn* than in the word *degeneration*.

But these long comfortable words that save modern people the toil of reasoning have one particular aspect in which they are especially ruinous and confusing. This difficulty occurs when the same long word is used in different connections to mean quite different things. Thus, to take a well-known instance, the word *idealist* has one meaning as a piece of philosophy and quite another as a piece of moral rhetoric. In the same way the scientific materialists have had just reason to complain of people mixing up *materialist* as a term of cosmology with *materialist* as a moral taunt. So, to take a cheaper instance, the man who hates "progressives" in London always calls himself a "progressive" in South Africa.

A confusion quite as unmeaning as this has arisen in connection with the word *liberal* as applied to religion and as applied to politics and society. It is often suggested that all Liberals ought to be freethinkers, because they ought to love everything that is free. You might just as well say that all idealists ought to be High Churchmen, because they ought to love everything that is high. You might as well say that Low Churchmen ought to like Low Mass, or that Broad Churchmen ought to like broad jokes.

The thing is a mere accident of words. In actual modern Europe a freethinker does not mean a man who thinks for himself. It means a man who, having thought for himself, has come to one particular class of conclusions, the material origin of phenomena, the impossibility of miracles, the improbability of personal immortality and so on. And none of these ideas are particularly liberal. Nay, indeed almost all these ideas are definitely illiberal, as it is the purpose of this chapter to show.

In the few following pages I propose to point out as rapidly as possible that on every single one of the matters most strongly insisted on by liberalisers of theology their effect upon social practice would be definitely illiberal. Almost every contemporary proposal to bring freedom into the church is simply a proposal to bring tyranny into the world. For freeing the church now does not even mean freeing it in all directions. It means freeing that peculiar set of dogmas loosely called scientific, dogmas of monism,* of pantheism,* or of Arianism,* or of necessity. And every one of these (and we will take them one by one) can be shown to be the natural ally of oppression. In fact, it is a remarkable circumstance (indeed not so very remarkable when one comes to think of it) that most things are the allies of oppression. There is only one thing that can never go past a certain point in its alliance with oppression—and that is **orthodoxy***. I may, it is true, twist orthodoxy so as partly to justify a tyrant. But I can easily make up a German philosophy to justify him entirely.

Now let us take in order the innovations that are the notes of the new theology or the modernist church. We concluded the last chapter with the discovery of one of them. The very doctrine which is called the most old-fashioned was found to be the only safeguard of the new democracies of the earth. The doctrine seemingly most unpopular was found to be the only strength of the people. In short, we found that the only logical negation of oligarchy was in the affirmation of original sin. So it is, I maintain, in all the other cases.

I take the most obvious instance first, the case of miracles. For some extraordinary reason, there is a fixed notion that it is more liberal to disbelieve in miracles than to believe in them. Why, I cannot imagine, nor can anybody tell me. For some inconceivable cause a "broad" or "liberal" clergyman always means a man who wishes at least to diminish the number of miracles; it never means a man who wishes to increase that number. It always means a man who is free to disbelieve that Christ came out of His grave; it never means a man who is free to believe that his own aunt came out of her grave. It is common to find trouble in a parish because the parish priest cannot admit that St.

Peter walked on water; yet how rarely do we find trouble in a parish because the clergyman says that his father walked on the Serpentine? And this is not because (as the swift secularist debater would immediately retort) miracles cannot be believed in our experience. It is not because "miracles do not happen," as in the dogma which Matthew Arnold recited with simple faith. More supernatural things are ALLEGED to have happened in our time than would have been possible eighty years ago. Men of science believe in such marvels much more than they did: the most perplexing, and even horrible, prodigies of mind and spirit are always being unveiled inmodern psychology.

Things that the old science at least would frankly have rejected as miracles are hourly being asserted by the new science. The only thing which is still old-fashioned enough to reject miracles is the New Theology. But in truth this notion that it is "free" to deny miracles has nothing to do with the evidence for or against them. It is a lifeless verbal prejudice of which the original life and beginning was not in the freedom of thought, but simply in the dogma of materialism. The man of the nineteenth century did not disbelieve in the Resurrection because his liberal Christianity allowed him to doubt it. He disbelieved in it because his very strict materialism did not allow him to believe it. Tennyson, a very typical nineteenth century man, uttered one of the instinctive truisms* of his contemporaries when he said that there was faith in their honest doubt. There was indeed. Those words have a profound and even a horrible truth. In their doubt of miracles there was a faith in a fixed and godless fate; a deep and sincere faith in the incurable routine of the cosmos. The doubts of the agnostic were only the dogmas of the monist.

Of the fact and evidence of the supernatural I will speak afterwards. Here we are only concerned with this clear point; that in so far as the liberal idea of freedom can be said to be on either side in the discussion about miracles, it is obviously on the side of miracles. Reform or (in the only tolerable sense) progress means simply the gradual control of matter by mind. A miracle simply means the swift control of matter by mind. If you wish to feed the people, you may think that feeding them miraculously in the wilderness is impossible—but you cannot think it illiberal. If you really want poor children to go to the seaside, you cannot think it illiberal that they should go there on flying dragons; you can only think it unlikely. A holiday, like Liberalism, only means the liberty of man. A miracle only means the liberty of God. You may conscientiously deny either of them, but you cannot call your denial a triumph of the liberal idea. The

Catholic Church believed that man and God both had a sort of spiritual freedom. Calvinism took away the freedom from man, but left it to God. Scientific materialism binds the Creator Himself; it chains up God as the Apocalypse chained the devil. It leaves nothing free in the universe. And those who assist this process are called the "liberal theologians."

This, as I say, is the lightest and most evident case. The assumption that there is something in the doubt of miracles akin to liberality or reform is literally the opposite of the truth. If a man cannot believe in miracles there is an end of the matter; he is not particularly liberal, but he is perfectly honourable and logical, which are much better things. But if he can believe in miracles, he is certainly the more liberal for doing so; because they mean first, the freedom of the soul, and secondly, its control over the tyranny of circumstance. Sometimes this truth is ignored in a singularly naive way, even by the ablest men. For instance, Mr. Bernard Shaw speaks with hearty old-fashioned contempt for the idea of miracles, as if they were a sort of breach of faith on the part of nature: he seems strangely unconscious that miracles are only the final flowers of his own favourite tree, the doctrine of the omnipotence of will. Just in the same way he calls the desire for immortality a paltry selfishness, forgetting that he has just called the desire for life a healthy and heroic selfishness. How can it be noble to wish to make one's life infinite and yet mean to wish to make it immortal? No, if it is desirable that man should triumph over the cruelty of nature or custom, then miracles are certainly desirable; we will discuss afterwards whether they are possible.

But I must pass on to the larger cases of this curious error; the notion that the "liberalising" of religion in some way helps the liberation of the world. The second example of it can be found in the question of pantheism—or rather of a certain modern attitude which is often called immanentism,* and which often is Buddhism. But this is so much more difficult a matter that I must approach it with rather more preparation.

The things said most confidently by advanced persons to crowded audiences are generally those quite opposite to the fact; it is actually our truisms that are untrue. Here is a case. There is a phrase of facile* liberality uttered again and again at ethical societies and parliaments of religion: "the religions of the earth differ in rites and forms, but they are the same in what they teach." It is false; it is the opposite of the fact. The religions of the earth do not greatly differ in rites and forms; they do greatly differ in what they teach. It is as if a man were to say, "Do not be misled by the fact that the *CHURCH TIMES* and the *FREETHINKER* look

utterly different, that one is painted on vellum and the other carved on marble, that one is triangular and the other hectagonal; read them and you will see that they say the same thing." The truth is, of course, that they are alike in everything except in the fact that they don't say the same thing. An atheist stockbroker in Surbiton looks exactly like a Swedenborgian* stockbroker in Wimbledon. You may walk round and round them and subject them to the most personal and offensive study without seeing anything Swedenborgian in the hat or anything particularly godless in the umbrella. It is exactly in their souls that they are divided. So the truth is that the difficulty of all the creeds of the earth is not as alleged in this cheap maxim: that they agree in meaning, but differ in machinery. It is exactly the opposite. They agree in machinery; almost every great religion on earth works with the same external methods, with priests, scriptures, altars, sworn brotherhoods, special feasts. They agree in the mode of teaching; what they differ about is the thing to be taught. Pagan optimists and Eastern pessimists would both have temples, just as Liberals and Tories would both have newspapers. Creeds that exist to destroy each other both have scriptures, just as armies that exist to destroy each other both have guns.

The great example of this alleged identity of all human religions is the alleged spiritual identity of Buddhism and Christianity. Those who adopt this theory generally avoid the ethics of most other creeds, except, indeed, Confucianism, which they like because it is not a creed. But they are cautious in their praises of Mahommedanism,* generally confining themselves to imposing its morality only upon the refreshment of the lower classes. They seldom suggest the Mahommedan view of marriage (for which there is a great deal to be said), and towards Thugs and fetish worshippers their attitude may even be called cold. But in the case of the great religion of Gautama they feel sincerely a similarity.

Students of popular science, like Mr. Blatchford, are always insisting that Christianity and Buddhism are very much alike, especially Buddhism. This is generally believed, and I believed it myself until I read a book giving the reasons for it. The reasons were of two kinds: resemblances that meant nothing because they were common to all humanity, and resemblances which were not resemblances at all. The author solemnly explained that the two creeds were alike in things in which all creeds are alike, or else he described them as alike in some point in which they are quite obviously different. Thus, as a case of the first class, he said that both Christ and Buddha were called by the divine voice coming out of the sky, as if you would expect the divine voice to come out of the coal-cellar. Or, again, it was gravely urged that these two Eastern teachers, by a singular coincidence, both had to do with the washing of feet. You might as well say that it was a remarkable coincidence that they both had feet to wash. And the other class of similarities were those which simply were not similar. Thus this reconciler of the two religions draws earnest attention to the fact that at certain religious feasts the robe of the Lama is rent in pieces out of respect, and the remnants highly valued. But this is the reverse of a resemblance, for the garments of Christ were not rent in pieces out of respect, but out of derision; and the remnants were not highly valued except for what they would fetch in the rag shops. It is rather like alluding to the obvious connection between the two ceremonies of the sword: when it taps a man's shoulder, and when it cuts off his head. It is not at all similar for the man. These scraps of puerile pedantry would indeed matter little if it were not also true that the alleged philosophical resemblances are also of these two kinds, either proving too much or not proving anything. That Buddhism approves of mercy or of self-restraint is not to say that it is specially like Christianity; it is only to say that it is not utterly unlike all human existence. Buddhists disapprove in theory of cruelty or excess because all sane human beings disapprove in theory of cruelty or excess. But to say that Buddhism and Christianity give the same philosophy of these things is simply false. All humanity does agree that we are in a net of sin. Most of humanity agrees that there is some way out. But as to what is the way out, I do not think that there are two institutions in the universe which contradict each other so flatly as Buddhism and Christianity.

Even when I thought, with most other well-informed, though unscholarly, people, that Buddhism and Christianity were alike, there was one thing about them that always perplexed me; I mean the startling difference in their type of religious art. I do not mean in its technical style of representation, but in the things that it was manifestly meant to represent. No two ideals could be more opposite than a Christian saint in a Gothic cathedral and a Buddhist saint in a Chinese temple. The opposition exists at every point; but perhaps the shortest statement of it is that the Buddhist saint always has his eyes shut, while the Christian saint always has them very wide open. The Buddhist saint has a sleek and harmonious body, but his eyes are heavy and sealed with sleep. The mediaeval saint's body is wasted to its crazy bones, but his eyes are frightfully alive. There cannot be any real community of spirit between forces that produced symbols so different as that. Granted that both images are extravagances, are perversions of the pure creed, it must be a real divergence which could produce such opposite extravagances. The Buddhist

is looking with a peculiar intentness inwards. The Christian is staring with a frantic intentness outwards. If we follow that clue steadily we shall find some interesting things.

A short time ago Mrs. Besant,* in an interesting essay, announced that there was only one religion in the world, that all faiths were only versions or perversions of it, and that she was quite prepared to say what it was. According to Mrs. Besant this universal Church is simply the universal self. It is the doctrine that we are really all one person; that there are no real walls of individuality between man and man. If I may put it so, she does not tell us to love our neighbours; she tells us to be our neighbours. That is Mrs. Besant's thoughtful and suggestive description of the religion in which all men must find themselves in agreement. And I never heard of any suggestion in my life with which I more violently disagree. I want to love my neighbour not because he is I, but precisely because he is not I. I want to adore the world, not as one likes a looking-glass, because it is one's self, but as one loves a woman, because she is entirely different. If souls are separate love is possible. If souls are united love is obviously impossible. A man may be said loosely to love himself, but he can hardly fall in love with himself, or, if he does, it must be a monotonous courtship. If the world is full of real selves, they can be really unselfish selves. But upon Mrs. Besant's principle the whole cosmos is only one enormously selfish person.

It is just here that Buddhism is on the side of modern pantheism and **immanence***. And it is just here that Christianity is on the side of humanity and liberty and love. Love desires personality; therefore love desires division. It is the instinct of Christianity to be glad that God has broken the universe into little pieces, because they are living pieces. It is her instinct to say "little children love one another" rather than to tell one large person to love himself. This is the intellectual abyss between Buddhism and Christianity; that for the Buddhist or Theosophist personality is the fall of man, for the Christian it is the purpose of God, the whole point of his cosmic idea. The world-soul of the Theosophists* asks man to love it only in order that man may throw himself into it. But the divine centre of Christianity actually threw man out of it in order that he might love it. The oriental deity is like a giant who should have lost his leg or hand and be always seeking to find it; but the Christian power is like some giant who in a strange generosity should cut off his right hand, so that it might of its own accord shake hands with him. We come back to the same tireless note touching the nature of Christianity; all modern philosophies are chains which connect and fetter; Christianity is a sword which separates and sets free. No other philosophy makes God actually rejoice in the separation of the universe into living souls. But according to orthodox Christianity this separation between God and man is sacred, because this is eternal. That a man may love God it is necessary that there should be not only a God to be loved, but a man to love him. All those vague theosophical minds for whom the universe is an immense melting-pot are exactly the minds which shrink instinctively from that earthquake saying of our Gospels, which declare that the Son of God came not with peace but with a sundering sword. The saying rings entirely true even considered as what it obviously is; the statement that any man who preaches real love is bound to beget hate. It is as true of democratic fraternity as a divine love; sham love ends in compromise and common philosophy; but real love has always ended in bloodshed. Yet there is another and yet more awful truth behind the obvious meaning of this utterance of our Lord. According to Himself the Son was a sword separating brother and brother that they should for an aeon hate each other. But the Father also was a sword, which in the black beginning separated brother and brother, so that they should love each other at last.

This is the meaning of that almost insane happiness in the eyes of the mediaeval saint in the picture. This is the meaning of the sealed eyes of the superb Buddhist image. The Christian saint is happy because he has verily been cut off from the world; he is separate from things and is staring at them in astonishment. But why should the Buddhist saint be astonished at things? —since there is really only one thing, and that being impersonal can hardly be astonished at itself. There have been many pantheist poems suggesting wonder, but no really successful ones. The pantheist cannot wonder, for he cannot praise God or praise anything as really distinct from himself. Our immediate business here, however, is with the effect of this Christian admiration (which strikes outwards, towards a deity distinct from the worshipper) upon the general need for ethical activity and social reform. And surely its effect is sufficiently obvious. There is no real possibility of getting out of pantheism, any special impulse to moral action. For pantheism implies in its nature that one thing is as good as another; whereas action implies in its nature that one thing is greatly preferable to another. Swinburne* in the high summer of his scepticism tried in vain to wrestle with this difficulty. In *Songs before Sunrise*, written under the inspiration of Garibaldi* and the revolt of Italy he proclaimed the newer religion and the purer God which should wither up all the priests of the world:

What doest thou now
Looking Godward to cry
I am I, thou art thou,

I am low, thou art high,
I am thou that thou seekest to find him,
find thou but thyself,
thou art I.

Of which the immediate and evident deduction is that tyrants are as much the sons of God as Garibald is; and that King Bomba of Naples having, with the utmost success, "found himself" is identical with the ultimate good in all things. The truth is that the western energy that dethrones tyrants has been directly due to the western theology that says "I am I, thou art thou." The same spiritual separation which looked up and saw a good king in the universe looked up and saw a bad king in Naples. The worshippers of Bomba's god dethroned Bomba. The worshippers of Swinburne's god have covered Asia for centuries and have never dethroned a tyrant. The Indian saint may reasonably shut his eyes because he is looking at that which is I and Thou and We and They and It. It is a rational occupation: but it is not true in theory and not true in fact that it helps the Indian to keep an eye on Lord Curzon. That external vigilance which has always been the mark of Christianity (the command that we should WATCH and pray) has expressed itself both in typical western orthodoxy and in typical western politics: but both depend on the idea of a divinity transcendent,* different from ourselves, a deity that disappears. Certainly the most sagacious creeds may suggest that we should pursue God into deeper and deeper rings of the labyrinth of our own ego. But only we of Christendom have said that we should hunt God like an eagle upon the mountains: and we have killed all monsters in the chase.

Here again, therefore, we find that in so far as we value democracy and the self-renewing energies of the west, we are much more likely to find them in the old theology than the new. If we want reform, we must adhere to orthodoxy: especially in this matter (so much disputed in the counsels of Mr. R. J.Campbell), the matter of insisting on the immanent or the transcendent deity. By insisting specially on the immanence of God we get introspection, self-isolation, quietism, social indifference—Tibet. By insisting specially on the transcendence of God we get wonder, curiosity, moral and political adventure, righteous indignation—Christendom. Insisting that God is inside man, man is always inside himself. By insisting that God transcends man, man has transcended himself.

If we take any other doctrine that has been called old-fashioned we shall find the case the same. It is the same, for instance, in the deep matter of the Trinity. Unitarians (a sect never to be mentioned without a special respect for their distinguished intellectual dignity and high intellectual honour) are often reformers by the accident that throws so many small sects into such an attitude. But there is nothing in the least liberal or akin to reform in the substitution of pure monotheism for the Trinity. The complex God of the Athanasian Creed may be an enigma for the intellect; but He is far less likely to gather the mystery and cruelty of a Sultan than the lonely god of Omar or Mahomet. The god who is a mere awful unity is not only a king but an Eastern king. The HEART of humanity, especially of European humanity, is certainly much more satisfied by the strange hints and symbols that gather round the Trinitarian idea, the image of a council at which mercy pleads as well as justice, the conception of a sort of liberty and variety existing even in the inmost chamber of the world. For Western religion has always felt keenly the idea "it is not well for man to be alone." The social instinct asserted itself everywhere as when the Eastern idea of hermits was practically expelled by the Western idea of monks. So even asceticism became brotherly; and the Trappists were sociable even when they were silent. If this love of a living complexity be our test, it is certainly healthier to have the Trinitarian religion than the Unitarian. For to us Trinitarians (if I may say it with reverence)—to us God Himself is a society. It is indeed a fathomless mystery of theology, and even if I were theologian enough to deal with it directly, it would not be relevant to do so here. Suffice it to say here that this triple enigma is as comforting as wine and open as an English fireside; that this thing that bewilders the intellect utterly quiets the heart: but out of the desert, from the dry places and the dreadful suns, come the cruel children of the lonely God; the real Unitarians who with scimitar in hand have laid waste the world. For it is not well for God to be alone.

Again, the same is true of that difficult matter of the danger of the soul, which has unsettled so many just minds. To hope for all souls is imperative; and it is quite tenable that their salvation is inevitable. It is tenable, but it is not specially favourable to activity or progress. Our fighting and creative society ought rather to insist on the danger of everybody, on the fact that every man is hanging by a thread or clinging to a precipice. To say that all will be well anyhow is a comprehensible remark: but it cannot be called the blast of a trumpet. Europe ought rather to emphasize possible perdition; and Europe always has emphasized it. Here its highest religion is at one with all its cheapest romances. To the Buddhist or the eastern fatalist existence is a science or a plan, which must end up in a certain way. But to a Christian existence is a STORY, which may end up in any way. In a thrilling novel (that purely Christian product) the hero is not eaten by cannibals; but it is essential to the existence of the thrill that he MIGHT be eaten by cannibals. The hero must (so to speak) be an eatable hero. So Christian morals have always said to the man, not that he would lose his soul, but that he must take care that he didn't. In Christian morals, in short, it is wicked to call a man "damned": but it is strictly religious and philosophic to call him damnable.

All Christianity concentrates on the man at the cross-roads. The vast and shallow philosophies, the huge syntheses of humbug, all talk about ages and evolution and ultimate developments. The true philosophy is concerned with the instant. Will a man take this road or that? —that is the only thing to think about, if you enjoy thinking. The aeons are easy enough to think about, any one can think about them. The instant is really awful: and it is because our religion has intensely felt the instant, that it has in literature dealt much with battle and in theology dealt much with hell. It is full of DANGER, like a boy's book: it is at an immortal crisis. There is a great deal of real similarity between popular fiction and the religion of the western people. If you say that popular fiction is vulgar and tawdry, you only say what the dreary and well-informed say also about the images in the Catholic churches. Life (according to the faith) is very like a serial story in a magazine: life ends with the promise (or menace) "to be continued in our next." Also, with a noble vulgarity, life imitates the serial and leaves off at the exciting moment. For death is distinctly an exciting moment.

But the point is that a story is exciting because it has in it so strong an element of will, of what theology calls free-will. You cannot finish a sum how you like. But you can finish a story how you like. When somebody discovered the Differential Calculus there was only one Differential Calculus he could discover. But when Shakespeare killed Romeo he might have married him to Juliet's old nurse if he had felt inclined. And Christendom has excelled in the narrative romance exactly because it has insisted on the theological free-will. It is a large matter and too much to one side of the road to be discussed adequately here; but this is the real objection to that torrent of modern talk about treating crime as disease, about making a prison merely a hygienic environment like a hospital, of healing sin by slow scientific methods. The fallacy of the whole thing is that evil is a matter of active choice whereas disease is not. If you say that you are going to cure a profligate as you cure an asthmatic, my cheap and obvious answer is, "Produce the people who want to be asthmatics as many people want to be profligates."* A man may lie still and be cured of a malady. But he must not lie still if he wants to be cured of a sin; on the contrary, he must get up and jump about violently. The whole point indeed is perfectly expressed in the very word which we use for a man in hospital; *patient* is in the passive mood; *sin-*

ner is in the active. If a man is to be saved from influenza, he may be a patient. But if he is to be saved from forging, he must be not a patient but an IMPATIENT. He must be personally impatient with forgery. All moral reform must start in the active not the passive will.

Here again we reach the same substantial conclusion. In so far as we desire the definite reconstructions and the dangerous revolutions which have distinguished European civilization, we shall not discourage the thought of possible ruin; we shall rather encourage it. If we want, like the Eastern saints, merely to contemplate how right things are, of course we shall only say that they must go right. But if we particularly want to MAKE them go right, we must insist that they may go wrong.

Lastly, this truth is yet again true in the case of the common modern attempts to diminish or to explain away the divinity of Christ. The thing may be true or not; that I shall deal with before I end. But if the divinity is true it is certainly terribly revolutionary. That a good man may have his back to the wall is no more than we knew already; but that God could have his back to the wall is a boast for all insurgents for ever. Christianity is the only religion on earth that has felt that omnipotence made God incomplete. Christianity alone has felt that God, to be wholly God, must have been a rebel as well as a king. Alone of all creeds, Christianity has added courage to the virtues of the Creator. For the only courage worth calling courage must necessarily mean that the soul passes a breaking point—and does not break. In this indeed I approach a matter more dark and awful than it is easy to discuss; and I apologise in advance if any of my phrases fall wrong or seem irreverent touching a matter which the greatest saints and thinkers have justly feared to approach. But in that terrific tale of the Passion there is a distinct emotional suggestion that the author of all things (in some unthinkable way) went not only through agony, but through doubt. It is written, "Thou shalt not tempt the Lord thy God." No; but the Lord thy God may tempt Himself; and it seems as if this was what happened in Gethsemane. In a garden Satan tempted man: and in a garden God tempted God. He passed in some superhuman manner through our human horror of pessimism. When the world shook and the sun was wiped out of heaven, it was not at the crucifixion, but at the cry from the cross: the cry which confessed that God was forsaken of God. And now let the revolutionists choose a creed from all the creeds and a god from all the gods of the world, carefully weighing all the gods of inevitable recurrence and of unalterable power. They will not find another god who has himself been in revolt. Nay, (the matter grows too difficult for human speech,) but let the atheists themselves choose a god. They will find only one divinity who ever uttered their isolation; only one religion in which God seemed for an instant to be an atheist.

These can be called the essentials of the old orthodoxy, of which the chief merit is that it is the natural fountain of revolution and reform; and of which the chief defect is that it is obviously only an abstract assertion. Its main advantage is that it is the most adventurous and manly of all theologies. Its chief disadvantage is simply that it is a theology. It can always be urged against it that it is in its nature arbitrary and in the air. But it is not so high in the air but that great archers spend their whole lives in shooting arrows at it—yes, and their last arrows; there are men who will ruin themselves and ruin their civilization if they may ruin also this old fantastic tale. This is the last and most astounding fact about this faith; that its enemies will use any weapon against it, the swords that cut their own fingers, and the firebrands that burn their own homes. Men who begin to fight the Church for the sake of freedom and humanity end by flinging away freedom and humanity if only they may fight the Church. This is no exaggeration; I could fill a book with the instances of it. Mr. Blatchford set out, as an ordinary Bible-smasher, to prove that Adam was guiltless of sin against God; in manoeuvring so as to maintain this he admitted, as a mere side issue, that all the tyrants, from Nero to King Leopold, were guiltless of any sin against humanity. I know a man who has such a passion for proving that he will have no personal existence after death that he falls back on the position that he has no personal existence now. He invokes Buddhism and says that all souls fade into each other; in order to prove that he cannot go to heaven he proves that he cannot go to Hartlepool. I have known people who protested against religious education with arguments against any education, saying that the child's mind must grow freely or that the old must not teach the young. I have known people who showed that there could be no divine judgment by showing that there can be no human judgment, even for practical purposes. They burned their own corn to set fire to the church; they smashed their own tools to smash it; any stick was good enough to beat it with, though it were the last stick of their own dismembered furniture. We do not admire, we hardly excuse, the fanatic who wrecks this world for love of the other. But what are we to say of the fanatic who wrecks this world out of hatred of the other? He sacrifices the very existence of humanity to the non-existence of God. He offers his victims not to the altar, but merely to assert the idleness of the altar and the emptiness of the throne. He is ready to ruin even that primary ethic by which all things live, for his strange and eternal vengeance upon some one who never lived at all.

And yet the thing hangs in the heavens unhurt. Its opponents only succeed in destroying all that they themselves justly hold dear. They do not destroy orthodoxy; they only destroy political and common courage sense. They do not prove that Adam was not responsible to God; how could they prove it? They only prove (from their premises) that the Czar is not responsible to Russia. They do not prove that Adam should not have been punished by God; they only prove that the nearest sweater should not be punished by men. With their oriental doubts about personality they do not make certain that we shall have no personal life hereafter; they only make certain that we shall not have a very jolly or complete one here. With their paralysing hints of all conclusions coming out wrong they do not tear the book of the Recording Angel; they only make it a little harder to keep the books of Marshall & Snelgrove. Not only is the faith the mother of all worldly energies, but its foes are the fathers of all worldly confusion. The secularists have not wrecked divine things; but the secularists have wrecked secular things, if that is any comfort to them. The Titans did not scale heaven; but they laid waste the world.

Algernon C. Swinburne - (1837–1909) a major English poet with unorthodox religious beliefs
Annie Wood Besant (Mrs. Besant) - (1847–1933) leader of Theosophy
Arianism - the belief that Christ the Son is subordinate to God the Father because he was begotten and created by God
Athanasian Creed - a Christian profession of faith authored around A.D. 430, dealing primarily with the Trinity, the Incarnation, and Christ's two natures
epoch - a period of time; era
facile - easily done, requiring little effort
gaol - jail
Giuseppe Garibaldi - (1807–1882) an Italian military hero who fought to unite and free his country
immanentism - the belief in the pervading presence of God within His Creation
indolent - disliking work; idle; lazy
Mahommedanism - Islam
monism - the doctrine that reality is an irreversible, universal organism
pantheism - the belief that God and the universe are the same thing, God is an expression of nature
profligates - very wicked; shamelessly bad
quietism - religious mysticism requiring abandonment of the will, withdrawal from worldly interests, and passive meditation on divine things
Swedenborgian - based on the doctrine of leader Emmanuel Swedenborg; a doctrine that stresses the Trinity being within Christ Himself and New Jerusalem as symbolic of the ideal human society
truisms - self-evident truths
Theosophist - one who beleives in the fused teachings of Hinduism and Buddhism; began in 1875
Unitarians - those who hold to the moral teachings of Christ but do not believe that He was divine; they also deny the Trinity

Fill in each of the following blanks with the correct explanation or answer.

1.63   Why does Chesterton say that Liberal theologians are actually illiberal?

Because the term "free thinker" means something else and "Liberals" act very much according to rules.

1.64   Why do Liberal theologians reject the doctrine of miracles?

because it's not "realistic"

1.65   Explain Chesterton's statement that "The religions of the earth do *not* greatly differ in rites and forms; they do greatly differ in what they teach."

Most are very similar when it comes down to it.

1.66   What key point disproves the liberal idea that Buddhism and Christianity are essentially similar religions?

Buddism = pantheism + immance Christianity = liberty + love and how the religion views sin.

BRITISH LITERATURE LIFEPAC FIVE TEST

Name Camille Durdon

Date _____

Score _____

99 / 124

Underline the correct answer in each of the following statements (each answer, 3 points).

1. In his/her books and essays in support of the women's suffrage movement, (C. S. Lewis, T. S. Eliot, Virginia Woolf) articulated his/her belief that a society dominated by males will always lead to the oppression of women.

2. Woolf's "new" style incorporated the (<u>stream of consciousness</u>, colloquial, feeling) technique.

3. The two great apologists for orthodox religion in the twentieth century were (G. K. Chesterton and C. S. Lewis, George Bernard Shaw and T. S. Eliot, T. S. Eliot and C. S. Lewis).

4. At the outbreak of World War II, (Chesterton, Lewis, Eliot) was asked to give a series of radio lectures on basic Christian beliefs.

5. W. B. Yeats's first poems convey an interest in (English, <u>Irish,</u> Norse) folklore.

6. George Bernard Shaw's main purpose in writing plays was to make (socialism, capitalism, communism) seem more appealing.

7. According to Yeats's poem titled ("Adam's Curse," "Four Quartets," "Sailing to Byzantium"), the modern world thinks that creating poetry is worthless work.

8. In ("Adam's Curse," "Four Quartets," "Sailing to Byzantium"), the narrator sails to Byzantium to escape the degradation of old age.

9. The narrator's view of modern relationships in ("Four Quartets," <u>*The Love Song of J. Alfred Prufrock*</u>, "Sailing to Byzantium") is that they are empty and meaningless.

10. In his speech to the House of Commons on May 13, 1940, Churchill said that the aim of his administration was (defeat, defense, victory).

Answer *true* or *false* for each of the following statements (each answer, 2 points).

11. _____ In Virginia Woolf's story *The Duchess and the Jeweller*, Oliver Bacon is an upper-class nobleman who is trying to marry the duchess's daughter.

12. _____ Oliver has flashbacks to when he was a boy selling stolen dogs to fashionable women because he is a jewel thief.

13. _____ In James Joyce's *Araby*, the boy goes to the bazaar because he wants to hear a speech on Irish independence.

14. _____ The boy doesn't buy anything at the bazaar because he sees the emptiness in his pursuits.

15. _____ The boy eventually sees himself as a "creature driven and derided by vanity" because his desire for love and affection are fulfilled.

16. *true* "The absence of God" from society caused many intellectuals to become pessimistic about the meaning of man's existence.

17. *false* The stream of consciousness technique attempts to tell a story in strict chronological detail.

18. _false_ Joseph Conrad set his stories at sea and in foreign lands to add an element of adventure to his stories.

19. _____ After World War II, members of the ruling Labour Party created a "cradle-to-grave" welfare program.

20. _____ After Germany exceeded the limitations set forth by the Treaty of Versailles, Britain entered into an alliance with France to stop Hitler's advance across Europe.

21. _false_ The First World War caused people to trust the goodness of God and the goodness of technology.

22. _____ In Shaw's play *Pygmalion*, Eliza Doolittle behaves more kindly than the middle-class gentleman Professor Higgins.

23. _____ Alfred Doolittle tries to "sell" his daughter to Professor Higgins.

Circle the letter of the line that best answers each of the following questions (each answer, 4 points).

24. According to Huxley's *Brave New World*, how does Mustapha Mond think that God manifests himself to modern men?

   a. As an absence
   b. In the Scriptures
   c. In relationships
   d. In all religions

25. What does the Savage think makes man noble and heroic?

   a. The absence of God
   b. The indulgence of pleasures
   c. Romantic feelings
   d. Belief in the existence of God

26. In Chapter 10 of *The Screwtape Letters*, on what grounds does Screwtape encourage Wormwood to persuade the patient to maintain his new acquaintances?

   a. That he might get to know them better
   b. That he is being a witness to them, and not to associate with them would be "Puritanical"
   c. That he might share their desires
   d. That he might enjoy the pleasures of the world

27. In Chapter 20, Screwtape attributes the creation of fashionable sex types to demons. What is the purpose behind this cultural endeavor?

   a. To destroy the possibility of good marriages
   b. To create more evil-minded people
   c. To consume the world with lust
   d. To cause divorces to multiply

2

28. According to Hardy's poem "The Respectable Burgher," why do the "Reverend Doctors" think that the stories that include supernatural events are included in the Bible?

    a. The stories contain historical details that are not found anywhere else.

    b. The stories are romantic

    c. The stories are truthful.

    d. The stories are sentimental to the Jewish people.

29. In *Heart of Darkness*, what are Kurtz's last words?

    a. "Take me home, God!"

    b. "The jungle is the heart of darkness."

    c. "I am hollow at the core."

    d. "The horror. The horror."

30. In *The Love Song of J. Alfred Prufrock*, what does the narrator mean when he says, "I have measured out my life with coffee spoons"?

    a. Every aspect of his life has great significance and meaning.

    (b.) His life is full of trite acts that amount to nothing.

    c. He trusts in God for every detail in his life.

    d. Even the most mundane things have meaning and significance.

31. According G. K. Chesterton's book *Orthodoxy*, what is the "natural fountain of revolution and reform?"

    (a.) Old orthodoxy

    b. A healthy skepticism of traditional moral and beliefs

    c. Liberal politics

    d. Atheism

32. In its context, explain Chesterton's statement that "Not only is the faith the mother of all worldly energies but its foes are the fathers of all worldly confusion."

    a. Democracy is the firm foundation for world peace.

    b. Orthodox Christianity is no different from Buddhism.

    (c.) Orthodox Christianity is the only true basis of liberty, humanity, and love.

    d. Religious beliefs have no impact on society.

33. In *The Finest Hour* speech, what does Winston Churchill say depends on Britain's victory?

    a. The survival of materialism

    b. The survival of democracy

    c. The survival of Christian civilization

    d. The survival of Nazism

Fill in each of the blanks using items from the following word list (each answer, 4 points).

~~Aldous Huxley~~   ~~Winston Churchill~~   *Dubliners*

Brave New World   Thomas Hardy   ~~G. K. Chesterton~~

James Joyce

34. _____ rebelled against the Roman Catholic beliefs of middle-class society.

35. In 1914, Joyce published _____ , a collection of short stories containing symbolic meanings of the modern world.

36. **Aldous Huxley**_____ was the grandson of Thomas Huxley, the champion of Darwinism.

37. _____ is a "satirical fantasy" set in the seventh century A.F. (After [Henry] Ford) where humans are conditioned from conception to take their place in a caste system based on scientifically graded intelligence.

38. During the First World War, **G.K.Chesterton**_____ was asked to write pamphlets in support of England's efforts to stave off German aggression.

39. The writing style of **Winston Churchill**_____ can be characterized as grand.

40. In his poetry written during the twentieth century, _____ experimented with verse forms using a language of the common people.

Writing and Thinking:

1. Explain briefly G. K. Chesterton's thoughts on the modern view of religion. Be sure to explain his thoughts on "liberal thinkers" and their illiberal view of miracles. Also, explain why liberal thinkers are wrong when they conclude that all religions are essentially the same. Discuss Chesterton's insistence that a belief in the existence of the Triune God is western civilization's only hope for "humanity and liberty and love." How does a belief in God's transcendence spur us on to reform our world?

2. Explain the modern view of love as presented in T. S. Eliot's poem *The Love Song of J. Alfred Prufrock*. Discuss why this view of love is typical of modern relationships. Why is the "absence of love" symptomatic of "the absence of God" from society? According to 1 John 4:7–19, what is the "source and effect" of love?

3. Explain the premise of *The Screwtape Letters*. Be sure to explain who Screwtape is and his relationship to Wormwood. Discuss the implications of Screwtape's advice to Wormwood. If "the road to Hell is a gradual one," then why do you think that Screwtape encourages the use of "small" sins over "big" sins? Why is it important to compare our everyday motives and actions with Scripture (cf. 2 Corinthians 13:5; 1 John 2: 15–17)?

1.67   Why does Chesterton disagree with Mrs. Besant's belief that the "universal Church is simply the universal self?"

Because   the   exact   opposite   is   true

1.68   Why does Chesterton say that "there is no real possibility of getting out of pantheism any special impulse to moral action?"

According   to   Pantheism,   we   are   all   the   same   and one   being,   so   there's   no   reason   too

1.69   Upon what central doctrine of Christianity does typical western orthodoxy and typical western politics depend?

Transecendence   of   deity.

1.70   Why does Chesterton say that Eastern civilization is prone to the oppression of tyrants?

_____

1.71   Why has Christendom excelled in the narrative romance?

it   has   been   based   on   free   will.

1.72   What does Chesterton say is the beginning of moral reform?

The   means   or   want   to   change   things.

1.73   What is the "natural fountain of revolution and reform?"

Old   Orthodoxy

1.74   In its context, explain Chesterton's statement that "Not only is the faith the mother of all worldly energies, but its foes are the fathers of all worldly confusion."

Because   people   will   do   anything   to   try   and prove   Christianity   to   be   false.

Review the material in this section in preparation for the Self Test, which will check your mastery of this particular section. The items missed on this Self Test will indicate specific areas where restudy is needed for mastery.

SELF TEST 1

Answer *true* **or** *false* **for each of the following statements** (each answer, 2 points).

1.01   _true_   The First World War caused people to doubt the goodness of God and the goodness of technology.

1.02   _false_   The Treaty of Versailles imposed limitations on England's military forces after World War I.

1.03   _true_   The economic depression after World War I caused many Britons to put their faith in socialism.

1.04   _false_   "The absence of God" from society caused many to adopt an optimistic outlook.

1.05   _true_   Britain refuses to grant Ireland total independence because many Protestants living in Northern Ireland wish to remain under British rule.

1.06   _false_   During World War II, Britain entered an alliance with Italy to stop Hitler's advance across Europe.

1.07   _false_   After World War II, members of the ruling Labour Party cut benefits for the poor and lower class to pay for war debts owed to the United States.

1.08   *false*   The influence of Freud's theories caused many writers to be more concerned about factual details of a story than about a character's feelings and thoughts.

1.09   *true*   The stream of consciousness technique attempts to tell a story through the natural flow of a character's thoughts.

1.010   *true*   Yeats's poetry helped to encourage the desire for Irish independence.

1.011   *true*   Joseph Conrad set his novels and short stories at sea and in foreign lands to supply a world removed from the influence of western civilization.

1.012   *false*   Conrad's typical narrative style uses an omniscient narrative to tell the story.

1.013   *false*   Conrad was optimistic about the human condition.

Underline the correct answer in each of the following statements (each answer, 3 points).

1.014   The "disappearance of God" from Victorian culture caused Thomas Hardy to write poetry and novels that are considered (optimistic, hopeful, <u>pessimistic</u>).

1.015   After receiving much criticism for (*Far From the Madding Crowd*, <u>*Jude the Obscure*</u>, *Tess of the D'Urbervilles*), Hardy gave up his career as a(n) (<u>poet</u>, novelist, architect).

1.016   In his poetry written during the twentieth century, Hardy experimented with (<u>verse forms</u>, prose forms, dramatic monologues), using a language of the (upper class, <u>common people</u>, clergy).

1.017   During the (Second World War, <u>First World War</u>, Vietnam War), G. K. Chesterton was asked to write pamphlets in support of England's efforts to stave off (French, American, <u>German</u>) aggression.

1.018   An able proponent of (conservative politics, capitalism, <u>orthodox Christianity</u>), Chesterton wrote religious essays that have commanded the respect of some of the most ardent skeptics.

1.019   Chesterton's religious essays have been (<u>appreciated</u>, condemned, banned) by both Catholics and Protestants.

Circle the letter of the line that best answers each of the following questions (each answer, 4 points).

1.020   According to "The Respectable Burgher," what is the major cause for "God's disappearance" from religion?

    a. Theologians and preachers who have questioned the truth of Scripture

    b. Liberal politics

    c. Immoral behavior

    d. Unlearned parishioners

1.021   If the stories of Adam and David are not true, then why do the "Reverend Doctors" of higher criticism think that they included in the Bible?

    a. The stories contain historical details not found anywhere else.

    b. The stories add a romantic air to religion.

    c. The stories are truthful.

    d. The stories were inspired by the Holy Spirit.

1.022   In the poem "Neutral Tones," what does the poet's conclusion that "love deceives" convey about a world without God?

    a.   The world does not need God.

    b.   The world is brimming with life and meaning.

    (c.)   Without God, everything is meaningless.

    d.   The existence of God has nothing to do with whether love is possible.

1.023   In *Heart of Darkness*, why does Marlow refer to the Roman conquest of England before he begins his tale?

    a.   He is drawing a comparison between himself and the Roman soldiers who conquered England thousands of years ago.

    b.   He believes that he is destined to become a great world leader.

    c.   He thinks that England is still as uncivilized as Africa.

    d.   He thinks England should be under the authority of the Pope.

1.024   Why does Marlow describe the heart of Africa as the "heart of darkness?"

    a.   It is a dark and sinister place.

    b.   It has no electricity for light.

    c.   The foliage is so thick that sunshine cannot reach the floor of the jungle.

    d.   The Congo is shaped like a snake.

1.025   After realizing that Kurtz has participated in barbaric ceremonies to win the admiration of the natives, why does Marlow describe him as "hollow at the core?"

    a.   Kurtz was always hungry.

    b.   Kurtz held to a strict moral standard.

    c.   Although he was in the "heart of darkness," Kurtz continued to act like a civilized European.

    d.   Kurtz was utterly depraved.

1.026   What are Kurtz's last words?

    a.   "My love. My love."

    b.   "The horror. The horror."

    c.   "Take me back."

    d.   "Save me from this horror."

1.027   According to G. K. Chesterton's book *Orthodoxy*, why do Liberal theologians reject the doctrine of miracles?

    (a.)   Their strict materialistic view of the world does not allow them to think freely about the possibility of the supernatural.

    b.   They believe that God has more liberty than man.

    c.   They believe that miracles will cause people to fall into sin.

    d.   They believe that God cannot be bound by the limitations of His own Creation.

1.028   What is the meaning of Chesterton's statement that, "The religions of the earth do *not* greatly differ in rites and forms; they do greatly differ in what they teach?"

     a.   All religions of the earth use similar external methods of worship, devotion, and community. They are also similar in their beliefs on salvation.

     (b.)   All religions of the earth use similar external methods of worship, devotion, and community. However, they differ greatly in their beliefs, especially on the means of salvation.

     c.   All religions worship the same God, just in different ways. The only important thing about religion is that you are sincere about what you believe.

     d.   The various religions of the earth are unique in external methods of worship, devotion, and community. However, they all lead to the same destination.

1.029   Upon what central doctrine of Christianity does typical western orthodoxy and typical western politics depend?

     a.   The immanence of God

     (b.)   The transcendence of God

     c.   The indwelling of the Holy Spirit

     (d.)   The free will of man

1.030   What is the "natural fountain of revolution and reform?"

     a.   A skepticism of traditional morals and beliefs

     b.   Liberal theology

     c.   Atheism

     (d.)   Old orthodoxy

1.031   In its context, explain Chesterton's statement that "Not only is the faith the mother of all worldly energies, but its foes are the fathers of all worldly confusion."

     (a.)   Orthodox Christianity is the only true basis of liberty, humanity, and love.

     b.   All religions supply a firm foundation for world peace.

     c.   Orthodox Christianity is not the only basis for liberty, humanity, and community.

     d.   Religious beliefs have no impact on society.

For Thought and Discussion:

Explain to a teacher/parent G. K. Chesterton's views on the modern view of religion. Be sure to explain his thoughts on "liberal thinkers" and their illiberal view of miracles. Also, explain why liberal thinkers are wrong when they conclude that all religions are essentially the same. Discuss Chesterton's insistence that a belief in the existence of the Triune God is western civilization's only hope for "humanity and liberty and love." How does a belief in God's transcendence spur us on to reform our world?

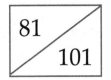

Score   _____

Adult Check   _____
                   Initial   Date

81 / 101

II. MODERN POETRY, DRAMA, AND PROSE

William Butler Yeats (1865–1939). William Butler Yeats was born in Dublin, Ireland. His father, John Butler Yeats, was a well-known portrait painter who rejected his family's fervent Protestant faith. The elder Yeats instead put his trust in the power of art to fulfill his religious longings. Yeats himself turned to the occult for answers that strict rationalism could not provide.

In 1874 J. B. Yeats moved his family to London. The younger Yeats was educated at the Godolphin School, London, and then at the High School when his family returned to Dublin in 1883. He attended the School of Art, Dublin, for a time, intending to become an artist, but he soon decided to develop his skills as a poet.

In 1891 Yeats helped found the Rhymers' Club, members of which cultivated his interest in medieval myths and legends. His first poems convey an interest in Irish folklore and the works of William Blake and Edmund Spenser. Yeats edited *The Poems of William Blake* in 1893 and the *Poems of Spenser* in 1906.

Yeats did much to promote a renewed interest in Irish culture. Along with the help of the nationalist Lady Gregory, Yeats established the Abbey Theatre, Ireland's first national theatre, in Dublin in 1904. Inspired by his unrequited love for the fiery Irish revolutionary Maud Gonne, Yeats wrote several plays that were performed by the National Theater Company. Portraits of Maud also appear in some of Yeats's most notable poems, which are included in *The Wanderings of Oisin and other Poems* (1889), *The Wind among the Reeds* (1899), *In the Seven Woods* (1903), and *The Green Hamlet and other Poems* (1910).

Abbey Theatre–Dublin

However, after he had suffered much frustration over his relationship with Maud and the political efforts of the Irish nationalists, Yeats's poetic style began to change. Leaving behind his dreamy, romantic verse, he wrote in an increasingly realistic style. His most notable poem of this time is "Easter 1916," which recalls the violence of the Easter Rebellion.

Yeats's marriage to Georgie Hyde-Lees in 1917 marked another turning point in his poetic style and interests. His wife's active involvement with the occult encouraged Yeats to work out a mystical system of belief. The system, which Yeats claimed was communicated to his wife by spirits, is explained in his book *A Vision*, first published in 1925. His later poetry is highly symbolic, dependent upon his complex mystical beliefs.

During his lifetime, Yeats was considered an icon of Irish culture. After the establishment of Irish independence in 1922, he was awarded an honorary seat in the senate of the Irish Free State. In 1923 he was awarded the Noble Prize for literature. While living in the south of France with his wife, he died in 1939. His *Collected Poems* were published posthumously in 1950. Many people consider Yeats to be the greatest British poet of the twentieth century.

Like many people who turn from the truth of orthodox Christianity, Yeats attempted to develop an elaborate system that would somehow shield him from his own conscience. His interest in the occult demonstrates modern society's longing for the otherworldly; abstracted from the acknowledgment of God Himself. In the twilight of his years, Yeats acknowledged the hardened state of his heart when he wrote to a friend, "I shall be a sinful man to the end." Yeats, like many of his contemporaries, was unwilling to fear God's wrath, and thus opted for a life in which truth and peace constantly eluded him.

➡ **Fill in each of the following blanks with the correct answer.**

2.1   William Butler Yeats was born in _Dublin, Ireland_ .

2.2   In 1891 Yeats helped to organize the _Rhymer's Club_ , which cultivated his interest in medieval _myths_ and _legends_ .

2.3   Yeats's first poems convey an interest in _Irish_ folklore and the works of _Blake_ and _Spenser_ .

2.4   In 1904 Yeats helped to establish Ireland's first _national_ theater in Dublin.

2.5   Yeats's unrequited love for _Maud Gonne_ inspired many poems and plays.

2.6   Yeats's frustration with the Irish nationalistic movement led him to write poetry that was _realistic_ .

2.7   Yeats's later poetry is concerned mainly with explaining his _mystical_ system of belief.

2.8   In 1923 Yeats was awarded the _Nobel Prize_ .

What to Look For:

Like his father, Yeats rejected the doctrines of his Christian forefathers. Instead, he attempted to find spiritual meaning in mysticism. As you read, notice Yeats's exalted view of art. What divine attributes does Yeats associate with art? Is it unchanging? Is it holy?

Adam's Curse

The poem refers to Yeats's failed courtship of Maud Gonne and the hollowness of modern life, which is unconcerned with the "old high way of love."

We sat together at one summer's end,
That beautiful mild woman, your close friend,
And you and I, and talked of poetry.

I said: "A line will take us hours maybe;
5   Yet if it does not seem a moment's thought,
Our stitching and unstitching has been naught.
Better go down upon your marrow-bones
And scrub a kitchen pavement, or break stones
Like an old pauper, in all kinds of weather;
10   For to articulate sweet sounds together
Is to work harder than all these and yet
Be thought an idler by the noisy set
Of bankers, schoolmasters, and clergymen
The martyrs call the world."

15   And thereupon
That beautiful mild woman for whose sake
There's many a one shall find out all heartache
On finding that her voice is sweet and low
Replied: "To be born woman is to know—
20   Although they do not talk of it at school—
That we must labour to be beautiful."

I said: "It's certain there is no fine thing
Since Adam's fall but needs much labouring.
There have been lovers who thought love should be
25   So much compounded of high courtesy
That they would sigh and quote with learned looks

Precedents out of beautiful old books;
Yet now it seems an idle trade enough."

    We sat grown quiet at the name of love;
30 We saw the last embers of daylight die,
    And in the trembling blue-green of the sky
    A moon, worn as if it had been a shell
    Washed by time's waters as they rose and fell
    About the stars and broke in days and years.

35 I had a thought for no one's but your ears;
    That you were beautiful, and that I strove
    To love you in the old high way of love;
    That it had all seemed happy, and yet we'd grown
    As weary-hearted as that hollow moon.

Sailing to Byzantium

Yeats envisioned early Byzantium [ca. A.D. 550] as a place where artists and craftsmen were the chief communicators of spiritual truths.

I

    That is no country for old men. The young
    In one another's arms, birds in the trees
    —Those dying generations—at their song,
    The salmon-falls, the mackerel-crowded seas,
5 Fish, flesh, or fowl, commend all summer long
    Whatever is begotten, born, and dies.
    Caught in that sensual music all neglect
    Monuments of unaging intellect.

II

    An aged man is but a paltry thing,
10 A tattered coat upon a stick, unless
    Soul clap its hands and sing, and louder sing
    For every tatter in its mortal dress;
    Nor is there singing school but studying
    Monuments of its own magnificence;
15 And therefore I have sailed the seas and come
    To the holy city of Byzantium.

III

    O sages standing in God's holy fire
    As in the gold mosaic of a wall,
    Come from the holy fire, perne in a gyre,
20 And be the singing-masters of my soul.
    Consume my heart away—sick with desire
    And fastened to a dying animal
    It knows not what it is—and gather me
    Into the artifice of eternity.

IV

25 Once out of nature I shall never take
    My bodily form from any natural thing,
    But such a form as Grecian goldsmiths make
    Of hammered gold and gold enameling
    To keep a drowsy emperor awake;
30 Or set upon a golden bough to sing
    To lords and ladies of Byzantium
    Of what is past, or passing, or to come.

Fill in each of the following blanks with the correct explanation or answer.

2.9 According to "Adam's Curse," what does the poet say the world will think of the hard work that goes into a poem that can "articulate sweet sounds together?"
they will just brush it off.

2.10 According to lines 22 and 23, why does good poetry require much work?
_____

2.11 According to lines 22–28, what other "fine thing" that requires much hard labor has also become an "idle trade?"
_____

2.12 According to line 39, what has the poet reaped after much hard labor in poetry and love?
_____

2.13 According to stanzas I and II of "Sailing to Byzantine," describe the way the poet's country views old age.
_____

2.14 According to stanza II, why has the poet sailed to Byzantium?
_____

2.15 Why do you think the poet describes Byzantium as a "holy city?"
_____

2.16 According to stanzas III and IV, why does the poet ask to be made into an artifice?
_____

2.17 What are some of the negative consequences of being a piece of art for all eternity?
_____

T. S. Eliot (1888–1965). Thomas Stearns Eliot was an extremely influential poet and literary critic during the 1920s and 1930s. As one writer has noted, "Eliot single-handedly changed the course of modern poetry—it has become more fragmented, less pretty, and more difficult." Before his conversion to Christianity in 1927, Eliot was the most read expounder of modernism. His poems captured the hopelessness and sterility of society during the modern era.

Eliot was born in St. Louis, Missouri, into a family of intellectual and social prominence. He earned his bachelor's and master's degrees from Harvard University. He also studied abroad at the Sorbonne in Paris and at Oxford. Deciding against a career as a college professor, Eliot remained in England to develop his skills as a poet.

While in England, Eliot befriended Ezra Pound. Pound carefully read Eliot's poems, helping him to develop his modern techniques. *The Love Song of J. Alfred Prufrock*, a long poem that he began at Harvard, was published in 1917. It focuses on the sterility of modern society while introducing a new form of poetry. Eliot adopted a fragmented form of expression (stream of consciousness technique) to illustrate more fully the lack of cohesion within society. His verses read like jumbled thoughts. At times, they seem to have no logical flow or organization. The narrator's thoughts are expressed "naturally."

In 1922 Eliot published what would be his most famous poem, *The Waste Land*. Similar to what he did in *Prufrock*, Eliot contrasted the spiritual desolation of modern society with societies of the past.

In 1927 Eliot became a citizen of Great Britain. The following year, he became a devout member of the Church of England. In a collection of essays titled *For Lancelot Andrewes* (1928), Eliot described his hedging conservatism by exclaiming, "[I am a] classicist in literature, royalist in politics, and anglo-catholic in religion." For many of the admirers of his earlier works, this declaration was a shock. His works increasingly revealed a man who believed that the answers to individual and societal problems are in the tenets of orthodox Christianity. *The Journey of the Magi* (1927), *Ash Wednesday* (1930), and *Four Quartets* (1943) are poems that were written after his conversion. *Four Quartets* consists of four individual poems that carry the theme "redeem the time." It is his message of salvation to the modern world.

The Delights of A Poet– Chirico

Eliot also wrote plays and critical essays. His plays carried religious themes and were produced both on Broadway and in London. As a literary critic, Eliot toured the United States, drawing sizable crowds to his lectures. He was awarded the Nobel Prize for literature in 1948 and the Presidential Medal of Freedom by the United States in 1964.

Fill in each of the following blanks with the correct answer.

2.18   T. S. Eliot was born in **Missouri**.

2.19   Eliot earned his bachelor's and master's degrees from **Harvard**.

2.20   **Ezra Pound** helped Eliot develop his modern techniques.

2.21   In 1917 Eliot published **The Love Song of J. Alfred Prufrock**

2.22   In 1922 Eliot published **The Waste Land**

2.23   In *The Love Song of J. Alfred Prufrock* and *The Waste Land,* Eliot used the **Stream of consciousness** technique to illustrate more fully the lack of cohesion within society.

2.24   In 1927 Eliot became a citizen of **Great Britain**

2.25   Published in 1944, **Four Quartets** consists of four individual poems that carry the theme "redeem the time."

2.26   Eliot was awarded the **Nobel Prize** Prize for literature in **1964**.

What to Look For:

Before Eliot's conversion, he addressed the problems of the modern age in a profound way. *The Love Song of J. Alfred Prufrock* is the best of his early work. It uses the stream of consciousness technique to convey the frustrations of an idealistic individual in a society that does not value beauty or love. As you read, pay attention to Prufrock's view of love. Why does his view of love cause him to be frustrated? How is Prufrock's situation typical of modern relationships? Do you think that the "absence of love" is symptomatic of "the absence of God" in a society? According to 1 John 4:7–19, what is the "source and effect" of love?

THE LOVE SONG OF J. ALFRED PRUFROCK

The poem conveys the narrator's thoughts in anticipation of telling a woman at a tea party that he loves her.

> S'io credesse che mia risposta fosse
> A persona che mai tornasse al mondo,
> Questa fiamma staria senza piu scosse.
> Ma percioche giammai di questo fondo
> Non torno vivo alcun, s'i'odo il vero,
> Senza tema d'infamia ti rispondo.

> *If I think my answer would be spoken*
> *To one who could ever return into the world,*
> *This flame would sleep unmoved.*
> *But since never, if true be told me, any from this depth*
> *Has found his way upward way, I answer thee,*
> *Nor fear lest infamy record my words.*

–from Dante's Inferno, XXVII, 61-6

Let us go then, you and I,
When the evening is spread out against the sky
Like a patient etherized upon a table;
Let us go, through certain half-deserted streets,
5   The muttering retreats
Of restless nights in one-night cheap hotels
And sawdust restaurants with oyster-shells:
Streets that follow like a tedious argument
Of insidious intent
10   To lead you to an overwhelming question...
Oh, do not ask, "What is it?"
Let us go and make our visit.
In the room the women come and go
Talking of Michelangelo.

15   The yellow fog that rubs its back upon the window-panes,
The yellow smoke that rubs its muzzle on the window-panes,
Licked its tongue into the corners of the evening,
Lingered upon the pools that stand in drains,
Let fall upon its back the soot that falls from chimneys,

20   Slipped by the terrace, made a sudden leap,
And seeing that it was a soft October night,
    Curled once about the house, and fell asleep.

And indeed there will be time
For the yellow smoke that slides along the street,
25   Rubbing its back upon the window-panes;
There will be time, there will be time
To prepare a face to meet the faces that you meet;
There will be time to murder and create,
And time for all the works and days of hands
30   That lift and drop a question on your plate;
Time for you and time for me,
And time yet for a hundred indecisions,
And for a hundred visions and revisions,
Before the taking of a toast and tea.

35   In the room the women come and go
Talking of Michelangelo.

And indeed there will be time
To wonder, "Do I dare?" and, "Do I dare?"
Time to turn back and descend the stair,
40   With a bald spot in the middle of my hair—
(They will say: 'How his hair is growing thin!')
My morning coat, my collar mounting firmly to the chin,
My necktie rich and modest, but asserted by a simple pin—
(They will say: "But how his arms and legs are thin!")
45   Do I dare
Disturb the universe?
In a minute there is time
For decisions and revisions which a minute will reverse.

For I have known them all already, known them all:—
50   Have known the evenings, mornings, afternoons,
I have measured out my life with coffee spoons;
I know the voices dying with a dying fall
Beneath the music from a farther room.
    So how should I presume?

55   And I have known the eyes already, known them all—
The eyes that fix you in a formulated phrase,
And when I am formulated, sprawling on a pin,
When I am pinned and wriggling on the wall,
Then how should I begin

60   To spit out all the butt-ends of my days and
      ways?
          And how should I presume?

      And I have known the arms already,
      known them all—
      Arms that are braceleted and white
      and bare
      (But in the lamplight, downed with
      light brown hair!)
65   Is it perfume from a dress
      That makes me so digress?
      Arms that lie along a table, or wrap
      about a shawl.
          And should I then presume?
          And how should I begin?

70   Shall I say, I have gone at dusk through narrow
      streets
      And watched the smoke that rises from the
      pipes
      Of lonely men in shirt-sleeves, leaning out of
      windows?...

      I should have been a pair of ragged claws
      Scuttling across the floors of silent seas.

75   And the afternoon, the evening, sleeps so peace-
      fully!
      Smoothed by long fingers,
      Asleep...tired...or it malingers,
      Stretched on the floor, here beside you and me.
      Should I, after tea and cakes and ices,
80   Have the strength to force the moment to its
      crisis?
      But though I have wept and fasted, wept and
      prayed,
      Though I have seen my head (grown slightly
      bald) brought in upon a platter,
      I am no prophet—and here's no great matter;
      I have seen the moment of my greatness flicker,
85   And I have seen the eternal Footman hold my
      coat, and snicker,
      And in short, I was afraid.
      And would it have been worth it, after all,
      After the cups, the marmalade, the tea,
      Among the porcelain, among some talk of you
      and me,
90   Would it have been worth while,
      To have bitten off the matter with a smile,
      To have squeezed the universe into a ball
      To roll it towards some overwhelming question,
      To say: "I am Lazarus, come from the dead,

95   Come back to tell you all, I shall tell you all"—
      If one, settling a pillow by her head
          Should say: "That is not what I meant at all;
          That is not it, at all."

      And would it have been worth it, after all,
100   Would it have been worth while,
      After the sunsets and the dooryards and the
      sprinkled streets,
      After the novels, after the teacups, after the
      skirts that trail along the floor—
      And this, and so much more?—
      It is impossible to say just what I mean!
105   But as if a magic lantern threw the nerves in
      patterns on a screen:
      Would it have been worth while
      If one, settling a pillow or throwing off a shawl,
      And turning toward the window, should say:
          "That is not it at all,
110   That is not what I meant, at all."

      No! I am not Prince Hamlet, nor was meant to
      be;
      Am an attendant lord, one that will do
      To swell a progress, start a scene or two,
      Advise the prince; no doubt, an easy tool,
115   Deferential, glad to be of use,
      Politic, cautious, and meticulous;
      Full of high sentence, but a bit obtuse;
      At times, indeed, almost ridiculous—
      Almost, at times, the Fool.

120   I grow old...I grow old...
      I shall wear the bottoms of my trousers rolled.

      Shall I part my hair behind? Do I dare to eat a
      peach?
      I shall wear white flannel trousers, and walk
      upon the beach.
      I have heard the mermaids singing, each to
      each.

125   I do not think that they will sing to me.

      I have seen them riding seaward on the waves
      Combing the white hair of the waves blown
      back
      When the wind blows the water white and
      black.
      We have lingered in the chambers of the sea
130   By sea-girls wreathed with seaweed red and
      brown
      Till human voices wake us, and we drown.

✤ **Fill in each of the following blanks with the correct explanation or answer.**

2.27 From which piece of literature is the epigraph at the beginning of the poem taken?

Dante's "Inferno"

2.28 Who is the *I* in the poem?

J. Alfred Prufrock.

2.29 In lines 1–12, what is the narrator's view of modern relationships?

They are short, apathetic, and meaningless

2.30 Why does the narrator repeatedly tell himself "there will be time?"

He's trying to convince himself that there's an abundance of time for him to gain courage.

2.31 On what basis is the narrator afraid that he will be judged by the ladies in the room?

His external appearance

2.32 Is the narrator confident that he will measure up to the likes of Michelangelo?

Not at all.

2.33 What does the narrator mean when he says, "I have measured out my life with coffee spoons?"

He has no collosal achievements.

2.34 Why does the narrator decide not to tell the woman of his love for her?

He is petrified of rejection.

2.35 How does the narrator excuse his own cowardice?

_____

2.36 What mythical figures has the narrator fantasized about?

mermaids

2.37 In the last lines of the poem, what brings the narrator back to reality?

_____

2.38 Explain the narrator's words *we drown.*

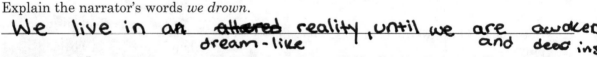
We live in an ~~altered~~ dream-like reality, until we are awoken and dead ins

George Bernard Shaw (1856–1950). George Bernard Shaw was born in Dublin. His father was a lower-class worker who spent what little money he earned on alcohol. Financially unable to attend university, Shaw educated himself and moved to London, where his mother and sister lived. During the next couple of years, Shaw wrote five novels, all of them unsuccessful. He also worked as a journalist and music critic for the *Pall Mall Gazette*. His enthusiasm for music can be attributed to his mother, who was a music teacher.

Poor, unappreciated, and "morally" passionate, Shaw was drawn to the work of Karl Marx. He soon became a member of the Social Democratic Federation, believing that wealth should be equally distributed and that no one should own private property. In 1884, Shaw joined the Fabian Society. The society believed that capitalism was the root cause of societal ills. Disease, poverty, immorality, and social inequalities were all related to a free economic market. Shaw hated the economic system of the middle class and associated its success with the triumph of hypocrisy and injustice. Like other members of the Fabian society, Shaw sought to usher in socialism "as painless and effective as possible," unlike other socialistic societies that sought to effect change by force. He wrote tracts and gave lectures in an attempt to move society toward socialism. Included among his pamphlets on socialism are *The Fabian*

Manifesto (1884), *The Impossibilities of Anarchism* (1893), and *Socialism for Millionaires* (1901).

Shaw also sought to inculcate the culture with his socialistic ideas by writing plays. Included among his plays that were meant to expose the ill effects of capitalism are *Man and Superman* (1902), *John Bull's Other Island* (1904), and *Major Barbara* (1905). After the war, Shaw's wit, known as "Shavian," began to gain him popular success. *Heartbreak House* (1919), *Back to Methuselah* (1921), and *Saint Joan* (1923) all won him critical acclaim and led to his award of the Noble Prize for literature in 1925. As one writer has noted, Shaw was a master of paradox. He often turned conventional views of society inside out to reveal to his audiences the foolishness of their hypocrisies. Other of Shaw's more notable plays include *Mrs. Warren's Profession* (1893); *Pygmalion* (1913), which was later rewritten as the musical *My Fair Lady*; *The Apple Cart* (1929); and *Too True to be Good* (1932). Shaw was also interested in the women's rights movement and the formation of the Labour Party, for which he wrote such works as *The Intelligent Woman's Guide to Socialism and Capitalism* (1928) and *A Plan on Campaign for Labour.*

In the prefaces to his *Collected Plays,* published in seven volumes from 1970 to 1974, Shaw articulated his belief in the "Life Force," a nonpersonal spiritual energy that enables mankind to transform himself into a greater being. Shaw was attracted to Nietzsche's concept of the will to power, believing that Christianity, as an outdated religion, was powerless to change society. He believed instead that man could make the world a better place. Writing to Henry James on January 17, 1909, Shaw outlined his reason for writing: "I, as a Socialist, have had to preach, as much as anyone, the enormous power of the environment. We can change it; we must change it; there is absolutely no other sense in life than the task of changing it. What is the use of writing plays, what is the use of writing anything, if there is not a will which finally moulds chaos itself into a race of gods." Shaw died at the age of 94, still convinced that man had no need for God and was able to perfect himself.

Fill in each of the following blanks with the correct answer.

2.39 George Bernard Shaw was born in ___Dublin___ .

2.40 As a member of the ___Fabian Society___ , Shaw hoped to usher in socialism "as painless and effective as possible" by writing tracts and giving lectures.

2.41 As a Socialist, Shaw believed that ___capitalism___ was the root of all societal ills, including disease, poverty, immorality, and social inequality.

2.42 Shaw's main purpose in writing ___plays___ was to inculcate the culture with his socialistic ideas.

2.43 In 1925 Shaw was awarded the ___Nobel Prize___ for literature.

2.44 Shaw's belief in the ___enviornment___ led him to think that man could transform himself into a greater being.

What to Look For:

Shaw hated the hypocrisy of the middle class. In many of his plays, he seeks to change middle-class prejudices by making people see the folly of their ways. As you read, notice the hypocrisy of Professor Higgins. Although from all appearances Higgins is a respected member of the middle class, is he truly a gentleman? Who treats people with more respect, Higgins or Eliza? With this comparison in mind, what message do you think that Shaw is trying to convey about class distinctions?

From: *Pygmalion*.

The title of the play is derived from an ancient Greek tale about a sculptor, Pygmalion, who created his vision of the perfect woman out of stone and then has Aphrodite, the goddess of love, bring his creation to life.

In Act I, a poor flower girl becomes the professional interest of Professor Higgins. Higgins is an expert in phonetics who attempts to record the flower girl's speech patterns. But the purpose of his notetaking is misperceived. He is accused of being an undercover cop. The flower girl becomes hysterical, insisting that she is a good girl. Colonel Pickering, a man who she tried to sell some flowers, defends her honor, claiming that she did nothing wrong. Higgins admits to his profession and discovers that Pickering has come to London to meet him. The two men leave the flower girl behind to discuss their shared interest.

Next day at 11 a.m. Higgins's laboratory in Wimpole Street. It is a room on the first floor, looking on the street, and was meant for the drawing-room. The double doors are in the middle of the back wall; and persons entering find in the corner to their right two tall file cabinets at right angles to one another against the walls. In this corner stands a flat writing-table, on which are a phonograph, a laryngoscope, a row of tiny organ pipes with a bellows, a set of lamp chimneys for singing flames with burners attached to a gas plug in the wall by an indiarubber tube, several tuning-forks of different sizes, a life-size image of half a human head, showing in section the vocal organs, and a box containing a supply of wax cylinders for the phonograph.

**Peasant Girl Drinking Her Coffee–
Art Institute of Chicago**

Further down the room, on the same side, is a fireplace, with a comfortable leather-covered easy-chair at the side of the hearth nearest the door, and a coal-scuttle. There is a clock on the mantelpiece. Between the fireplace and the phonograph table is a stand for newspapers.

On the other side of the central door, to the left of the visitor, is a cabinet of shallow drawers. On it is a telephone and the telephone directory. The corner beyond, and most of the side wall, is occupied by a grand piano, with the keyboard at the end furthest from the door, and a bench for the player extending the full length of the keyboard. On the piano is a dessert dish heaped with fruit and sweets, mostly chocolates.

The middle of the room is clear. Besides the easy-chair, the piano bench, and two chairs at the phonograph table, there is one stray chair. It stands near the fireplace. On the walls, engravings; mostly Piranesis and mezzotint portraits. No paintings.

Pickering is seated at the table, putting down some cards and a tuning-fork which he has been using. Higgins is standing up near him, closing two or three file drawers which are hanging out. He appears in the morning light as a robust, vital, appetizing sort of man of forty or thereabouts, dressed in a professional-looking black frock-coat with a white linen collar and black silk tie. He is of the energetic, scientific type, heartily, even violently interested in everything that can be studied as a scientific subject, and careless about himself and other people, including their feelings. He is, in fact, but for his years and size, rather like a very impetuous baby "taking notice" eagerly and loudly, and requiring almost as much watching to keep him out of unintended mischief. His manner varies from genial bullying when he is in a good humor to stormy petulance when anything goes wrong; but he is so entirely frank and void of malice that he remains likeable even in his least reasonable moments.

From: Act II

HIGGINS

[*as he shuts the last drawer*] Well, I think that's the whole show.

PICKERING

It's really amazing. I haven't taken half of it in, you know.

HIGGINS

Would you like to go over any of it again?

PICKERING

[*rising and coming to the fireplace, where he plants himself with his back to the fire*] No, thank you; not now. I'm quite done up for this morning.

HIGGINS

[*following him, and standing beside him on his left*] Tired of listening to sounds?

PICKERING

Yes. It's a fearful strain. I rather fancied myself because I can pronounce twenty-four distinct vowel sounds; but your hundred and thirty beat me. I can't hear a bit of difference between most of them.

HIGGINS

[*chuckling, and going over to the piano to eat sweets*] Oh, that comes with practice. You hear no difference at first; but you keep on listening, and presently you find they're all as different as A from B. [*Mrs. Pearce looks in: she is Higgins's housekeeper*] What's the matter?

MRS. PEARCE

[*hesitating, evidently perplexed*] A young woman wants to see you, sir.

HIGGINS

A young woman! What does she want?

MRS. PEARCE

Well, sir, she says you'll be glad to see her when you know what she's come about. She's quite a common girl, sir. Very common indeed. I should have sent her away, only I thought perhaps you wanted her to talk into your machines. I hope I've not done wrong; but really you see such queer people sometimes—you'll excuse me, I'm sure, sir—

HIGGINS

Oh, that's all right, Mrs. Pearce. Has she an interesting accent?

MRS. PEARCE

Oh, something dreadful, sir, really. I don't know how you can take an interest in it.

HIGGINS

[*to Pickering*] Let's have her up. Shew her up, Mrs. Pearce [*he rushes across to his working table and picks out a cylinder to use on the phonograph*].

MRS. PEARCE

[*only half resigned to it*] Very well, sir. It's for you to say. [*She goes downstairs*].

HIGGINS

This is rather a bit of luck. I'll shew you how I make records. We'll set her talking; and I'll take it down first in Bell's visible Speech; then in broad Romic; and then we'll get her on the phonograph so that you can turn her on as often as you like with the written transcript before you.

MRS. PEARCE

[*returning*] This is the young woman, sir.

The flower girl enters in state. She has a hat with three ostrich feathers, orange, sky-blue, and red. She has a nearly clean apron, and the shoddy coat has been tidied a little. The pathos of this deplorable figure, with its innocent vanity and consequential air, touches Pickering, who has already straightened himself in the presence of Mrs. Pearce. But as to Higgins, the only distinction he makes between men and women is that when he is neither bullying nor exclaiming to the heavens against some featherweight cross, he coaxes women as a child coaxes its nurse when it wants to get anything out of her.*

HIGGINS

[*brusquely, recognizing her with unconcealed disappointment, and at once, babylike, making an intolerable grievance of it*] Why, this is the girl I jotted down last night. She's no use: I've got all the records I want of the Lisson Grove lingo; and I'm not going to waste another cylinder on it [*To the girl*] Be off with you: I don't want you.

THE FLOWER GIRL

Don't you be so saucy. You ain't heard what I come for yet. [*To Mrs. Pearce, who is waiting at the door for further instruction*] Did you tell him I come in a taxi?

MRS. PEARCE

Nonsense, girl! What do you think a gentleman like Mr. Higgins cares what you came in?

THE FLOWER GIRL

Oh, we are proud! He ain't above giving lessons, not him: I heard him say so. Well, I ain't come here to ask for any compliment; and if my money's not good enough I can go elsewhere.

HIGGINS

Good enough for what?

THE FLOWER GIRL

Good enough for ye-oo. Now you know, don't you? I'm come to have lessons, I am. And to pay for 'em too: make no mistake.

HIGGINS

[*stupent*] Well! [*Recovering his breath with a gasp*] What do you expect me to say to you?

THE FLOWER GIRL

Well, if you was a gentleman, you might ask me to sit down, I think. Don't I tell you I'm bringing you business?

HIGGINS

Pickering; shall we ask this baggage to sit down, or shall we throw her out of the window?

THE FLOWER GIRL

[*running away in terror to the piano, where she turns at bay*] Ah-ah-ah-ow-ow-ow-oo! [*Wounded and whimpering*] I won't be called a baggage when I've offered to pay like any lady.

Motionless, the two men stare at her from the other side of the room, amazed.

PICKERING

[*gently*] What is it you want, my girl?

THE FLOWER GIRL

I want to be a lady in a flower shop stead of selling at the corner of Tottenham Court Road. But they won't take me unless I can talk more genteel. He said he could teach me. Well, here I am ready to pay him—not asking any favor—and he treats me as if I was dirt.

MRS. PEARCE

How can you be such a foolish ignorant girl as to think you could afford to pay Mr. Higgins?

THE FLOWER GIRL

Why shouldn't I? I know what lessons cost as well as you do; and I'm ready to pay.

HIGGINS

How much?

THE FLOWER GIRL

[*coming back to him, triumphant*] Now you're talking! I thought you'd come off it when you saw a chance of getting back a bit of what you chucked at me last night. [*Confidentially*] You'd had a drop in, hadn't you?

HIGGINS

[*peremptorily*] Sit down.

THE FLOWER GIRL

Oh, if you're going to make a compliment of it—

HIGGINS

[*thundering at her*] Sit down.

MRS. PEARCE

[*severely*] Sit down, girl. Do as you're told. [*She places the stray chair near the hearthrug between Higgins and Pickering, and stands behind it waiting for the girl to sit down*].

THE FLOWER GIRL

Ah-ah-ah-ow-ow-oo! [*She stands, half rebellious, half bewildered*].

PICKERING

[*very courteous*] Won't you sit down?

THE FLOWER GIRL

[*coyly*] Don't mind if I do. [*She sits down. Pickering returns to the hearthrug*].

HIGGINS

What's your name?

THE FLOWER GIRL

Liza Doolittle.

HIGGINS

[*declaiming gravely*] Eliza, Elizabeth, Betsy and Bess, They went to the woods to get a bird nes:'

PICKERING

They found a nest with four egg in it:

HIGGINS

They took one apiece, and left three in it.

They laugh heartily at their own wit.

LIZA

Oh, don't be silly.

MRS. PEARCE

You mustn't speak to the gentleman like that.

LIZA

Well, why won't he speak sensible to me?

HIGGINS

Come back to business. How much do you propose to pay me for the lessons?

LIZA

Oh, I know what's right. A lady friend of mine gets French lessons for eighteenpence an hour from a real French gentleman. Well, you wouldn't have the face to ask me the same for teaching me my own language as you would for French; so I won't give more than a shilling. Take it or leave it.

HIGGINS

[*walking up and down the room, rattling his keys and his cash in his pockets*] You know, Pickering, if you consider a shilling, not as a simple shilling, but as a percentage of this girl's income, it works out as fully equivalent to sixty or seventy guineas from a millionaire.

PICKERING

How so?

HIGGINS

Figure it out. A millionaire has about £150 a day. She earns about half-a-crown.

LIZA

[*haughtily*] Who told you I only—

HIGGINS

[*continuing*] She offers me two-fifths of her day's income for a lesson. Two-fifths of a millionaire's income for a day would be somewhere about £60. It's handsome. By George, it's enormous! it's the biggest offer I ever had.

LIZA

[*rising, terrified*] Sixty pounds! What are you talking about? I never offered you sixty pounds. Where would I get—

HIGGINS

Hold your tongue.

LIZA

[*weeping*] But I ain't got sixty pounds. Oh—

MRS. PEARCE

Don't cry, you silly girl. Sit down. Nobody is going to touch your money.

HIGGINS

Somebody is going to touch you, with a broomstick, if you don't stop snivelling. Sit down.

LIZA

[obeying slowly] Ah-ah-ah-ow-oo-o! One would think you was my father.

HIGGINS

If I decide to teach you, I'll be worse than two fathers to you. Here [he offers her his silk handkerchief]!

LIZA

What's this for?

HIGGINS

To wipe your eyes. To wipe any part of your face that feels moist. Remember: that's your handkerchief; and that's your sleeve. Don't mistake the one for the other if you wish to become a lady in a shop.

Liza, utterly bewildered, stares helplessly at him.

MRS. PEARCE

It's no use talking to her like that, Mr. Higgins: she doesn't understand you. Besides, you're quite wrong: she doesn't do it that way at all [she takes the handkerchief].

LIZA

[snatching it] Here! You give me that handkerchief. He give it to me, not to you.

PICKERING

[laughing] He did. I think it must be regarded as her property, Mrs. Pearce.

MRS. PEARCE

[resigning herself] Serve you right, Mr. Higgins.

PICKERING

Higgins, I'm interested. What about the ambassador's garden party? I'll say you're the greatest teacher alive if you make that good. I'll bet you all the expenses of the experiment you can't do it. And I'll pay for the lessons.

LIZA

Oh, you are real good. Thank you, Captain.

HIGGINS

[tempted, looking at her] It's almost irresistible. She's so deliciously low—so horribly dirty—

LIZA

[protesting extremely] Ah-ah-ah-ah-ow-ow-oo-oo!!! I ain't dirty: I washed my face and hands afore I come, I did.

PICKERING

You're certainly not going to turn her head with flattery, Higgins.

MRS. PEARCE

[uneasy] Oh, don't say that, sir: there's more ways than one of turning a girl's head; and nobody can do it better than Mr. Higgins, though he may not always mean it. I do hope, sir, you won't encourage him to do anything foolish.

HIGGINS

[becoming excited as the idea grows on him] What is life but a series of inspired follies? The difficulty is to find them to do. Never lose a chance: it doesn't come every day. I shall make a duchess of this draggle-tailed guttersnipe.*

LIZA

[strongly deprecating this view of her] Ah-ah-ah-ow-ow-oo!

HIGGINS

[carried away] Yes: in six months—in three if she has a good ear and a quick tongue—I'll take her anywhere and pass her off as anything. We'll start today: now! this moment! Take her away and clean her, Mrs. Pearce. Monkey Brand, if it won't come off any other way. Is there a good fire in the kitchen?

MRS. PEARCE

[protesting]. Yes; but—

HIGGINS

[storming on] Take all her clothes off and burn them. Ring up Whiteley or somebody for new ones. Wrap her up in brown paper 'til they come.

LIZA

You're no gentleman, you're not, to talk of such things. I'm a good girl, I am; and I know what the like of you are, I do.

HIGGINS

We want none of your Lisson Grove prudery here, young woman. You've got to learn to behave like a duchess. Take her away, Mrs. Pearce. If she gives you any trouble wallop her.

LIZA

[springing up and running between Pickering and Mrs. Pearce for protection] No! I'll call the police, I will.

MRS. PEARCE

But I've no place to put her.

HIGGINS

Put her in the dustbin.

LIZA

Ah-ah-ah-ow-ow-oo!

PICKERING

Oh come, Higgins! Be reasonable.

MRS. PEARCE

[resolutely] You must be reasonable, Mr. Higgins: really you must. You can't walk over everybody like this.

Higgins, thus scolded, subsides. The hurricane is succeeded by a zephyr* of amiable surprise.

HIGGINS

[with professional exquisiteness of modulation] I walk over everybody! My dear Mrs. Pearce, my dear Pickering, I never had the slightest intention of walking over anyone. All I propose is that we should be kind to this poor girl. We must help her to prepare and fit herself for her new station in life. If I did not express myself clearly it was because I did not wish to hurt her delicacy, or yours.

Liza, reassured, steals back to her chair.

MRS. PEARCE

[*to Pickering*] Well, did you ever hear anything like that, sir?

PICKERING

[*laughing heartily*] Never, Mrs. Pearce: never.

HIGGINS

[*patiently*] What's the matter?

MRS. PEARCE

Well, the matter is, sir, that you can't take a girl up like that as if you were picking up a pebble on the beach.

HIGGINS

Why not?

MRS. PEARCE

Why not! But you don't know anything about her. What about her parents? She may be married.

LIZA

Garn!

HIGGINS

There! As the girl very properly says, Garn! Married indeed! Don't you know that a woman of that class looks a worn out drudge of fifty a year after she's married.

LIZA

Who'od marry me?

HIGGINS

[*suddenly resorting to the most thrillingly beautiful low tones in his best elocutionary* style*] By George, Eliza, the streets will be strewn with the bodies of men shooting themselves for your sake before I've done with you.

MRS. PEARCE

Nonsense, sir. You mustn't talk like that to her.

LIZA

[*rising and squaring herself determinedly*] I'm going away. He's off his chump, he is. I don't want no balmies teaching me.

HIGGINS

[*wounded in his tenderest point by her insensibility to his elocution*] Oh, indeed! I'm mad, am I? Very well, Mrs. Pearce: you needn't order the new clothes for her. Throw her out.

LIZA

[*whimpering*] Nah-ow. You got no right to touch me.

MRS. PEARCE

You see now what comes of being saucy. [*Indicating the door*] This way, please.

LIZA

[*almost in tears*] I didn't want no clothes. I wouldn't have taken them [*she throws away the handkerchief*]. I can buy my own clothes.

HIGGINS

[*deftly retrieving the handkerchief and intercepting her*

on her reluctant way to the door] You're an ungrateful wicked girl. This is my return for offering to take you out of the gutter and dress you beautifully and make a lady of you.

MRS. PEARCE

Stop, Mr. Higgins. I won't allow it. It's you that are wicked. Go home to your parents, girl; and tell them to take better care of you.

LIZA

I ain't got no parents. They told me I was big enough to earn my own living and turned me out.

MRS. PEARCE

Where's your mother?

LIZA

I ain't got no mother. Her that turned me out was my sixth stepmother. But I done without them. And I'm a good girl, I am.

HIGGINS

Very well, then, what on earth is all this fuss about? The girl doesn't belong to anybody—is no use to anybody but me. [*He goes to Mrs. Pearce and begins coaxing*]. You can adopt her, Mrs. Pearce: I'm sure a daughter would be a great amusement to you. Now don't make any more fuss. Take her downstairs; and—

MRS. PEARCE

But what's to become of her? Is she to be paid anything? Do be sensible, sir.

HIGGINS

Oh, pay her whatever is necessary: put it down in the housekeeping book. [*Impatiently*] What on earth will she want with money? She'll have her food and her clothes. She'll only drink if you give her money.

LIZA

[*turning on him*] Oh you are a brute. It's a lie: nobody ever saw the sign of liquor on me. [*She goes back to her chair and plants herself there defiantly*].

PICKERING

[*in good-humored remonstrance*] Does it occur to you, Higgins, that the girl has some feelings?

HIGGINS

[*looking critically at her*] Oh no, I don't think so. Not any feelings that we need bother about. [*Cheerily*] Have you, Eliza?

LIZA

I got my feelings same as anyone else.

HIGGINS

[*to Pickering, reflectively*] You see the difficulty?

PICKERING

Eh? What difficulty?

HIGGINS

To get her to talk grammar. The mere pronunciation is easy enough.

LIZA

I don't want to talk grammar. I want to talk like a lady.

MRS. PEARCE

Will you please keep to the point, Mr. Higgins. I want to know on what terms the girl is to be here. Is she to have any wages? And what is to become of her when youve finished your teaching? You must look ahead a little.

HIGGINS

[*impatiently*] What's to become of her if I leave her in the gutter? Tell me that, Mrs. Pearce.

MRS. PEARCE

That's her own business, not yours, Mr. Higgins.

HIGGINS

Well, when I've done with her, we can throw her back into the gutter; and then it will be her own business again; so that's all right.

LIZA

Oh, you've no feeling heart in you: you don't care for nothing but yourself [*she rises and takes the floor resolutely*]. Here! I've had enough of this. I'm going [*making for the door*]. You ought to be ashamed of yourself, you ought.

HIGGINS

[*snatching a chocolate cream from the piano, his eyes suddenly beginning to twinkle with mischief*] Have some chocolates, Eliza.

LIZA

[*halting, tempted*] How do I know what might be in them? I've heard of girls being drugged by the like of you.

Higgins whips out his penknife; cuts a chocolate in two; puts one half into his mouth and bolts it; and offers her the other half.

HIGGINS

Pledge of good faith, Eliza. I eat one half: you eat the other. [*Liza opens her mouth to retort: he pops the half chocolate into it*]. You shall have boxes of them, barrels of them, every day. You shall live on them. Eh?

LIZA

[*who has disposed of the chocolate after being nearly choked by it*] I wouldn't have ate it, only I'm too lady-like to take it out of my mouth.

HIGGINS

Listen, Eliza. I think you said you came in a taxi.

LIZA

Well, what if I did? I've as good a right to take a taxi as anyone else.

HIGGINS

You have, Eliza; and in future you shall have as many taxis as you want. You shall go up and down and round the town in a taxi every day. Think of that, Eliza.

MRS. PEARCE

Mr. Higgins, you're tempting the girl. It's not right. She should think of the future.

HIGGINS

At her age! Nonsense! Time enough to think of the future when you haven't any future to think of. No, Eliza: do as this lady does: think of other people's futures; but never think of your own. Think of chocolates, and taxis, and gold, and diamonds.

LIZA

No: I don't want no gold and no diamonds. I'm a good girl, I am. [*She sits down again, with an attempt at dignity*].

HIGGINS

You shall remain so, Eliza, under the care of Mrs. Pearce. And you shall marry an officer in the Guards, with a beautiful moustache: the son of a marquis,* who will disinherit him for marrying you, but will relent when he sees your beauty and goodness—

PICKERING

Excuse me, Higgins; but I really must interfere. Mrs. Pearce is quite right. If this girl is to put herself in your hands for six months for an experiment in teaching, she must understand thoroughly what she's doing.

HIGGINS

How can she? She's incapable of understanding anything. Besides, do any of us understand what we are doing? If we did, would we ever do it?

PICKERING

Very clever, Higgins; but not sound sense. [*To Eliza*] Miss Doolittle—

LIZA

[*overwhelmed*] Ah-ah-ow-oo!

HIGGINS

There! That's all you get out of Eliza. Ah-ah-ow-oo! No use explaining. As a military man you ought to know that. Give her her orders: that's what she wants. Eliza: you are to live here for the next six months, learning how to speak beautifully, like a lady in a florist's shop. If you're good and do whatever you're told, you shall sleep in a proper bedroom, and have lots to eat, and money to buy chocolates and take rides in taxis. If you're naughty and idle you will sleep in the back kitchen among the black beetles, and be walloped by Mrs. Pearce with a broomstick. At the end of six months you shall go to Buckingham Palace in a carriage, beautifully dressed. If the King finds out you're not a lady, you will be taken by the police to the Tower of London, where your head will be cut off as a warning to other presumptuous flower girls. If you are not found out, you shall have a present of seven-and-sixpence to start life with as a lady in a shop. If you refuse this offer you will be a most ungrateful and wicked girl; and the angels will weep for you. [*To Pickering*] Now are you satisfied, Pickering? [*To Mrs. Pearce*] Can I put it more plainly and fairly, Mrs. Pearce?

MRS. PEARCE

[*patiently*] I think you'd better let me speak to the girl properly in private. I don't know that I can take charge of her or consent to the arrangement at all. Of course I know you don't mean her any harm; but when you get what you call interested in people's accents, you never think or care what may happen to them or you. Come with me, Eliza.

HIGGINS

That's all right. Thank you, Mrs. Pearce. Bundle her off to the bath-room.

LIZA

[*rising reluctantly and suspiciously*] You're a great bully, you are. I won't stay here if I don't like. I won't let nobody wallop me. I never asked to go to Bucknam Palace, I didn't. I was never in trouble with the police, not me. I'm a good girl—

MRS. PEARCE

Don't answer back, girl. You don't understand the gentleman. Come with me. [*She leads the way to the door, and holds it open for Eliza*].

LIZA

[*as she goes out*] Well, what I say is right. I won't go near the king, not if I'm going to have my head cut off. If I'd known what I was letting myself in for, I wouldn't have come here. I always been a good girl; and I never offered to say a word to him; and I don't owe him nothing; and I don't care; and I won't be put upon; and I have my feelings the same as anyone else—

Mrs. Pearce shuts the door; and Eliza's plain'ts are no longer audible. Pickering comes from the hearth to the chair and sits astride it with his arms on the back.

Mrs. Pearce opens the door. She has Eliza's hat in her hand. Pickering retires to the easy-chair at the hearth and sits down.

HIGGINS

[*eagerly*] Well, Mrs. Pearce: is it all right?

MRS. PEARCE

[*at the door*] I just wish to trouble you with a word, if I may, Mr. Higgins.

HIGGINS

Yes, certainly. Come in. [*She comes forward*]. Don't burn that, Mrs. Pearce. I'll keep it as a curiosity. [*He takes the hat*].

MRS. PEARCE

Handle it carefully, sir, please. I had to promise her not to burn it; but I had better put it in the oven for a while.

HIGGINS

[*putting it down hastily on the piano*] Oh! thank you. Well, what have you to say to me?

PICKERING

Am I in the way?

MRS. PEARCE

Not at all, sir. Mr. Higgins: will you please be very particular what you say before the girl?

HIGGINS

[*sternly*] Of course. I'm always particular about what I say. Why do you say this to me?

MRS. PEARCE

[*unmoved*] No, sir: you're not at all particular when you've mislaid anything or when you get a little impatient. Now it doesn't matter before me: I'm used to it. But you really must not swear before the girl.

HIGGINS

[*indignantly*] I swear! [*Most emphatically*] I never swear. I detest the habit. What the devil do you mean?

MRS. PEARCE

[*stolidly*] That's what I mean, sir. You swear a great deal too much. I don't mind your damning and blasting, and what the devil and where the devil and who the devil—

HIGGINS

Mrs. Pearce: this language from your lips! Really!

MRS. PEARCE

[*not to be put off*]—but there is a certain word I must ask you not to use. The girl has just used it herself because the bath was too hot. It begins with the same letter as bath. She knows no better: she learnt it at her mother's knee. But she must not hear it from your lips.

HIGGINS

[*loftily*] I cannot charge myself with having ever uttered it, Mrs. Pearce. [*She looks at him steadfastly. He adds, hiding an uneasy conscience with a judicial air*] Except perhaps in a moment of extreme and justifiable excitement.

MRS. PEARCE

Only this morning, sir, you applied it to your boots, to the butter, and to the brown bread.

HIGGINS

Oh, that! Mere alliteration, Mrs. Pearce, natural to a poet.

MRS. PEARCE

Well, sir, whatever you choose to call it, I beg you not to let the girl hear you repeat it.

HIGGINS

Oh, very well, very well. Is that all?

MRS. PEARCE

No, sir. We shall have to be very particular with this girl as to personal cleanliness.

HIGGINS

Certainly. Quite right. Most important.

MRS. PEARCE

I mean not to be slovenly about her dress or untidy in leaving things about.

HIGGINS

[*going to her solemnly*] Just so. I intended to call your attention to that [*He passes on to Pickering, who is enjoying the conversation immensely*]. It is these little things that matter, Pickering. "Take care of the pence and the pounds will take care of themselves" is as true of personal habits as of money. [*He comes to anchor on the hearthrug, with the air of a man in an unassailable position*].

MRS. PEARCE

Yes, sir. Then might I ask you not to come down to breakfast in your dressing-gown, or at any rate not to use it as a napkin to the extent you do, sir. And if you would be so good as not to eat everything off the same plate, and to remember not to put the porridge saucepan out of your hand on the clean tablecloth, it would be a better example to the girl. You know you nearly choked yourself with a fishbone in the jam only last week.

HIGGINS

[*routed from the hearthrug and drifting back to the piano*] I may do these things sometimes in absence of mind; but surely I don't do them habitually. [*Angrily*] By the way: my dressing-gown smells most damnably of benzine.

MRS. PEARCE

No doubt it does, Mr. Higgins. But if you will wipe your fingers—

HIGGINS

[*yelling*] Oh very well, very well: I'll wipe them in my hair in future.

MRS. PEARCE

I hope you're not offended, Mr. Higgins.

HIGGINS

[*shocked at finding himself thought capable of an unamiable sentiment*] Not at all, not at all. You're quite right, Mrs. Pearce: I shall be particularly careful before the girl. Is that all?

MRS. PEARCE

No, sir. Might she use some of those Japanese dresses you brought from abroad? I really can't put her back into her old things.

HIGGINS

Certainly. Anything you like. Is that all?

MRS. PEARCE

Thank you, sir. That's all. [*She goes out*].

HIGGINS

You know, Pickering, that woman has the most extraordinary ideas about me. Here I am, a shy, diffident sort of man. I've never been able to feel really grown-up and tremendous, like other chaps. And yet she's firmly persuaded that I'm an arbitrary overbearing bossing kind of person. I can't account for it.

Mrs. Pearce returns.

MRS. PEARCE

If you please, sir, the trouble's beginning already. There's a dustman* downstairs, Alfred Doolittle, wants to see you. He says you have his daughter here.

PICKERING

[*rising*] Phew! I say! [*He retreats to the hearthrug*].

HIGGINS

[*promptly*] Send the blackguard up.

MRS. PEARCE

Oh, very well, sir. [*She goes out*].

PICKERING

He may not be a blackguard, Higgins.

HIGGINS

Nonsense. Of course he's a blackguard.

PICKERING

Whether he is or not, I'm afraid we shall have some trouble with him.

HIGGINS

[*confidently*] Oh no: I think not. If there's any trouble he shall have it with me, not I with him. And we are sure to get something interesting out of him.

PICKERING

About the girl?

HIGGINS

No. I mean his dialect.

PICKERING

Oh!

MRS. PEARCE

[*at the door*] Doolittle, sir. [*She admits Doolittle and retires*].

Alfred Doolittle is an elderly but vigorous dustman, clad in the costume of his profession, including a hat with a back brim covering his neck and shoulders. He has well marked and rather interesting features, and seems equally free from fear and conscience. He has a remarkably expressive voice, the result of a habit of giving vent to his feelings without reserve. His present pose is that of wounded honor and stern resolution.

DOOLITTLE

[*at the door, uncertain which of the two gentlemen is his man*] Professor Higgins?

HIGGINS

Here. Good morning. Sit down.

DOOLITTLE

Morning, Governor. [*He sits down magisterially*] I come about a very serious matter, Governor.

HIGGINS

[*to Pickering*] Brought up in Hounslow. Mother Welsh, I should think. [*Doolittle opens his mouth, amazed. Higgins continues*] What do you want, Doolittle?

DOOLITTLE

[*menacingly*] I want my daughter: that's what I want. See?

HIGGINS

Of course you do. You're her father, aren't you? You don't suppose anyone else wants her, do you? I'm glad to see you have some spark of family feeling left. She's upstairs. Take her away at once.

DOOLITTLE

[*rising, fearfully taken aback.*] What!

81

HIGGINS

Take her away. Do you suppose I'm going to keep your daughter for you?

DOOLITTLE

[*remonstrating*] Now, now, look here, Governor. Is this reasonable? Is it fairity to take advantage of a man like this? The girl belongs to me. You got her. Where do I come in? [*He sits down again*].

HIGGINS

Your daughter had the audacity to come to my house and ask me to teach her how to speak properly so that she could get a place in a flower-shop. This gentleman and my housekeeper have been here all the time. [*Bullying him*] How dare you come here and attempt to blackmail me? You sent her here on purpose.

DOOLITTLE

[*protesting*] No, Governor.

HIGGINS

You must have. How else could you possibly know that she is here?

DOOLITTLE

Don't take a man up like that, Governor.

HIGGINS

The police shall take you up. This is a plant—a plot to extort money by threats. I shall telephone for the police [*he goes resolutely to the telephone and opens the directory*].

DOOLITTLE

Have I asked you for a brass farthing? I leave it to the gentleman here: have I said a word about money?

HIGGINS

[*throwing the book aside and marching down on Doolittle with a poser*] What else did you come for?

DOOLITTLE

[*sweetly*] Well, what would a man come for? Be human, Governor.

HIGGINS

[*disarmed*] Alfred: did you put her up to it?

DOOLITTLE

So help me, Governor, I never did. I take my Bible oath I ain't seen the girl these two months past.

HIGGINS

Then how did you know she was here?

DOOLITTLE

[*"most musical, most melancholy"*] I'll tell you, Governor, if you'll only let me get a word in. I'm willing to tell you. I'm wanting to tell you. I'm waiting to tell you.

HIGGINS

Pickering: this chap has a certain natural gift of rhetoric. Observe the rhythm of his native woodnotes wild. "I'm willing to tell you: I'm wanting to tell you: I'm waiting to tell you." Sentimental rhetoric! that's the Welsh strain in him. It also accounts for his mendacity and dishonesty.

PICKERING

Oh, p l e a s e, Higgins: I'm west country myself. [*To Doolittle*] How did you know the girl was here if you didn't send her?

DOOLITTLE

It was like this, Governor. The girl took a boy in the taxi to give him a jaunt. Son of her landlady, he is. He hung about on the chance of her giving him another ride home. Well, she sent him back for her luggage when she heard you was willing for her to stop here. I met the boy at the corner of Long Acre and Endell Street.

HIGGINS

Public house. Yes?

DOOLITTLE

The poor man's club, Governor: why shouldn't I?

PICKERING

Do let him tell his story, Higgins.

DOOLITTLE

He told me what was up. And I ask you, what was my feelings and my duty as a father? I says to the boy, "You bring me the luggage," I says—

PICKERING

Why didn't you go for it yourself?

DOOLITTLE

Landlady wouldn't have trusted me with it, Governor. She's that kind of woman: you know. I had to give the boy a penny afore he trusted me with it, the little swine. I brought it to her just to oblige you like, and make myself agreeable. That's all.

HIGGINS

How much luggage?

DOOLITTLE

Musical instrument, Governor. A few pictures, a trifle of jewelry, and a bird-cage. She said she didn't want no clothes. What was I to think from that, Governor? I ask you as a parent what was I to think?

HIGGINS

So you came to rescue her from worse than death, eh?

DOOLITTLE

[*appreciatively: relieved at being so well understood*] Just so, Governor. That's right.

PICKERING

But why did you bring her luggage if you intended to take her away?

DOOLITTLE

Have I said a word about taking her away? Have I now?

HIGGINS

[*determinedly*] You're going to take her away, double quick. [*He crosses to the hearth and rings the bell*].

DOOLITTLE

[*rising*] No, Governor. Don't say that. I'm not the man to stand in my girl's light. Here's a career opening for her, as you might say; and—

Mrs. Pearce opens the door and awaits orders.

HIGGINS

Mrs. Pearce: this is Eliza's father. He has come to take her away. Give her to him. [*He goes back to the piano, with an air of washing his hands of the whole affair*].

DOOLITTLE

No. This is a misunderstanding. Listen here—

MRS. PEARCE

He can't take her away, Mr. Higgins: how can he? You told me to burn her clothes.

DOOLITTLE

That's right. I can't carry the girl through the streets like a blooming monkey, can I? I put it to you.

HIGGINS

You have put it to me that you want your daughter. Take your daughter. If she has no clothes go out and buy her some.

DOOLITTLE

[*desperate*] Where's the clothes she come in? Did I burn them or did your missus here?

MRS. PEARCE

I am the housekeeper, if you please. I have sent for some clothes for your girl. When they come you can take her away. You can wait in the kitchen. This way, please.

Doolittle, much troubled, accompanies her to the door; then hesitates; finally turns confidentially to Higgins.

DOOLITTLE

Listen here, Governor. You and me is men of the world, ain't we?

HIGGINS

Oh! Men of the world, are we? Shouldn't you better go, Mrs. Pearce?

MRS. PEARCE

I think so, indeed, sir. [*She goes, with dignity*].

PICKERING

The floor is yours, Mr. Doolittle.

DOOLITTLE

[*to Pickering*] I thank you, Governor. [*To Higgins, who takes refuge on the piano bench, a little overwhelmed by the proximity of his visitor; for Doolittle has a professional flavor of dust about him*]. Well, the truth is, I've taken a sort of fancy to you, Governor; and if you want the girl, I'm not so set on having her back home again but what I might be open to an arrangement. Regarded in the light of a young woman, she's a fine handsome girl. As a daughter she's not worth her keep; and so I tell you straight. All I ask is my rights as a father; and you're the last man alive to expect me to let her go for nothing; for I can see you're one of the straight sort, Governor. Well, what's a five pound note to you? And what's Eliza to me? [*He returns to his chair and sits down judicially*].

PICKERING

I think you ought to know, Doolittle, that Mr. Higgins's intentions are entirely honorable.

DOOLITTLE

Course they are, Governor. If I thought they wasn't, I'd ask fifty.

HIGGINS

[*revolted*] Do you mean to say, you callous rascal, that you would sell your daughter for £50?

DOOLITTLE

Not in a general way I wouldn't; but to oblige a gentleman like you I'd do a good deal, I do assure you.

PICKERING

Have you no morals, man?

DOOLITTLE

[*unabashed*] Can't afford them, Governor. Neither could you if you was as poor as me. Not that I mean any harm, you know. But if Liza is going to have a bit out of this, why not me, too?

HIGGINS

[*troubled*] I don't know what to do, Pickering. There can be no question that as a matter of morals it's a positive crime to give this chap a farthing. And yet I feel a sort of rough justice in his claim.

DOOLITTLE

That's it, Governor. That's all I say. A father's heart, as it were.

PICKERING

Well, I know the feeling; but really it seems hardly right—

DOOLITTLE

Don't say that, Governor. Don't look at it that way. What am I, Governors both? I ask you, what am I? I'm one of the undeserving poor: that's what I am. Think of what that means to a man. It means that he's up agen middle-class morality all the time. If there's anything going, and I put in for a bit of it, it's always the same story: "You're undeserving; so you can't have it." But my needs is as great as the most deserving widow's that ever got money out of six different charities in one week for the death of the same husband. I don't need less than a deserving man: I need more. I don't eat less hearty than him; and I drink a lot more. I want a bit of amusement, cause I'm a thinking man. I want cheerfulness and a song and a band when I feel low. Well, they charge me just the same for everything as they charge the deserving. What is middle-class morality? Just an excuse for never giving me anything. Therefore, I ask you, as two gentlemen, not to play that game on me. I'm playing straight with you. I ain't pretending to be deserving. I'm undeserving; and I mean to go on being undeserving. I like it; and that's the truth. Will you take advantage of a man's nature to do him out of the price of his own daughter what he's brought up and fed and clothed by the sweat of his brow until she's growed big enough to be interesting to you two gentlemen? Is five pounds unreasonable? I put it to you; and I leave it to you.

HIGGINS

[*rising, and going over to Pickering*] Pickering, if we were to take this man in hand for three months, he could choose between a seat in the Cabinet and a popular pulpit in Wales.

PICKERING

What do you say to that, Doolittle?

DOOLITTLE

Not me, Governor, thank you kindly. I've heard all the preachers and all the prime ministers—for I'm a thinking man and game for politics or religion or social reform same as all the other amusements—and I tell you it's a dog's life anyway you look at it. Undeserving poverty is my line. Taking one station in society with another, it's—it's—well, it's the only one that has any ginger in it, to my taste.

HIGGINS

I suppose we must give him a fiver.

PICKERING

He'll make a bad use of it, I'm afraid.

DOOLITTLE

Not me, Governor, so help me I won't. Don't you be afraid that I'll save it and spare it and live idle on it. There won't be a penny of it left by Monday: I'll have to go to work same as if I'd never had it. It won't pauperize me, you bet. Just one good spree for myself and the missus, giving pleasure to ourselves and employment to others, and satisfaction to you to think it's not been throwed away. You couldn't spend it better.

HIGGINS

[*taking out his pocket book and coming between Doolittle and the piano*] This is irresistible. Let's give him ten. [*He offers two notes to the dustman*].

DOOLITTLE

No, Governor. She wouldn't have the heart to spend ten; and perhaps I shouldn't neither. Ten pounds is a lot of money: it makes a man feel prudent like; and then goodbye to happiness. You give me what I ask you, Governor: not a penny more, and not a penny less.

PICKERING

Why don't you marry that missus of yours? I rather draw the line at encouraging that sort of immorality.

DOOLITTLE

Tell her so, Governor: tell her so. I'm willing. It's me that suffers by it. I've no hold on her. I got to be agreeable to her. I got to give her presents. I got to buy her clothes something sinful. I'm a slave to that woman, Governor, just because I'm not her lawful husband. And she knows it too. Catch her marrying me! Take my advice, Governor: marry Eliza while she's young and don't know no better. If you don't you'll be sorry for it after. If you do, she'll be sorry for it after; but better you than her, because you're a man, and she's only a woman and don't know how to be happy anyhow.

HIGGINS

Pickering: if we listen to this man another minute, we shall have no convictions left. [*To Doolittle*] Five pounds I think you said.

DOOLITTLE

Thank you kindly, Governor.

HIGGINS

You're sure you won't take ten?

DOOLITTLE

Not now. Another time, Governor.

HIGGINS

[*handing him a five-pound note*] Here you are.

DOOLITTLE

Thank you, Governor. Good morning. [*He hurries to the door, anxious to get away with his booty. When he opens it he is confronted with a dainty and exquisitely clean young Japanese lady in a simple blue cotton kimono printed cunningly with small white jasmine blossoms. Mrs. Pearce is with her. He gets out of her way deferentially and apologizes*]. Beg pardon, miss.

THE JAPANESE LADY

Garn! Don't you know your own daughter?

DOOLITTLE \ *exclaiming* / Bly me! it's Eliza!
HIGGINS > *simultaneously* < What's that! This!
PICKERING / \ By Jove!

LIZA

Don't I look silly?

HIGGINS

Silly?

MRS. PEARCE

[*at the door*] Now, Mr. Higgins, please don't say anything to make the girl conceited about herself.

HIGGINS

[*conscientiously*] Oh! Quite right, Mrs. Pearce. [*To Eliza*] Yes, damned silly.

MRS. PEARCE

Please, sir.

HIGGINS

[*correcting himself*] I mean extremely silly.

LIZA

I should look all right with my hat on. [*She takes up her hat; puts it on; and walks across the room to the fireplace with a fashionable air*].

HIGGINS

A new fashion, by George! And it ought to look horrible!

DOOLITTLE

[*with fatherly pride*] Well, I never thought she'd clean up as good looking as that, Governor. She's a credit to me, ain't she?

LIZA

I tell you, it's easy to clean up here. Hot and cold water on tap, just as much as you like, there is. Woolly towels, there is; and a towel horse so hot, it burns your fingers. Soft brushes to scrub yourself, and a wooden bowl of soap smelling like primroses. Now I know why ladies is so clean. Washing's a treat for them. Wish they saw what it is for the like of me!

HIGGINS

I'm glad the bath-room met with your approval.

LIZA

It didn't: not all of it; and I don't care who hears me say it. Mrs. Pearce knows.

HIGGINS

What was wrong, Mrs. Pearce?

MRS. PEARCE

[*blandly*] Oh, nothing, sir. It doesn't matter.

LIZA

I had a good mind to break it. I didn't know which way to look. But I hung a towel over it, I did.

HIGGINS

Over what?

MRS. PEARCE

Over the looking-glass, sir.

HIGGINS

Doolittle, you have brought your daughter up too strictly.

DOOLITTLE

Me! I never brought her up at all, except to give her a lick of a strap now and again. Don't put it on me, Governor. She ain't accustomed to it, you see, that's all. But she'll soon pick up your free and easy ways.

LIZA

I'm a good girl, I am; and I won't pick up no free and easy ways.

HIGGINS

Eliza, if you say again that you're a good girl, your father shall take you home.

LIZA

Not him. You don't know my father. All he come here for was to touch you for some money to get drunk on.

DOOLITTLE

Well, what else would I want money for? To put into the plate in church, I suppose. [*She puts out her tongue at him. He is so incensed by this that Pickering presently finds it necessary to step between them*]. Don't you give me none of your lip; and don't let me hear you giving this gentleman any of it neither, or you'll hear from me about it. See?

HIGGINS

Have you any further advice to give her before you go, Doolittle? Your blessing, for instance.

DOOLITTLE

No, Governor: I ain't such a mug as to put up my children to all I know myself. Hard enough to hold them in without that. If you want Eliza's mind improved, Governor, you do it yourself with a strap. So long, gentlemen. [*He turns to go*].

HIGGINS

[*impressively*] Stop. You'll come regularly to see your daughter. It's your duty, you know. My brother is a clergyman; and he could help you in your talks with her.

DOOLITTLE

[*evasively*] Certainly. I'll come, Governor. Not just this week, because I have a job at a distance. But later on you may depend on me. Afternoon, gentlemen. Afternoon, ma'am. [*He takes off his hat to Mrs. Pearce, who disdains the salutation and goes out. He winks at Higgins, thinking him probably a fellow-sufferer from Mrs. Pearce's difficult disposition, and follows her*].

LIZA

Don't you believe the old liar. He'd as soon you set a bull-dog on him as a clergyman. You won't see him again in a hurry.

HIGGINS

I don't want to, Eliza. Do you?

LIZA

Not me. I don't want never to see him again, I don't. He's a disgrace to me, he is, collecting dust, instead of working at his trade.

PICKERING

What is his trade, Eliza?

LIZA

Talking money out of other people's pockets into his own. His proper trade's a navvy;* and he works at it sometimes too—for exercise—and earns good money at it. Ain't you going to call me Miss Doolittle any more?

PICKERING

I beg your pardon, Miss Doolittle. It was a slip of the tongue.

LIZA

Oh, I don't mind; only it sounded so genteel. I should just like to take a taxi to the corner of Tottenham Court Road and get out there and tell it to wait for me, just to put the girls in their place a bit. I wouldn't speak to them, you know.

PICKERING

Better wait 'til we get you something really fashionable.

HIGGINS

Besides, you shouldn't cut your old friends now that you have risen in the world. That's what we call snobbery.

LIZA

You don't call the like of them my friends now, I should hope. They've took it out of me often enough with their ridicule when they had the chance; and now I mean to get a bit of my own back. But if I'm to have fashionable clothes, I'll wait. I should like to have some. Mrs. Pearce says you're going to give me some to wear in bed at night different to what I wear in the daytime; but it do seem a waste of money when you could get something to shew. Besides, I never could fancy changing into cold things on a winter night.

MRS. PEARCE

[*coming back*] Now, Eliza. The new things have come for you to try on.

LIZA

Ah-ow-oo-ooh! [*She rushes out*].

MRS. PEARCE

[*following her*] Oh, don't rush about like that, girl [*She shuts the door behind her*].

HIGGINS

Pickering: we have taken on a stiff job.

PICKERING

[*with conviction*] Higgins, we have.

dustman - garbage collector
elocutionary - as if spoken in a public speech
guttersnipe - a street urchin
marquis - a nobleman ranking below a duke but above an earl or a count
navvy - unskilled laborer employed in the excavation and construction of canals, roads, etc.
pathos - pathetic expression or utterance
zephyr - soft gentle wind; mild breeze

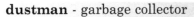

♠ **Answer** *true* **or** *false* **for each of the following statements.**

2.45 _____ Higgins allows Mrs. Pearce to let the "common girl" into his laboratory so that he can record her unusual accent.

2.46 _____ Eliza Doolittle asks Higgins to teach her to speak proper English so that she can get a job in a flower shop and rise above her lower-class upbringing.

2.47 _____ After Higgins decides to teach Eliza, Mrs. Pearce warns him to think about her future when his experiment is complete.

2.48 _____ Pickering wagers that Higgins will not be able to pass Eliza off as a lady in six months time.

2.49 _____ Higgins asks Pickering to be more sensitive to Eliza's feelings despite her detestable appearance.

2.50 _____ Mrs. Pearce asks Higgins to watch his language and manners around Eliza.

2.51 _____ Alfred Doolittle, Eliza's father, comes to Higgins to demand the return of his daughter.

2.52 _____ Doolittle calls himself the "undeserving poor" and asks Higgins to give him a five pound note.

2.53 _____ Doolittle refuses to take more than five pounds from Higgins because he wishes to spend the money irresponsibly and without guilt.

2.54 _____ After the use of middle-class conveniences, a bath and clean clothes, Eliza no longer appears like a poor flower girl.

2.55 _____ Eliza greets her father with adoring affection.

2.56 _____ Eliza's father is a politican.

2.57 _____ After Eliza expresses a wish to show off in front of her old friends, Pickering informs her that that would be snobbish and improper to do.

Winston Churchill (1874–1965). Sir Winston Leonard Spencer Churchill was born in Blenheim Palace, Woodstock. His father was Lord Randolph Churchill and his grandfather was the seventh Duke of Marlborough. Educated at Harrow and the Royal Military College, Sandhurst, Churchill became an officer in the army, serving in India, Egypt, and the Sudan, where he fought in the Battle of Omduman (1898). While serving as a war correspondent during the Boer War, he was taken captive but escaped. The feat established his reputation for bravery and determination, virtues that would later serve him as prime minister during the Second World War. Before entering politics, Churchill had published several books about the military and his experiences, including *The Story of the Malakand Field Force* (1898), *The River War* (1899), *London to Ladysmith via Pretoria* (1900), and *Ian Hamilton's March* (1900).

In 1900 Churchill was elected to Parliament as a member of the Conservative Party. From 1906–1908, he served as undersecretary of state for the colonies. In 1908, he was appointed to the Prime Minister's cabinet as the President of the Board of Trade. From 1911–1915, he served as the First Lord of the Admiralty, establishing the Royal Naval Air Service. After the resignation of Neville Chamberlain during the early days of World War II, Churchill was appointed Prime Minister. As one writer has noted, Churchill "used English literature as a weapon of war." His wartime speeches were an incalucable source of hope and determination for the war-weary British and their allies. Churchill's *War Speeches* (1940–1945) were published in 1946.

An eloquent orator, Churchill wrote in a grand style. After the publication of *The Second World War* (6 vols., 1948–1954), he was awarded the Nobel Prize for literature. As an able historian, Churchill published *A History of the English-Speaking Peoples* (4 vols, 1956–1958). It is recognized as a classic. Other works by Churchill include *Liberalism and the Social Problem* (1909), *The World Crisis* (4 vols, 1923–1929), *My Early Life* (1930), and *Marlborough: His life and Times* (1933–1938).

Circle the letter of the line that best answers each of the following questions.

2.58   Who was Winston Churchill's grandfather?

    (a.) The seventh Duke of Marlborough   c.   An officer in the Royal Air Force

    b. The king of England   d.   The prime minister of England

2.59   What was Churchill's first career?

    a. Naval officer   c.   Politician

    (b.) Army officer   d.   War correspondent

2.60   While serving as the First Lord of the Admiralty, Churchill established what department of the military?

    a. The Royal Navy SEALs   (c.) The Royal Naval Air Force

    b. The Royal Marines   d.   The Royal War Department

2.61.   Churchill was appointed Prime Minister during World War II after whose resignation?

    a. Lord Randolph Churchill's   c.   Benjamin Disreali's

    b. William Gladstone's   (d.) Neville Chamberlain's

2.62   What did Churchill's war-time speeches cause the English people to do?

    a. To have feelings of despair and regret for entering the war

    (b.) To have the hope and determination that the Allies would win the war

    c. To abandon their war efforts

    d. To decry the Liberals' plans to allow Irish independence

2.63   How may Churchill's writing style be characterized?

    a. as common   c. as grand

    b. as modern   (d.) as colloquial

What to Look For:

One writer has noted that Winston Churchill "used English literature as a weapon of war." As you read, notice Churchill's choice of words. How are they more effective in stopping fear of German aggression in the hearts of the English people than any sword, bomb, or gun could ever be? How does his eloquent style add power to his words?

First Speech as Prime Minister to the House of Commons
May 13, 1940

I beg to move,

> That this House welcomes the formation of a Government representing the united and inflexible resolve of the nation to prosecute the war with Germany to a victorious conclusion.

> On Friday evening last I received His Majesty's commission to form a new Administration. It was the evident wish and will of Parliament and the nation that this should be conceived on the broadest possible basis and that it should include all parties, both those who supported the late Government and also the parties of the Opposition. I have completed the most important part of this task. A War Cabinet has been formed of five Members, representing, with the Opposition Liberals, the unity of the nation. The three party Leaders have agreed to serve, either in the War Cabinet or in high executive office. The three Fighting Services have been filled. It was necessary that this should be done in one single day, on account of the extreme urgency and rigour of events. A number of other positions, key positions, were filled yesterday, and I am submitting a further list to His Majesty tonight. I hope to complete the appointment of the principal Ministers during tomorrow. The appointment of the other Ministers usually takes a little longer, but I trust that, when Parliament meets again, this part of my task will be completed, and that the administration will be complete in all respects.

> I considered it in the public interest to suggest that the House should be summoned to meet today. Mr. Speaker agreed, and took the necessary steps, in accordance with the powers conferred upon him by the Resolution of the House. At the end of the proceedings today, the Adjournment of the House will be proposed until Tuesday, 21st May, with, of course, provision for earlier meeting, if need be. The business to be considered during that week will be notified to Members at the earliest opportunity. I now invite the House, by the Motion which stands in my name, to record its approval of the steps taken and to declare its confidence in the new Government.

> To form an Administration of this scale and complexity is a serious undertaking in itself, but it must be remembered that we are in the preliminary stage of one of the greatest battles in history, that we are in action at many other points in Norway and in Holland, that we have to be prepared in the Mediterranean, that the air battle is continuous and that many preparations, such as have been indicated by my hon. Friend below the Gangway, have to be made here at home. In this crisis I hope I may be pardoned if I do not address the House at any length today. I hope that any of my friends and colleagues, or former colleagues, who are affected by the political reconstruction, will make allowance, all allowance, for any lack of ceremony with which it has been necessary to act. I would say to the House, as I said to those who have joined this government: "I have nothing to offer but blood, toil, tears, and sweat."

We have before us an ordeal of the most grievous kind. We have before us many, many long months of struggle and of suffering. You ask, what is our policy? I can say: It is to wage war, by sea, land and air, with all our might and with all the strength that God can give us; to wage war against a monstrous tyranny, never surpassed in the dark, lamentable catalogue of human crime. That is our policy. You ask, what is our aim? I can answer in one word: It is victory, victory at all costs, victory in spite of all terror, victory, however long and hard the road may be; for without victory, there is no survival. Let that be realised; no survival for the British Empire, no survival for all that the British Empire has stood for, no survival for the urge and impulse of the ages, that mankind will move forward towards its goal. But I take up my task with buoyancy and hope. I feel sure that our cause will not be suffered to fail among men. At this time I feel entitled to claim the aid of all, and I say, "Come then, let us go forward together with our united strength."

From: *Their Finest Hour*
June 18, 1940 – House of Commons

Punishment–
George Grosz

I have thought it right upon this occasion to give the House and the country some indication of the solid, practical grounds upon which we base our inflexible resolve to continue the war. There are a good many people who say, "Never mind. Win or lose, sink or swim, better die than submit to tyranny—and such a tyranny." And I do not dissociate myself from them. But I can assure them that our professional advisers of the three Services unitedly advise that we should carry on the war, and that there are good and reasonable hopes of final victory. We have fully informed and consulted all the self-governing Dominions, these great communities far beyond the oceans who have been built up on our laws and on our civilization, and who are absolutely free to choose their course, but are absolutely devoted to the ancient Motherland, and who feel themselves inspired by the same emotions which lead me to stake our all upon duty and honor. We have fully consulted them, and I have received from their prime ministers, Mr. Mackenzie King of Canada, Mr. Menzies of Australia, Mr. Fraser of New Zealand, and General Smuts of South Africa—that wonderful man, with his immense profound mind, and his eye watching from a distance the whole panorama of European affairs—I have received from all these eminent men, who all have Governments behind them elected on wide franchises, who are all there because they represent the will of their people, messages couched in the most moving terms in which they endorse our decision to fight on, and declare themselves ready to share our fortunes and to persevere to the end. That is what we are going to do.

We may now ask ourselves: In what way has our position worsened since the beginning of the war? It has worsened by the fact that the Germans have conquered a large part of the coast line of Western Europe, and many small countries have been overrun by them. This aggravates the possibilities of air attack and adds to our naval preoccupations. It in no way diminishes, but on the contrary definitely increases, the power of our long-distance blockade. Similarly, the entrance of Italy into the war increases the power of our long-distance blockade. We have stopped the worst leak by that. We do not know whether military resistance will come to an end in France or not, but should it do so, then of course the Germans will be able to concentrate their forces, both military and industrial, upon us. But for the reasons I have given to the House these will not be found so easy to apply. If invasion has become more imminent, as no doubt it has, we, being relieved from the task of maintaining a large army in France, have far larger and more efficient forces to meet it.

If Hitler can bring under his despotic control the industries of the countries he has conquered, this will add greatly to his already vast armament output. On the other hand, this will not happen immediately, and we are now assured of immense, continuous and increasing support in supplies and munitions of all kinds from the United States; and especially of aeroplanes and pilots from the Dominions and across the oceans coming from regions which are beyond the reach of enemy bombers.

I do not see how any of these factors can operate to our detriment on balance before the winter comes; and the winter will impose a strain upon the Nazi regime, with almost all Europe writhing and starving under its cruel heel, which, for all their ruthlessness, will run them very hard. We must not forget that from the moment when we declared war on the 3rd September it was always possible for Germany to turn all her Air Force upon this country, together with any other devices of invasion she might conceive, and that France could have done little or nothing to prevent her doing so. We have, therefore, lived under this danger, in principle and in a slightly modified form, during all these six months. In the meanwhile, however, we have enormously improved our methods of defense, and we have learned what we had no right to assume at the beginning, namely, that the individual aircraft and the individual British pilot have a sure and definite superiority. Therefore, in casting up this dread balance sheet and contemplating our dangers with a disillusioned eye, I see great reason for intense vigilance and exertion, but none whatever for panic or despair.

During the first four years of the last war the Allies experienced nothing but disaster and disappointment. That was our constant fear: one blow after another, terrible losses, frightful dangers. Everything miscarried. And yet at the end of those four years the morale of the Allies was higher than that of the Germans, who had moved from one aggressive triumph to another, and who stood everywhere triumphant invaders of the lands into which they had broken. During that war we repeatedly asked ourselves the question: How are we going to win? and no one was able ever to answer it with much precision, until at the end, quite suddenly, quite unexpectedly, our terrible foe collapsed before us, and we were so glutted with victory that in our folly we threw it away.

We do not yet know what will happen in France or whether the French resistance will be prolonged, both in France and in the French Empire overseas. The French Government will be throwing away great opportunities and casting adrift their future if they do not continue the war in accordance with their Treaty obligations, from which we have not felt able to release them. The House will have read the historic declaration in which, at the desire of many Frenchmen—and of our own hearts—we have proclaimed our willingness at the darkest hour in French history to conclude a union of common citizenship in this struggle. However matters may go in France or with the French Government, or other French Governments, we in this Island and in the British Empire will never lose our sense of comradeship with the French people. If we are now called upon to endure what they have been suffering, we shall emulate their courage, and if final victory rewards our toils they shall share the gains, aye, and freedom shall be restored to all. We abate nothing of our just demands; not one jot or tittle do we recede. Czechs, Poles, Norwegians, Dutch, Belgians have joined their causes to our own. All these shall be restored.

What General Weygand called the Battle of France is over. I expect that the Battle of Britain is about to begin. Upon this battle depends the survival of Christian civilization. Upon it depends our own British life, and the long continuity of our institutions and our Empire. The whole fury and might of the

90

enemy must very soon be turned on us. Hitler knows that he will have to break us in this Island or lose the war. If we can stand up to him, all Europe may be free and the life of the world may move forward into broad, sunlit uplands. But if we fail, then the whole world, including the United States, including all that we have known and cared for, will sink into the abyss of a new Dark Age made more sinister, and perhaps more protracted, by the lights of perverted science. Let us therefore brace ourselves to our duties, and so bear ourselves that, if the British Empire and its Commonwealth last for a thousand years, men will still say, "This was their finest hour."

Fill in each of the following blanks with the correct explanation or answer.

2.64   What "serious undertaking" was Churchill outlining to the House of Commons in his May 13, 1940, speech?

_____

2.65   Why does Churchill say to the House, "I have nothing to offer but blood, toil, tears, and sweat?"

_____

2.66   What does Churchill say is the policy of his administration?

_____

2.67   What is the aim of his administration?

_____

2.68   How does Churchill motivate his listeners to strive "at all costs" for victory?

_____

2.69   In *The Finest Hour* speech, what reasons does Churchill give for continuing the war?

_____

2.70   Why does Churchill not see any great reason for panic or despair despite the imminent possibility of a German air attack?

_____

2.71   What depends on the battle of Britain?

_____

2.72   Why is it crucial that Hitler conquer England?

_____

2.73   How does Churchill describe the consequences of a Nazi victory as compared with a British [Allied] victory? What images of good and evil does he use?

_____

2.74   What final encouragement to duty does Churchill present to the English people in anticipation of "the whole fury and might of the enemy?"

_____

Review the material in this section in preparation for the Self Test, which will check your mastery of this particular section as well as your knowledge of the previous section.

SELF TEST 2

Fill in each of the blanks using items from the following word list (each answer, 4 points).

~~"redeem the time"~~	~~George Bernard Shaw~~	~~William Blake~~
~~Irish~~	~~realistic~~	~~Edmund Spenser~~
~~National~~	~~"stream of consciousness"~~	~~socialism~~
~~Ezra Pound~~	~~T. S. Eliot~~	~~mystical~~

2.01   Yeats's first poems convey an interest in ___Irish___ folklore and the works of ___Blake___ and ___Spenser___.

2.02   In 1904 Yeats helped to establish Ireland's first ___national___ theater in Dublin.

2.03   Yeats's frustration with the Irish nationalistic movement led him to write poetry that was ___realistic___.

2.04   Yeats's later poetry is mainly concerned with explaining his ___mystical___ system of belief.

2.05   ___Ezra Pound___ helped Eliot develop his modern techniques.

2.06   In *The Love Song of J. Alfred Prufrock* and *The Waste Land*, Eliot used the ___stream of consciousness___ technique to illustrate more fully the lack of cohesion within society.

2.07   Born in St. Louis, Missouri, ___T.S. Eliot___ became a citizen of Great Britain in 1927.

2.08   Published in 1944, *Four Quartets* consists of four individual poems that carry the theme "___redeem the time___."

2.09   As a member of the Fabian Society, ___G. B. Shaw___ hoped to usher in socialism "as painless and effective as possible" by writing tracts and giving lectures.

2.010   Shaw's main purpose in writing plays was to make ___socialism___ seem more appealing.

Underline the correct answer in each of the following statements (each answer, 3 points).

2.011   Before Winston Churchill entered politics, he served as an officer in the Royal (navy, <u>army</u>, air force).

2.012   Churchill was appointed prime minister during World War II after the resignation of (William Gladstone, Benjamin Disreali, <u>Neville Chamberlain</u>).

2.013   Churchill's war-time speeches caused the English people to feel (hopeless, <u>courageous</u>, defeated).

2.014   Churchill's writing style can be characterized as (modern, grand, <u>colloquial</u>).

2.015   During the (Second World War, <u>First World War</u>, Vietnam War), G. K. Chesterton was asked to write pamphlets in support of England's efforts to stave off (French, American, <u>German</u>) aggression.

2.016   Chesterton's religious essays have been (<u>appreciated</u>, condemned, banned) by both Catholics and Protestants.

92

Circle the letter of the line that best answers each of the following questions (each answer, 4 points).

2.017   According to "Adam's Curse," what does the modern world think of the work that goes into creating poetry?

     a. It is worthless work.

     b. It is to be valued more than the work of bankers and merchants.

     c. It is a fun pastime.

     d. It is the highest calling a man can receive.

2.018   According to line 39 of "Adam's Curse," what has the poet reaped after much hard labor in poetry and love?

     a. Lasting peace and happiness

     b. The recognition that hard work deserves

     c. Nothing

     d. Religious significance

2.019   According to stanza II of "Sailing to Byzantium," why has the poet sailed to Byzantium?

     a. To escape the degradation of old age

     b. To go on vacation

     c. To worship God

     d. To be resurrected

2.020   According to stanzas III and IV, why does the poet ask to be made into an artifice?

     a. So that he can die with dignity

     b. So that he can remain in the form of a man forever

     c. So that he can be a thing of beauty forever

     d. So that his faith in God will not waver

2.021   In lines 1–12 of *The Love Song of J. Alfred Prufrock*, what is the narrator's view of modern relationships?

     a. They are full and meaningful.

     b. They are godly.

     c. They are tradition conscious.

     d. They are empty and meaningless.

2.022   What does the narrator mean when he says, "I have measured out my life with coffee spoons?"

     a. Every aspect of his life has great significance and meaning.

     b. His life is full of trite acts that amount to nothing.

     c. He trusts in God in every aspect of his life.

     d. Even the simple things of life have meaning.

2.023   Why does the narrator decide not to tell the woman of his love for her?

     a. He fears rejection and has feelings of inadequacy.

     b. He doesn't have the time to talk to her.

     c. He realizes that she is not the one for him.

     d. He is humiliated by the other women in the tea room.

2.024　In the last lines of the poem, what reminds the narrator that his thoughts about mermaids and their love are just a delusion?

 a. Voices from the tea room

 b. The coldness of the water

 c. His feelings of rejection

 d. The taste of oysters

2.025　In his speech to the House of Commons on May 13, 1940, what does Churchill say is the aim of his administration?

 a. Defeat

 b. Surrender

 c. Peace

 d. Victory

2.026　How does Churchill motivate his listeners to strive "at all costs" for victory?

 a. He tells them that if they are not victorious then all that the British Empire has stood for will not survive.

 b. He tells them that the German air force has the power to destroy most of England's major cities.

 c. He tells them that they must take loans out from the United States to win the war.

 d. He tells them that God will give them the victory.

2.027　In *The Finest Hour* speech, what reason does Churchill give for continuing the war?

 a. There is hope for final victory.

 b. There is no hope for final victory.

 c. He is determined to win no matter what the costs.

 d. It is not honorable to surrender.

2.028　What depends on the battle of Britain?

 a. The survival of materialism

 b. The survival of democracy

 c. The survival of Christian civilization

 d. The survival of Nazism

2.029　What final encouragement to duty does Churchill present to the English people in anticipation of "the whole fury and might of the enemy?"

 a. Their faithful efforts will be remembered as the "finest hour" in British history.

 b. Their devotion to country is expected as British citizens.

 c. They are not true Christians if they abandon their duties.

 d. They will all be killed or imprisoned if they do not remain faithful.

2.030　According to Hardy's poem "The Respectable Burgher," what is the major cause for "God's disappearance" from religion?

 a. Theologians and preachers who have questioned the truth of Scripture

 b. Liberal politics

 c. Immoral behavior

 d. Unlearned parishioners

2.031   In *Heart of Darkness*, why does Marlow describe Kurtz as "hollow at the core?"

    a. Kurtz was always hungry in the jungle.

    b. Kurtz held to a strict moral standard.

    c. Although he was in the "heart of darkness," Kurtz did not participate in barbaric ceremonies.

    d. Kurtz was utterly depraved.

2.032   In its context, explain Chesterton's statement that "Not only is the faith the mother of all worldly energies, but its foes are the fathers of all worldly confusion."

    a. Orthodox Christianity is the only true basis for liberty, humanity, and love.

    b. All religions supply a firm foundation for world peace.

    c. Orthodox Christianity is not the only basis for liberty, humanity, and love.

    d. Religious beliefs have no impact on society.

Answer *true* or *false* for each of the following statements (each answer, 2 points).

2.033   _____   In *Pygmalion*, Eliza Doolittle asks Professor Higgins to teach her to speak proper English so that she can get a job in a flower shop and rise above her lower-class upbringing.

2.034   _____   Higgins does not act toward Eliza like a middle-class gentleman.

2.035   _____   Alfred Doolittle comes to Higgins to demand the return of his daughter, Eliza.

2.036   _____   A simple bath and clean clothes makes Eliza look like a middle-class girl.

2.037   *true*   The First World War caused people to doubt the goodness of God and the goodness of technology.

2.038   *false*   "The absence of God" from society caused many people to adopt an optimistic outlook on the world.

2.039   *true*   The influence of Freud's theories on society caused many writers to be more concerned about the factual details of a story rather than about a character's feelings and thoughts.

2.040   *true*   The stream of consciousness technique attempts to tell a story through the natural flow of a character's thoughts.

For Thought and Discussion:

Explain to a teacher/parent the modern view of love presented in T. S. Eliot's poem *The Love Song of J. Alfred Prufrock*. Discuss why this view of love is typical of modern relationships. Why is the "absence of love" symptomatic of "the absence of God" in a society? According to 1 John 4:7–19, what is the "source and effect" of love?

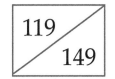

119 / 149

Score   _____

Adult Check   _____

         Initial   Date

III. MODERN FICTION

Virginia Woolf (1882–1941). Adeline Virginia Woolf was born to Sir Leslie Stephen and Julia Duckworth in London at Hyde Park Gate. Her father was an eminent Victorian critic and biographer who exposed his sons and daughters to the cultural movers and shakers of the day. Virginia was educated largely at home in her father's vast library.

After her father's death in 1904 (her mother had died when Virginia was thirteen), Virginia went to live with her sister, Vanessa, and two brothers in the Bloomsbury district of London. Seeking to discuss their progressive but often degenerate ideas about art, literature, politics, and religion with other intellectuals, the Stephen children formed the Bloomsbury Group. Included in the group's lively discussions were such avant-garde figures as E. M. Forester, the modern novelist; Clive Bell, art critic and husband of Virginia's sister, Vanessa; John Maynard Keynes, economist; Leonard Woolf, author, social reformer, and Virginia's husband; Roger Fry, art critic; and Duncan Grant, painter.

The Bloomsbury Group's hostile attitude toward Victorian standards of morality encouraged Virginia in her profligate pursuits, which most probably contributed to her frequent bouts with nervous depression. Although she was married, Woolf actively supported the women's suffrage movement on the grounds that a male-dominated society would always lead to the oppression of women. Her books and essays on the subject include *Night and Day* (1919), *A Room of One's Own* (1929), and *Three Guineas* (1938).

Woolf's first novel, *The Voyage Out*, which she had begun before she was married to Leonard in 1912, was published in 1915. In 1917, the Woolfs founded Hogarth Press. The press subsequently published many of Woolf's works, which were written in what she called the "new" style. Fellow modernists hailed *Jacob's Room*, published in 1922, as an innovative development in fiction. As one writer has noted, "Woolf rejected the traditional framework of narrative, description, and rational exposition in prose and made considerable use of the stream of consciousness technique (recording the flow of thoughts and feelings as they pass through the character's mind)." Also used by James Joyce, the stream of consciousness technique was influenced by Freud's theories, which emphasized man's need to release or satisfy unconscious desires. Woolf's other novels in which she uses experimental techniques include *Mrs. Dalloway* (1925), *To the Lighthouse* (1927), *Orlando* (1928), *The Waves* (1931), and *Between Two Acts* (1941).

Woolf was also a literary critic. Her essays were published in several volumes, including *The Common Reader* (1925), *The Death of the Moth* (1942), and *The Captain's Death Bed* (1950). A collection of her *Letters* was published posthumously in six volumes from 1975–1980. Her *Diary* (1977–1984), offers an intimate look at a woman and a writer who is plagued by personal turmoil brought on and fostered by the absence of God in her life and in a world wrought with war and unbelief. While in an utterly hopeless state of mind, Woolf committed suicide by drowning herself in a river near her home in Sussex.

 Fill in each of the following blanks with the correct answer.

3.1 Virginia Woolf was educated at ___home___ .

3.2 The Stephen children started the ___Bloomsbury group___ to discuss "progressive" ideas about art, literature, politics, and religion.

3.3 In her books and essays in support of the ___women's suffrage movent___ Woolf articulated her belief that a society dominated by males will always lead to the oppression of women.

3.4   In 1912, Virginia married ~~Leonard Keynes~~ Leonard Keynes, a member of the Bloomsbury Group.

3.5   In 1917, the Woolfs founded Hogarth Press.

3.6   Woolf's "new" style incorporated the Stream of consciousness technique.

What to Look For:

Virginia Woolf rejected traditional forms of narration. Instead, she used the stream of consciousness technique to create complex characters. As you read, pay attention to the thoughts and feelings of Oliver Bacon. What does the author reveal about Oliver Bacon that would otherwise never be revealed? How does this add greater depth and meaning to Oliver's actions?

The Duchess and the Jeweller

["The Duchess and the Jeweller" from A HAUNTED HOUSE AND OTHER SHORT STORIES by Virginia Woolf, copyright © 1944 and 1972 by Harcourt, Inc., reprinted by permission of the publisher.]

Oliver Bacon lived at the top of a house overlooking the Green Park. He had a flat; chairs jutted out at the right angles – chairs covered in hide. Sofas filled the bays of the windows – sofas covered in tapestry. The windows, the three long windows, had the proper allowance of discreet net and figured satin. The mahogany sideboard bulged discreetly with the right brandies, whiskeys and liqueurs. And from the middle window he looked down upon the glossy roofs of fashionable cars packed in the narrow straits of Piccadilly. A more central position could not be imagined. And at eight in the morning he would have his breakfast brought in on a tray by a man-servant: the man-servant would unfold his crimson dressing-gown; he would rip his letters open with his long pointed nails and would extract thick white cards of invitation upon which the engraving stood up roughly from duchesses, countesses, viscountesses and Honourable Ladies. Then he would wash; then he would eat his toast; then he would read his paper by the bright burning fire of electric coals.

"Behold Oliver," he would say, addressing himself. "You who began life in a filthy little alley, you who..." and he would look down at his legs, so shapely in their perfect trousers; at his boots; at his spats. They were all shapely, shining; cut from the best cloth by the best scissors in Savile Row. But he dismantled himself often and became again a little boy in a dark alley. He had once thought that the height of his ambition – selling stolen dogs to fashionable women in Whitechapel. And once he had been done. "Oh, Oliver," his mother had wailed. "Oh, Oliver! When will you have sense, my son?" ... Then he had gone behind a counter; had sold cheap watches; then he had taken a wallet to Amsterdam.... At that memory he would chuckle – old Oliver remembering the young. Yes, he had done well with the three diamonds; also there was the commission on the emerald. After that he went into the private room behind the shop in Hatton Garden; the room with the scales, the safe, the thick magnifying glasses. And then... and then... He chuckled. When he passed through the knots of jewellers in the hot evening who were discussing prices, gold mines, diamonds, reports from South Africa, one of them would lay a finger to the side of his nose and murmur, "Hum–m–m," as he passed. It was no more than a murmur; no more than a nudge on the shoulder, a finger on the nose, a buzz that ran through the cluster of jewellers in Hatton Garden on a hot afternoon – oh, many years ago now! But still Oliver felt it purring down his spine, the nudge, the murmur that meant, "Look at him – young Oliver, the young jeweller – there he goes." Young he was then. And he dressed better and better; and had, first a hansom cab; then a car; and first he went up to the dress circle, then down into the stalls. And he had a villa at Richmond, overlooking the river, with trellises of red roses; and Mademoiselle used to pick one every morning and stick it in his buttonhole.

"So," said Oliver Bacon, rising and stretching his legs. "So... "

And he stood beneath the picture of an old lady on the mantelpiece and raised his hands. "I have kept my word," he said, laying his hands together, palm to palm, as if he were doing homage to her. "I have won my bet." That was so; he was the richest jeweller in England; but his nose, which was long and flexible, like an elephant's trunk, seemed to say by its curious quiver at the nostrils (but it seemed as if the whole nose quivered, not only the nostrils) that he was not satisfied yet; still smelt something under the ground a little further off. Imagine a giant hog in a pasture rich with truffles; after unearthing this truffle and that, still it smells a bigger, a blacker truffle under the ground further off. So Oliver snuffed always in the rich earth of Mayfair another truffle, a blacker, a bigger further off.

Now then he straightened the pearl in his tie, cased himself in his smart blue overcoat; took his yellow gloves and his cane; and swayed as he descended the stairs and half snuffed, half sighed through his long sharp nose as he passed out into Piccadilly. For was he not still a sad man, a dissat-

97

isfied man, a man who seeks something that is hidden, though he had won his bet?

He swayed slightly as he walked, as the camel at the zoo sways from side to side when it walks along the asphalt paths laden with grocers and their wives eating from paper bags and throwing little bits of silver paper crumpled up on to the path. The camel despises the grocers; the camel is dissatisfied with its lot; the camel sees the blue lake and the fringe of palm trees in front of it. So the great jeweller, the greatest jeweller in the whole world, swung down Piccadilly, perfectly dressed, with his gloves, with his cane; but dissatisfied still, till he reached the dark little shop, that was famous in France, in Germany, in Austria, in Italy, and all over America – the dark little shop in the street off Bond Street.

As usual, he strode through the shop without speaking, though the four men, the two old men, Marshall and Spencer, and the two young men, Hammond and Wicks, stood straight and looked at him, envying him. It was only with one finger of the amber-coloured glove, waggling, that he acknowledged their presence. And he went in and shut the door of his private room behind him.

Then he unlocked the grating that barred the window. The cries of Bond Street came in; the purr of the distant traffic. The light from reflectors at the back of the shop struck upwards. One tree waved six green leaves, for it was June. But Mademoiselle had married Mr. Pedder of the local brewery – no one stuck roses in his buttonhole now.

"So," he half sighed, half snorted, "so—"

Then he touched a spring in the wall and slowly the panelling slid open, and behind it were the steel safes, five, no, six of them, all of burnished steel. He twisted a key; unlocked one; then another. Each was lined with a pad of deep crimson velvet; in each lay jewels—bracelets, necklaces, rings, tiaras, ducal coronets; loose stones in glass shells; rubies, emeralds, pearls, diamonds. All safe, shining, cool, yet burning, eternally, with their own compressed light.

"Tears!" said Oliver, looking at the pearls.

"Heart's blood!" he said, looking at the rubies.

"Gunpowder!" he continued, rattling the diamonds so that they flashed and blazed.

"Gunpowder enough to blow Mayfair – sky high, high, high!" He threw his head back and made a sound like a horse neighing as he said it.

The telephone buzzed obsequiously in a low muted voice on his table. He shut the safe.

"In ten minutes," he said. "Not before." And he sat down at his desk and looked at the heads of the Roman emperors that were graved on his sleeve links. And again he dismantled himself and became once more the little boy playing marbles in the alley where they sell stolen dogs on Sunday. He became that wily astute little boy, with lips like wet cherries. He dabbled his fingers in ropes of tripe; he dipped them in pans of frying fish; he dodged in and out among the crowds. He was slim, lissome, with eyes like licked stones. And now – now – hands of the clock ticked on, one, two, three, four.... The Duchess of Lambourne waited his pleasure; the Duchess of Lambourne, daughter of a hundred Earls. She would wait for ten minutes on a chair at the counter. She would wait his pleasure. She would wait till he was ready to see her. He watched the clock in its shagreen case. The hand moved on. With each tick the clock handed him – so it seemed – *pâté de foie gras*, a glass of champagne, another of fine brandy, a cigar costing one guinea. The clock laid them on the table beside him as the ten minutes passed. Then he heard soft slow footsteps approaching; a rustle in the corridor. The door opened. Mr. Hammond flattened himself against the wall.

"Her Grace!" he announced.

And he waited there, flattened against the wall.

And Oliver, rising, could hear the rustle of the dress of the Duchess as she came down the passage. Then she loomed up, filling the door, filling the room with the aroma, the prestige, the arrogance, the pomp, the pride of all the Dukes and Duchesses swollen in one wave. And as a wave breaks, she broke, as she sat down, spreading and splashing and falling over Oliver Bacon, the great jeweller, covering him with sparkling bright colours, green, rose, violet; and odours; and iridescences; and rays shooting from fingers, nodding from plumes, flashing from silk; for she was very large, very fat, tightly girt in pink taffeta, and past her prime. As a parasol with many flounces, as a peacock with many feathers, shuts its flounces, folds its feathers, so she subsided and shut herself as she sank down in the leather armchair.

"Good morning, Mr. Bacon," said the Duchess. And she held out her hand which came through the slit of her white glove. And Oliver bent low as he shook it. And as their hands touched the link was forged between them once more. They were friends, yet enemies; he was master, she was mistress; each cheated the other, each needed the other, each feared the other, each felt this and knew this every time they touched hands thus in the little back room with the white light outside, and the tree with its six leaves, and the sound of the street in the distance and behind them the safes.

"And to-day, Duchess – what can I do for you to-day?" said Oliver, very softly.

The Duchess opened her heart, her private heart, gaped wide. And with a sigh but no words she took from her bag a long washleather pouch – it looked like a lean yellow ferret. And from a slit in the ferret's belly she dropped pearls – ten pearls. They rolled from the slit in the ferret's belly – one, two, three, four – like the eggs of some heavenly bird.

"All's that's left me, dear Mr. Bacon," she moaned. Five, six, seven – down they rolled, down the slopes of the vast mountain sides that fell between her knees into one narrow valley – the eighth, the ninth, and the tenth. There they lay in the glow of the peach-blossom taffeta. Ten pearls.

"From the Appleby cincture," she mourned. "The last... the last of them all."

Oliver stretched out and took one of the pearls between finger and thumb. It was round, it was lustrous. But real was it, or false? Was she lying again? Did she dare?

She laid her plump padded finger across her lips. "If the Duke knew..." she whispered. "Dear Mr. Bacon, a bit of bad luck..."

Been gambling again, had she?

"That villain! That sharper!" she hissed.

The man with the chipped cheek bone? A bad 'un. And the Duke was straight as a poker; with side whiskers; would cut her off, shut her up down there if he knew – what I know, thought Oliver, and glanced at the safe.

"Araminta, Daphne, Diana," she moaned. "It's for *them*."

The ladies Araminta, Daphne, Diana – her daughters. He knew them; adored them. But it was Diana he loved.

"You have all my secrets," she leered. Tears slid; tears fell; tears, like diamonds, collecting powder in the ruts of her cherry blossom cheeks.

"Old friend," she murmured, "old friend."

"Old friend," he repeated, "old friend," as if he licked the words.

"How much?" he queried.

She covered the pearls with her hand.

"Twenty thousand," she whispered.

But was it real or false, the one he held in his hand? The Appleby cincture – hadn't she sold it already? He would ring for Spencer or Hammond. "Take it and test it," he would say. He stretched to the bell.

"You will come down to-morrow?" she urged, she interrupted. "The Prime Minister – His Royal Highness..." She stopped. "And Diana..." she added.

Oliver took his hand off the bell.

He looked past her, at the backs of the houses in Bond Street. But he saw, not the houses in Bond Street, but a dimpling river; and trout rising and salmon; and the Prime Minister; and himself, too, in white waistcoat; and then, Diana. He looked down at the pearl in his hand. But how could he test it, in the light of the river, in the light of the eyes of Diana? But the eyes of the Duchess were on him.

"Twenty thousand," she moaned. "My honour!"

The honour of the mother of Diana! He drew his cheque book towards him; he took out his pen.

"Twenty—" he wrote. Then he stopped writing. The eyes of the old woman in the picture were on him – of the old woman his mother.

"Oliver!" she warned him. "Have sense! Don't be a fool!"

"Oliver!" the Duchess entreated – it was "Oliver" now, not "Mr. Bacon." "You'll come for a long weekend?"

Alone in the woods with Diana! Riding alone in the woods with Diana!

"Thousand," he wrote, and signed it.

"Here you are," he said.

And there opened all the flounces of the parasol, all the plumes of the peacock, the radiance of the wave, the swords and spears of Agincourt, as she rose from her chair. And the two old men and the two young men, Spencer and Marshall, Wicks and Hammond, flattened themselves behind the counter envying him as he led her through the shop to the door. And he waggled his yellow glove in their faces, and she held her honour – a cheque for twenty thousand pounds with his signature – quite firmly in her hands.

"Are they false or are they real?" asked Oliver, shutting his private door. There they were, ten pearls on the blotting-paper on the table. He took them to the window. He held them under his lens to the light.... This, then, was the truffle he had routed out of the earth! Rotten at the centre – rotten at the core!

"Forgive me, oh, my mother!" he sighed, raising his hand as if he asked pardon of the old woman in the picture. And again he was a little boy in the alley where they sold dogs on Sunday.

"For," he murmured, laying the palms of his hands together, "it is to be a long week-end."

♦ Fill in each of the following blanks with the correct explanation or answer.

3.7   Describe Oliver Bacon.

_____

3.8   Is Oliver Bacon a member of the same social class as the Duchess?

_____

3.9   What childhood "occupation" does Oliver keep remembering?
       Selling dogs in an alleyway on Sundays.

3.10   What bet did he win with the "old lady?"

_____

3.11   Who is the "old lady?"

_____

3.12   What "secret" of the Duchess's does Oliver keep?

_____

3.13   What makes Oliver stop writing the check for the Duchess?

_____

3.14   What makes Oliver finish writing the check for the Duchess?

_____

3.15   What is significant about Oliver's flashbacks to when he was a boy selling stolen dogs to fashionable women?

_____

3.16   Are the pearls that the Duchess sells to Oliver real or fake?

_____

3.17   In light of Matthew 7:6, what is significant about the Duchess's appearance? How might she resemble a pig?
       She is a liar and a gambler.

3.18   In what ways might the Duchess tear Oliver to pieces if he reveals her secret?

_____

3.19   In light of Matthew 13:45,46, explain Oliver's grievous dissatisfaction with his dealings with the Duchess.

_____

James Joyce (1882–1941). James Augustine Aloysius Joyce was born in Dublin to an irresponsible father and a devout Catholic mother. His education at Clongowes Wood College and Belvedere College provided him with a Jesuit understanding of the Catholic faith and an opportunity to become a priest. But Joyce's disillusionment with Ireland's middle-class society caused him to rebel against its legalism. He graduated from University College, Dublin, in 1902 with an A.B. degree in modern languages. Before he finished his education, Joyce had determined to become a priest of another kind. As a writer and an artist, he believed that he could communicate a vision of life that was more real than that which middle-class religion had to offer.

Not long after his graduation, Joyce lived in Paris but returned home shortly before his mother's death. Joyce returned to the continent in 1904 with Nora Barnacle, a poor, uneducated girl who had a lively Irish demeanor. He lived with Nora for the rest of his life. The couple had two children and were finally married in 1931. In an attempt to support himself and his family, Joyce worked as a teacher and received funds from generous patrons. Joyce lived in Europe for the rest of his life. He died in Zurich in 1941.

While living in Paris, Joyce published *Dubliners* (1914), a collection of sketches of life in Dublin during the turn of the century. The stories are realistic tales with deep symbolic meanings. By using the things of ordinary life, Joyce said he was converting bread into art.

Joyce continued to write about Dublin and its people although he was far removed from the political difficulties and spiritual tyranny there. *A Portrait of the Artist as a Young Man* was published serially in Ezra Pound's magazine *The Egoist* from 1914–1915. The autobiographical novel represents Joyce as Stephen Dedalus, who must live in exile from middle-class Irish society to "encounter... the reality of experience and to forge in the smithy of my soul the uncreated conscience of my race."

Ulysses, considered to be Joyce's masterpiece, was published in Paris in 1922. Using the stream of consciousness technique, Joyce reveals the thoughts and feelings of the various characters on a given day in Dublin in 1904. The structure of the novel and its characters correspond to Homer's *Odyssey*. Initially, the novel was banned in the United States and Britain for obscenity. Joyce's last completed novel, *Finnegans Wake*, was published in 1939. Although it is difficult to read, Joyce considered it to be his masterpiece. It is written in several different languages in the form of a dream sequence.

Underline the correct answer in each of the following statements.

3.20   James Joyce was born and raised in (Dublin, Paris, London).

3.21   Joyce rebelled against the (Protestant, Roman Catholic, Muslim) beliefs of middle-class society.

3.22   In 1914 Joyce published (*A Portrait of the Artist as a Young Man*, *Ulysses*, *Dubliners*), a collection of short stories containing symbolic meanings of the modern world.

3.23   In 1916 Joyce published (*A Portrait of the Artist as a Young Man*, *Ulysses*, *Dubliners*), an autobiographical novel of his own self-exile from middle-class society in Ireland.

3.24   Published in Paris in 1922, (*A Portrait of the Artist as a Young Man*, *Ulysses*, *Dubliners*) uses the stream of consciousness technique to reveal the inner life of various characters on a given day in Dublin in 1904.

3.25   Published in 1939, (*Ulysses*, *Finnegans Wake*, *Dubliners*) is written in several different languages in the form of a dream sequence.

What to Look For:

James Joyce despised the effects of the modernization on Dublin. He believed that the modern world had paralyzed humanity. Life was cruel and meaningless. Love no longer existed. As you read, pay close attention to the realistic details. How do they symbolize the spiritual and emotional emptiness of modern life? Who or what is responsible for the boy's feelings of "anguish and anger?"

From: *Dubliners*

Araby

North Richmond Street, being blind, was a quiet street except at the hour when the Christian Brothers' School set the boys free. An uninhabited house of two storeys stood at the blind end, detached from its neighbours in a square ground. The other houses of the street, conscious of decent lives within them, gazed at one another with brown imperturbable faces.

The former tenant of our house, a priest, had died in the back drawing-room. Air, musty from having been long enclosed, hung in all the rooms, and the waste room behind the kitchen was littered with old useless papers. Among these I found a few paper-covered books, the pages of which were curled and damp: *The Abbot*, by Walter Scott, *The Devout Communicant*, and *The Memoirs of Vidocq*. I liked the last best because its leaves were yellow. The wild garden behind the house contained a central apple-tree and a few straggling bushes, under one of which I found the late tenant's rusty bicycle-pump. He had been a very charitable priest; in his will he had left all his money to institutions and the furniture of his house to his sister.

When the short days of winter came, dusk fell before we had well eaten our dinners. When we met in the street the houses had grown sombre. The space of sky above us was the colour of ever-changing violet and towards it the lamps of the street lifted their feeble lanterns. The cold air stung us and we played till our bodies glowed. Our shouts echoed in the silent street. The career of our play brought us through the dark muddy lanes behind the houses, where we ran the gauntlet of the rough tribes from the cottages, to the back doors of the dark dripping gardens where odours arose from the ashpits, to the dark odorous stables where a coachman smoothed and combed the horse or shook music from the buckled harness. When we returned to the street, light from the kitchen windows had filled the areas. If my uncle was seen turning the corner, we hid in the shadow until we had seen him safely housed. Or if Mangan's sister came out on the doorstep to call her brother in to his tea, we watched her from our shadow peer up and down the street. We waited to see whether she would remain or go in and, if she remained, we left our shadow and walked up to Mangan's steps resignedly. She was waiting for us, her figure defined by the light from the half-opened door. Her brother always teased her before he obeyed, and I stood by the railings looking at her. Her dress swung as she moved her body, and the soft rope of her hair tossed from side to side.

Every morning I lay on the floor in the front parlour watching her door. The blind was pulled down to within an inch of the sash so that I could not be seen. When she came out on the doorstep my heart leaped. I ran to the hall, seized my books and followed her. I kept her brown figure always in my eye and, when we came near the point at which our ways diverged, I quickened my pace and passed her. This happened morning after morning. I had never spoken to her, except for a few casual words, and yet her name was like a summons to all my foolish blood.

Her image accompanied me even in places the most hostile to romance. On Saturday evenings when my aunt went marketing I had to go to carry some of the parcels. We walked through the flaring streets, jostled by drunken men and bargaining women, amid the curses of labourers, the shrill litanies of shop-boys who stood on guard by the barrels of pigs' cheeks, the nasal chanting of street-singers, who sang a come-all-you about O'Donovan Rossa, or a ballad about the troubles in our native land. These noises converged in a single sensation of life for me: I imagined that I bore my chalice safely through a throng of foes. Her name sprang to my lips at moments in strange prayers and praises which I myself did not understand. My eyes were often full of tears (I could not tell why) and at times a flood from my heart seemed to pour itself out into my bosom. I thought little of the future. I did not know whether I would ever speak to her or not or, if I spoke to her, how I could tell her of my confused adoration. But my body was like a harp and her words and gestures were like fingers running upon the wires.

One evening I went into the back drawing-room in which the priest had died. It was a dark rainy evening and there was no sound in the house. Through one of the broken panes I heard the rain impinge upon the earth, the fine incessant needles of water playing in the sodden beds. Some distant lamp or lighted window gleamed below me. I was thankful that I could see so little. All my senses seemed to desire to veil themselves and, feeling that I was about to slip from them, I pressed the palms of my hands together until they trembled, murmuring: "O love! O love!" many times.

At last she spoke to me. When she addressed the first words to me I was so confused that I did not know what to answer. She asked me was I going to Araby. I forgot whether I answered yes or no. It would be a splendid bazaar; she said she would love to go.

"And why can't you?" I asked.

While she spoke she turned a silver bracelet round and round her wrist. She could not go, she said, because there would be a retreat that week in her convent. Her brother and two other boys were fighting for their caps, and I was alone at the railings. She held one of the spikes, bowing her head towards me. The light from the lamp opposite our door caught the white curve of her neck, lit up her hair that rested there and, falling, lit up the hand upon the railing. It fell over one side of her dress and caught the white border of a petticoat, just visible as she stood at ease.

"It's well for you," she said.

"If I go," I said, "I will bring you something."

What innumerable follies laid waste my waking and sleeping thoughts after that evening! I wished to annihilate the tedious intervening days. I chafed against the work of school. At night in my bedroom and by day in the classroom her image came between me and the page I strove to read. The syllables of the word *Araby* were called to me through the silence in which my soul luxuriated and cast an Eastern enchantment over me. I asked for leave to go to the bazaar on Saturday night. My aunt was surprised, and hoped it was not some Freemason* affair. I answered few questions in class. I watched my master's face pass from amiability to sternness; he hoped I was not beginning to idle. I could not call my wandering thoughts together. I had hardly any patience with the serious work of life which, now that it stood between me and my desire, seemed to me child's play, ugly monotonous child's play.

On Saturday morning I reminded my uncle that I wished to go to the bazaar in the evening. He was fussing at the hallstand, looking for the hat-brush, and answered me curtly:

"Yes, boy, I know."

As he was in the hall I could not go into the front parlour and lie at the window. I felt the house in bad humour and walked slowly towards the school. The air was pitilessly raw and already my heart misgave me.

When I came home to dinner my uncle had not yet been home. Still it was early. I sat staring at the clock for some time and, when its ticking began to irritate me, I left the room. I mounted the staircase and gained the upper part of the house. The high, cold, empty, gloomy rooms liberated me and I went from room to room singing. From the front window I saw my companions playing below in the street. Their cries reached me weakened and indistinct and, leaning my forehead against the cool glass, I looked over at the dark house where she lived. I may have stood there for an hour, seeing nothing but the brown-clad figure cast by my imagination, touched discreetly by the lamplight at the curved neck, at the hand upon the railings and at the border below the dress.

When I came downstairs again I found Mrs. Mercer sitting at the fire. She was an old, garrulous* woman, a pawnbroker's widow, who collected used stamps for some pious purpose. I had to endure the gossip of the tea-table. The meal was prolonged beyond an hour and still my uncle did not come. Mrs. Mercer stood up to go: she was sorry she couldn't wait any longer, but it was after eight o'clock and she did not like to be out late, as the night air was bad for her. When she had gone I began to walk up and down the room, clenching my fists. My aunt said:

"I'm afraid you may put off your bazaar for this night of Our Lord."

At nine o'clock I heard my uncle's latchkey in the hall door. I heard him talking to himself and heard the hallstand rocking when it had received the weight of his overcoat. I could interpret these signs. When he was midway through his dinner I asked him to give me the money to go to the bazaar. He had forgotten.

"The people are in bed and after their first sleep now," he said.

I did not smile. My aunt said to him energetically:

"Can't you give him the money and let him go? You've kept him late enough as it is."

My uncle said he was very sorry he had forgotten. He said he believed in the old saying: "All work and no play makes Jack a dull boy." He asked me where I was going and, when I told him a second time, he asked me did I know The *Arab's Farewell to his Steed*. When I left the kitchen he was about to recite the opening lines of the piece to my aunt.

I held a florin tightly in my hand as I strode down Buckingham Street towards the station. The sight of the streets thronged with buyers and glaring with gas recalled to me the purpose of my journey. I took my seat in a third-class carriage of a deserted train. After an intolerable delay the train moved out of the station slowly. It crept onward among ruinous houses and over the twinkling river. At Westland Row Station a crowd of people pressed to the carriage doors; but the porters moved them back, saying that it was a special train for the bazaar. I remained alone in the bare carriage. In a few minutes the train drew up beside an improvised wooden platform. I passed out on to the road and saw by the lighted dial of a clock that it was ten minutes to ten. In front of me was a large building which displayed the magical name.

I could not find any sixpenny entrance and, fearing that the bazaar would be closed, I passed in quickly through a turnstile, handing a shilling to a weary-looking man. I found myself in a big hall girded at half its height by a gallery. Nearly all the stalls were closed and the greater part of the hall was in darkness. I recognized a silence like that which pervades a church after a service. I walked into the centre of the bazaar timidly. A few people were gathered about the stalls which were still open. Before a curtain, over which the words Café Chantant were written in coloured lamps, two men were counting money on a salver. I listened to the fall of the coins.

Remembering with difficulty why I had come, I went over to one of the stalls and examined porcelain vases and flowered tea-sets. At the door of the stall a young lady was talking and laughing with two young gentlemen. I remarked their English accents and listened vaguely to their conversation.

"O, I never said such a thing!"

"O, but you did!"

"O, but I didn't!"

"Didn't she say that?"

"Yes. I heard her."

"O, there's a... fib!"

Observing me, the young lady came over and asked me did I wish to buy anything. The tone of her voice was not encouraging; she seemed to have spoken to me out of a sense of duty. I looked humbly at the great jars that stood like eastern guards at either side of the dark entrance to the stall and murmured:

'No, thank you.'

The young lady changed the position of one of the vases and went back to the two young men. They began to talk of the same subject. Once or twice the young lady glanced at me over her shoulder.

I lingered before her stall, though I knew my stay was useless, to make my interest in her wares seem the more real. Then I turned away slowly and walked down the middle of the bazaar. I allowed the two pennies to fall against the six-pence in my pocket. I heard a voice call from one end of the gallery that the light was out. The upper part of the hall was now completely dark.

Gazing up into the darkness I saw myself as a creature driven and derided by vanity; and my eyes burned with anguish and anger.

Freemason - having to do with the world-wide secret society whose purpose is mutual aid and fellowship
humour - state of mind, mood, disposition
garrulous - talking too much about trifles; talkative

✦ **Fill in each of the following blanks with the correct explanation or answer.**

3.26 How does the boy describe his neighborhood?

_____

3.27 What time of the year is it?

_____

3.28 How does light affect the boy's view of the girl?

_____

3.29 Why can't the girl go to the bazaar?

_____

3.30 Why does the boy go to the bazaar?

_____

3.31 Describe the boy's emotional reaction to the girl.

_____

3.32 Before going to the bazaar, why does the boy say of his "serious work" that it "seemed to me child's play, ugly monotonous child's play?"

_____

3.33 Why is the boy late to the bazaar?

_____

3.34 Describe the state of the big hall that houses the bazaar when the boy arrives.

_____

3.35 How does he describe the silence of the bazaar?

_____

3.36 What is perculiar about the nationality of the young people surrounding the stall in the bazaar?

_____

3.37 What stops the boy from buying something at the bazaar?

_____

3.38 In light of Joyce's modernistic view of the world, what does the darkness of the bazaar symbolize?

_____

3.39   Explain why the boy eventually sees himself as a "creature driven and derided by vanity?"

Aldous Leonard Huxley (1894–1963). Aldous Huxley was born in Godalming, Surrey, the son of Leonard Huxley, editor of *Cornhill Magazine,* and the grandson of Thomas Huxley (1825–1895), a champion of Darwinism and the originator of the philosophical term *agnostic*. While attending Eton, the elite prep school, Huxley developed a serious eye impairment. Unable to pursue a career in science, like his brother Sir Julian Huxley (1887–1975), Huxley instead read English at Balliol College, Oxford. While at Oxford, he wrote and published three volumes of poetry and contributed to *The Athenaeum*, a monthly journal that published the works of such thinkers and writers as Carlyle, Lamb, T. S. Eliot, and Virginia Woolf.

During the 1920s, Huxley published a collection of stories and several notable novels. *Crome Yellow*, published in 1921, established his reputation as an insightful satirist. Huxley also published three other novels, *Antic Hay* (1923), *Those Barren Leaves* (1925), and *Point Counter Point* (1928). *Those Barren Leaves* is set in Italy, where Huxley and his wife lived between the world wars. *Point Counter Point* features the character Mark Rampion, who is a depiction of Huxley's friend D. H. Lawrence. Many of Huxley's friends and literary acquaintances appear in his works.

In 1932 Huxley published his most read and discussed "novel of ideas," *Brave New World*. Described as a "satirical fantasy," it is set in seventh century A.F. (After [Henry] Ford) where humans are conditioned from conception to take their place in a caste system based on scientifically graded intelligence. Like George Orwell's *1984*, Huxley's vision of the future is prophetic. However, as Neil Postman has observed, Huxley did not believe that our undoing would be Big Brother but rather our "infinite appetite for distractions" or pleasures.

After the publication of *Eyeless in Gaza* in 1936, Huxley moved to California in search of alternative answers to the cold materialistic world that thinkers like his grandfather had helped to create. Unconvinced of his own **depravity***, Huxley attempted to experience the spiritual realm through drugs, mysticism, and encounters with the paranormal. Before his death in 1963, he published six more novels, which have been received with mixed reviews.

Underline the correct answer in each of the following statements.

3.40   Aldous Huxley was the grandson of Thomas Huxley, the champion of (Protestantism, Darwinism, mysticism).

3.41   Huxley was unable to pursue a career in science because of his poor (grades, background, eyesight).

3.42   (*Crome Yellow*, *Brave New World*, *Point Counter Point*) first established Huxley's reputation as an insightful satirist.

3.43   Many of Huxley's (family members, boyhood enemies, friends) and literary acquaintances appear in his works.

3.44   (*Crome Yellow*, *Brave New World*, *Point Counter Point*) is a "satirical fantasy" set in the seventh century A.F. (After [Henry] Ford) where humans are conditioned from conception to take their place in a caste system based on scientifically graded intelligence.

3.45   Later in life, Huxley turned to (mysticism, Christianity, philosophy) for the answers to the cold materialistic world.

What to Look For:

Huxley predicted that the instability and fragmentation of modern society caused by the Great War and the absence of God would cause many to seek peace by means of government control. As you read the chapter below, pay attention to the World Controller's reasons for God's absence in modern society. Why does he think that God is unnecessary in modern society? Does the Savage agree with him? Why or why not? How does the Savage's ideas compare with G. K. Chesterton's ideas on the "romance" of orthodoxy?

From *Brave New World*

John the Savage is the hero of the book. Unlike the members of modern society, he has been born and raised in a community that maintains a strict moral code based on a mixture of religious beliefs. His conversation with the World Controller (Mustapha Mond) reveals the stark differences between the "old world" and the "new world."

Chapter 17—*Brave New World*

"Art, science—you seem to have paid a fairly high price for your happiness," said the Savage, when they were alone. "Anything else?"

"Well, religion, of course," replied the Controller. "There used to be something called God–before the Nine Years' War. But I was forgetting; you know all about God, I suppose."

"Well…" The Savage hesitated. He would have liked to say something about solitude, about night, about the mesa lying pale under the moon, about the precipice, the plunge into shadowy darkness, about death. He would have liked to speak; but there were no words. Not even in Shakespeare.

The Controller, meanwhile, had crossed to the other side of the room and was unlocking a large safe set into the wall between the bookshelves. The heavy door swung open. Rummaging in the darkness within, "It's a subject," he said,
"that has always had a great interest for me." He pulled out a thick black volume. "You've never read this, for example."

The Savage took it. "The Holy Bible, containing the Old and New Testaments," he read aloud from the title page.

"Nor this." It was a small book and had lost its cover. *"The Imitation of Christ."*

"Nor this." He handed out another volume.

"The Varieties of Religious Experience. By William James."

"And I've got plenty more," Mustapha Mond continued, resuming his seat. "A whole collection of pornographic old books. God in the safe and Ford on the shelves." He pointed with a laugh to his avowed library–to the shelves of books, the rack full of reading-machine bobbins and sound-track rolls.

"But if you know about God, why don't you tell them?" asked the Savage indignantly. "Why don't you give them these books about God?"

"For the same reason as we don't give them Othello: they're old; they're about God hundreds of years ago. Not about God now."

"But God doesn't change."

"Men do, though."

"What difference does that make?"

"All the difference in the world," said Mustapha Mond. He got up again and walked

to the safe. "There was a man called Cardinal Newman," he said. "A cardinal," he exclaimed parenthetically, "was a kind of Arch-Community-Songster."

"'I Pandulph, of fair Milan, cardinal.' I've read about them in Shakespeare."

"Of course you have. Well, as I was saying, there was a man called Cardinal Newman. Ah, here's the book." He pulled it out. "And while I'm about it I'll take this one, too. It's by a man called Maine de Biran. He was a philosopher, if you know what that was."

"A man who dreams of fewer things than there are in heaven and earth," said the Savage promptly.

"Quite so. I'll read you one of the things he did dream of in a moment. Meanwhile, listen to what this old Arch-Community-Songster said." He opened the book at the place marked by a slip of paper and began to read. "'We are not our own any more than what we possess is our own. We did not make our selves, we cannot be supreme over ourselves. We are not our own masters. We are God's property. Is it not our happiness thus to view the matter? Is it any happiness or any comfort, to consider that we are our own? It may be thought so by the young and prosperous.

These may think it a great thing to have everything, as they suppose, their own way–to depend on no one–to have to think of nothing out of sight, to be without the irksomeness of continual acknowledgment, continual prayer, continual reference of what they do to the will of another. But as time goes on, they, as all men, will find that independence was not made for man–that it is an unnatural state–will do for a while, but will not carry us on safely to the end….'" Mustapha Mond paused, put down the first book and, picking up the other, turned over the pages. "Take this, for example," he said, and in his deep voice once more began to read: "'A man grows old; he feels in himself that radical sense of weakness, of listlessness, of discomfort, which accompanies the advance of age; and, feeling thus, imagines himself merely sick, lulling his fears with the notion that this distressing condition is due to some particular cause, from which, as from an illness, he hopes to recover. Vain imaginings! That sickness is old age; and a horrible disease it is. They say that it is the fear of death and of what comes after death that makes men turn to religion as they advance in years. But my own experience has given me the conviction that, quite apart from any such terrors or imaginings, the religious sentiment tends to develop as we grow older; to develop because, as the passions grow calm, as the fancy and sensibilities are less excited and less excitable, our reason becomes less troubled in its working, less obscured by the images, desires and distractions, in which it used to be absorbed; whereupon God emerges as from behind a cloud; our soul feels, sees, turns towards the source of all light; turns naturally and inevitably; for now that all that gave to the world of sensations its life and charms has begun to leak away from us, now that phenomenal existence is no more bolstered up by impressions from within or from without, we feel the need to lean on something that abides, something that will never play us false–a reality, an absolute and everlasting truth. Yes, we inevitably turn to God; for this religious sentiment is of its nature so pure, so delightful to the soul that experiences it, that it makes up to us for all our other losses.'" Mustapha Mond shut the book and leaned back in his chair. "One of the numerous things in heaven and earth that these philosophers didn't dream about was this" (he waved his hand), "us, the modern world. 'You can only be independent of God while you've got youth and prosperity; independence won't take you safely to the end.' Well, we've now got youth and prosperity right up to the end. What follows? Evidently, that we can be independent of God. 'The religious sentiment will compensate us for all our losses.' But there aren't any losses for us to compensate; religious sentiment is superfluous. And why should we go hunting for a substitute for youthful desires, when youthful desires never fail? A substitute for distractions, when we go on enjoying all the old fooleries to the very last? What need have we of repose when our minds and bodies continue to delight in activity? or consolation, when we have soma?* or something immovable, when there is the social order?"

"Then you think there is no God?"

"No, I think there quite probably is one."

"Then why?...."

Mustapha Mond checked him. "But he manifests himself in different ways to different men. In premodern times he manifested himself as the being that's described in these books. Now ..."

"How does he manifest himself now?" asked the Savage.

"Well, he manifests himself as an absence; as though he weren't there at all."

"That's your fault."

"Call it the fault of civilization. God isn't compatible with machinery and scientific medicine and universal happiness. You must make your choice. Our civilization has chosen machinery and medicine and happiness. That's why I have to keep these books locked up in the safe. They're smut. People would be shocked it...."

The Savage interrupted him. "But isn't it natural to feel there's a God?"

"You might as well ask if it's natural to do up one's trousers with zippers," said the Controller sarcastically. "You remind me of another of those old fellows called Bradley.* He defined philosophy as the finding of bad reason for what one believes by instinct. As if one believed anything by instinct! One believes things because one has been conditioned to believe them. Finding bad reasons for what one believes for other bad reasons–that's philosophy. People believe in God because they've been conditioned to."

"But all the same," insisted the Savage, "it is natural to believe in God when you're alone–quite alone, in the night, thinking about death...."

"But people never are alone now," said Mustapha Mond. "We make them hate solitude; and we arrange their lives so that it's almost impossible for them ever to have it."

The Savage nodded gloomily. At Malpais he had suffered because they had shut him out from the communal activities of the pueblo; in civilized London he was suffering because he could never escape from those communal activities, never be quietly alone.

"Do you remember that bit in King Lear?" said the Savage at last. "'The gods are just and of our pleasant vices make instruments to plague us; the dark and vicious place where thee he got cost him his eyes,' and Edmund answers–you remember, he's wounded, he's dying– 'Thou hast spoken right; 'tis true. The wheel has come full circle; I am here.' What about that now? Doesn't there seem to be a God managing things, punishing, rewarding?"

"Well, does there?" questioned the Controller in his turn. "You can indulge in any number of pleasant vices with a freemartin* and run no risks of having your eyes put out by your son's mistress. 'The wheel has come full circle; I am here.' But where would Edmund be nowadays? Sitting in a pneumatic chair, with his arm round a girl's waist, sucking away at his sex-hormone chewing-gum and looking at the feelies. The gods are just. No doubt. But their code of law is dictated, in the last resort, by the people who organize society; Providence takes its cue from men."

"Are you sure?" asked the Savage. "Are you quite sure that the Edmund in that pneumatic chair hasn't been just as heavily punished as the Edmund who's wounded and bleeding to death? The gods are just. Haven't they used his pleasant vices as an instrument to degrade him?"

"Degrade him from what position? As a happy, hard-working, goods-consuming citizen he's perfect. Of course, if you choose some other standard than ours, then perhaps you might say he was degraded. But you've got to stick to one set of postulates. You can't play Electro-magnetic Golf according to the rules of Centrifugal Bumble-puppy."

"But value dwells not in particular will," said the Savage. "It holds his estimate and dignity as well wherein 'tis precious of itself as in the prizer."

"Come, come," protested Mustapha Mond, "that's going rather far, isn't it?"

"If you allowed yourselves to think of God, you wouldn't allow yourselves to be degraded by pleasant vices. You'd have a reason for bearing things patiently, for doing things with courage. I've seen it with the Indians."

"I'm sure you have," said Mustapha Mond. "But then we aren't Indians. There isn't any need for a civilized man to bear anything that's seriously unpleasant. And as for doing things—Ford forbid that he should get the idea into his head. It would upset the whole social order if men started doing things on their own."

"What about self-denial, then? If you had a God, you'd have a reason for self-denial."

"But industrial civilization is only possible when there's no self-denial. Self-indulgence up to the very limits imposed by hygiene and economics. Otherwise the wheels stop turning."

"You'd have a reason for chastity!" said the Savage, blushing a little as he spoke the words.

"But chastity means passion, chastity means neurasthenia.* And passion and neurasthenia mean instability. And instability means the end of civilization. You can't have a lasting civilization without plenty of pleasant vices."

"But God's the reason for everything noble and fine and heroic. If you had a God...."

"My dear young friend," said Mustapha Mond, "civilization has absolutely no need of nobility or heroism. These things are symptoms of political inefficiency. In a properly organized society like ours, nobody has any opportunities for being noble or heroic. Conditions have got to be thoroughly unstable before the occasion can arise. Where there are wars, where there are divided allegiances, where there are temptations to be resisted, objects of love to be fought for or defended—there, obviously, nobility and heroism have some sense. But there aren't any wars nowadays. The greatest care is taken to prevent you from loving any one too much. There's no such thing as a divided allegiance; you're so conditioned that you can't help doing what you ought to do. And what you ought to do is on the whole so pleasant, so many of the natural impulses are allowed free play, that there really aren't any temptations to resist. And if ever, by some unlucky chance, anything unpleasant should somehow happen, why, there's always soma to give you a holiday from the facts. And there's always soma to calm your anger, to reconcile you to your enemies, to make you patient and long-suffering. In the past you could only accomplish these things by making a great effort and after years of hard moral training. Now, you swallow two or three half-gramme tablets, and there you are. Anybody can be virtuous now. You can carry at least half your mortality about in a bottle. Christianity without tears—that's what soma is."

"But the tears are necessary. Don't you remember what Othello said? 'If after every tempest came such calms, may the winds blow till they have wakened death.' There's a story one of the old Indians used to tell us, about the Girl of Mátaski. The young men who wanted to marry her had to do a morning's hoeing in her garden. It seemed easy; but there were flies and mosquitoes, magic ones. Most of the young men simply couldn't stand the biting and stinging. But the one that could—he got the girl."

"Charming! But in civilized countries," said the Controller, "you can have girls without hoeing for them, and there aren't any flies or mosquitoes to sting you. We got rid of them all centuries ago."

The Savage nodded, frowning. "You got rid of them. Yes, that's just like you. Getting rid of everything unpleasant instead of learning to put up with it. Whether 'tis better in the mind to suffer the slings and arrows of outrageous fortune, or to take arms against a sea of troubles and by opposing end them ... But you don't do either. Neither suffer nor oppose. You just abolish the slings and arrows. It's too easy."

He was suddenly silent, thinking of his mother. In her room on the thirty-seventh floor, Linda had floated in a sea of singing lights and perfumed caresses—floated away, out of space, out of time, out of the prison of her memories, her habits, her aged and bloated body. And Tomakin, ex-Director of Hatcheries and Conditioning, Tomakin was still on holiday—on holiday from humiliation and pain, in a world where he could not hear those words, that derisive laughter, could not see that hideous face, feel those moist and flabby arms round his neck, in a beautiful world....

"What you need," the Savage went on, "is something with tears for a change. Nothing costs enough here."

("Twelve and a half million dollars," Henry Foster had protested when the Savage told him that. "Twelve and a half million—that's what the new Conditioning Centre cost. Not a cent less.")

"Exposing what is mortal and unsure to all that fortune, death and danger dare, even for an eggshell. Isn't there something in that?" he asked, looking up at Mustapha Mond. "Quite apart from God—though of course God would be a reason for it. Isn't there something in living dangerously?"

"There's a great deal in it," the Controller replied. "Men and women must have their adrenals stimulated from time to time."

"What?" questioned the Savage, uncomprehending.

"It's one of the conditions of perfect health. That's why we've made the V.P.S. treatments compulsory."

"V.P.S.?"

"Violent Passion Surrogate. Regularly once a month. We flood the whole system with adrenin. It's the complete physiological equivalent of fear and rage. All the tonic effects of murdering Desdemona and being murdered by Othello, without any of the inconveniences."

"But I like the inconveniences."

"We don't," said the Controller. "We prefer to do things comfortably."

"But I don't want comfort. I want God, I want poetry, I want real danger, I want freedom, I want goodness. I want sin."

"In fact," said Mustapha Mond, "you're claiming the right to be unhappy."

"All right then," said the Savage defiantly, "I'm claiming the right to be unhappy."

"Not to mention the right to grow old and ugly and impotent; the right to have syphilis and cancer; the right to have too little to eat; the right to be lousy; the right to live in constant apprehension of what may happen tomorrow; the right to catch typhoid; the right to be tortured by unspeakable pains of every kind." There was a long silence.

"I claim them all," said the Savage at last.

Mustapha Mond shrugged his shoulders. "You're welcome," he said.

Francis Herbert Bradley - (1846–1924) British idealistic philosopher who believed that reality is a suprapersonal being or absolute

freemartin - an imperfect or sterile female calf born twin with a male

neurasthenia - a neurosis accompanied by varying aches and pains with no discernable organic cause, and characterized by extreme mental and physical fatigue and chronic depression

soma - an intoxicating drink of ancient India used in religious rites

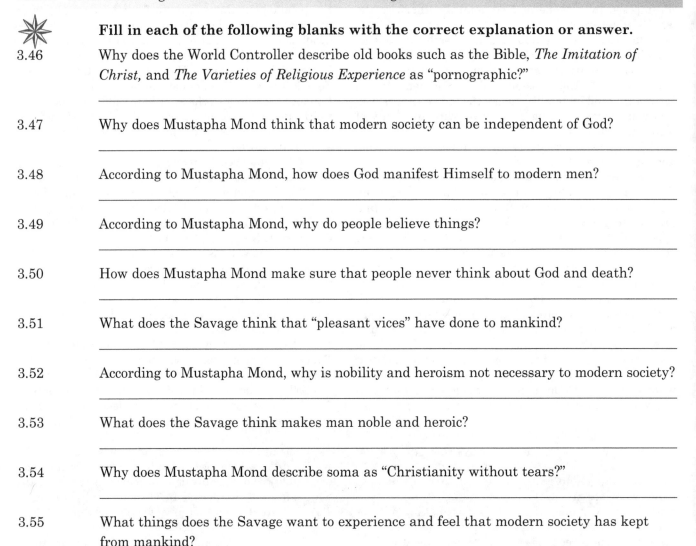

Fill in each of the following blanks with the correct explanation or answer.

3.46   Why does the World Controller describe old books such as the Bible, *The Imitation of Christ,* and *The Varieties of Religious Experience* as "pornographic?"

_____

3.47   Why does Mustapha Mond think that modern society can be independent of God?

_____

3.48   According to Mustapha Mond, how does God manifest Himself to modern men?

_____

3.49   According to Mustapha Mond, why do people believe things?

_____

3.50   How does Mustapha Mond make sure that people never think about God and death?

_____

3.51   What does the Savage think that "pleasant vices" have done to mankind?

_____

3.52   According to Mustapha Mond, why is nobility and heroism not necessary to modern society?

_____

3.53   What does the Savage think makes man noble and heroic?

_____

3.54   Why does Mustapha Mond describe soma as "Christianity without tears?"

_____

3.55   What things does the Savage want to experience and feel that modern society has kept from mankind?

_____

Clive Staples Lewis (1898–1963). During the first half of the twentieth century, two great apologists for orthodox religion did much to "maintain the existence of the important minority in the modern world"—G. K. Chesterton, and Clive Staples Lewis. Lewis was the one who first confronted the modern world with the statement: "You must make your choice. Either [Jesus] was, and is, the Son of God: or else a madman or something worse...let us not come with any patronising nonsense about His being a great human teacher. He has not left that open to us. He did not intend to."

C. S. Lewis was born in Belfast, Ireland, the son of a lawyer. He had an older brother, Warren, who remained his closest friend throughout his life. After his mother died of cancer when he was nine, Lewis and his brother Warren

were sent to boarding school. During this time of great grief, Lewis acquired a spiritual appreciation for Norse mythology. Subsequently, Lewis lost his faith in Anglicanism.

In 1916 Lewis won a scholarship to University College, Oxford. Not long after his enrollment, he was enlisted in the British army, serving as an officer on the front line in France. Discharged in 1918, Lewis resumed his studies at Oxford, graduating in 1922 with his bachelor's degree in Greek and Latin literature. In 1925, Lewis was appointed a Fellow of Magdalen College, Oxford. He served as Tutor in English for twenty-nine years, until he accepted the Chair of Medieval and Renaissance Literature at Magdalene College, Cambridge, in 1954. While at Oxford, Lewis met with a group of writers known as the Inklings. The group's membership included Lewis's brother Warren, J. R. R. Tolkien (author of *The Hobbit*), and Charles Williams.

Lewis's discussions with various members of the Inklings were not limited to literary matters. After a long discussion over dinner with J. R. R. Tolkein and Hugo Dyson in 1931, Lewis began to grasp the reality of Christ's atonement. The next day on the way to the zoo, Lewis believed that Jesus Christ was the Son of God. He described his conversion experience not as a sudden fervor of emotions, but "it was more like when a man, after long sleep, still lying motionless in bed, becomes aware that he is now awake."

The first literary fruits of Lewis's spiritual awakening was a prose book written in imitation of Bunyan's *Pilgrim's Progress*. Lewis's *The Pilgrim's Regress* was published in 1932. In that same year, Lewis's brother Warren retired from the military and came to live with him at "The Kilns," a home in Headington, functioning as his secretary. Warren Lewis had also come to faith in Jesus Christ in 1931.

In 1938 Lewis published his first novel, *Out of the Silent Planet*. It was the first in a science fiction trilogy in which Lewis "wished to conquer for my own (Christian) point of view what has been always hitherto been used by the other side." *Perelandra* (1943) and *That Hideous Strength* (1945) completed the set.

At the outbreak of World War II, the British Broadcasting Company asked Lewis to give a series of radio lectures on basic Christian beliefs. The talks were published in book form as *The Problem of Pain* (1940), *Beyond Personality* (1940), *Miracles* (1947), *Mere Christianity* (1952), and *The Four Loves* (1960). They established his reputation as "the apostle to the skeptics."

In 1942 Lewis published his most famous work, *The Screwtape Letters*. Organized into a series of letters between a senior demon and a junior tempter, the book rips back the cover on the material world to reveal, as Lewis said, that "there is no neutral ground in the universe: every square inch, every split second, is claimed by God and counterclaimed by Satan."

The first in his popular seven-part children's series, *The Chronicles of Narnia*, was published in 1950. *The Lion, the Witch, and the Wardrobe* was the first book in the series. In 1955 Lewis published an autobiography of the early part of his life, *Surprised by Joy*, which included an account of his conversion. After the death of his wife, Lewis wrote *A Grief Observed* (1961).

During his lifetime, Lewis wrote many other books on literary criticism and Christian apologetics, including *Allegory of Love: A Study in Medieval Tradition* (1936), *The Great Divorce* (1945), *The Abolition of Man* (1946), and *An Experiment in Criticism* (1961). For his efforts to give a "ready defense" of the faith, the University of St. Andrews awarded him an honorary doctor of divinity degree in 1946. He died the same day as John F. Kennedy and Aldous Huxley (November 22, 1963) and is buried at Holy Trinity Church in Headington Quarry, Oxford.

Fill in each of the following blanks with the correct answer.

3.56   The two great apologists for orthodox religion in the twentieth century were G. K. Chesterton and __C.S. Lewis__.

3.57   C. S. Lewis was born in __Belfast, Ireland__ .

3.58   After the death of his mother, he obtained a spiritual appreciation for Norse __mythology__ .

3.59   Lewis taught English at __Cambridge__ for twenty-nine years.

3.60   In 1954 he was appointed Chair of Medieval and Renaissance Literature at __Magdalene College__ .

3.61   In 1931 Lewis was converted to Christ after a dinner conversation with __J.R.R. Tolkien__ and Hugo Dyson.

3.62   The __Inklings__ was a group of writers that met in Oxford.

3.63   At the outbreak of World War II, Lewis was asked to give a series of radio lectures on __basic Christian beliefs__.

3.64   __The Screwtape Letters__ is organized into a series of letters between a senior demon and a junior tempter.

3.65   __Surprised by Joy__ is an autobiography of the early part of his life.

3.66   __The Chronicles of Narnia__ is his popular children's series.

What to Look For:

Modern thought encourages us to ignore the spiritual implications of our actions and to dismiss the possibility that the powers of darkness have any influence on our everyday lives. As you read, notice by what means Screwtape instructs Wormwood to separate his "patient" from the "Enemy." Does Screwtape encourage the use of "big" sins or "small" sins? Because "the safest road to Hell is a gradual one—the gentle slope, soft underfoot, without sudden turnings, without milestones, without signposts," why is it important to compare our everyday motives and actions with Scripture (cf. 2 Corinthians 13:5; 1 John 2: 15–17)?

From: *The Screwtape Letters*

Chapter X

MY DEAR WORMWOOD,

I was delighted to hear from Triptweeze that your patient has made some very desirable new acquaintances and that you seem to have used this event in a really promising manner. I gather that the middle-aged married couple who called at his office are just the sort of people we want him to know—rich, smart, superficially intellectual, and brightly sceptical about everything in the world. I gather they are even vaguely pacifist, not on moral grounds but from an ingrained habit of belittling anything that concerns the great mass of their fellow men and from a dash of purely fashionable and literary communism. This is excellent. And you seem to have made good use of all his social, sexual, and intellectual vanity. Tell me more. Did he commit himself deeply? I don't mean in words. There is a subtle play of looks and tones and laughs by which a mortal can imply that he is of the same party as those to whom he is speaking. That is the kind of betrayal you should specially encourage, because the man does not fully realise it himself; and by the time he does you will have made withdrawal difficult.

No doubt he must very soon realise that his own faith is in direct opposition to the assumptions on which all the conversation of his new frineds is based. I don't think that matters much, provided that you can persuade him to postpone any open acknowledgment of the fact, and this, with the aid of shame, pride, modesty, and vanity, will be easy to do. As long as the postponement lasts he will be in a false position. He will be silent when he ought to speak and laugh when he ought to be silent. He will assume, at first only by his manner, but presently by his words, all sorts of cynical and sceptical attitudes which are not really his. But if you play him well, they may become his. All mortals tend to turn into the thing they are pretending to be. This is elementary. The real question is how to prepare for the Enemy's counterattack.

The first thing is to delay as long as possible the moment at which he realises this new pleasure as a temptation. Since the Enemy's servants have been preaching about "the World" as one of the great standard temptations for two thousand years, this might seem difficult to do. But fortunately they have said very little about it for the last few decades. In modern Christian writings, though I see much (indeed more than I like) about Mammon, I see few of the old warnings about Worldly Vanities, the Choice of Friends, and the Value of Time. All that, your patient would probably classify as "Puritanism"— and may I remark in passing that the value we have given to that word is one of the really solid triumphs of the last hundred years? By it we rescue annually thousands of humans from temperance, chastity, and sobriety of life.

Sooner or later, however, the real nature of his new friends must become clear to him, and then your tactics must depend on the patient's intelligence. If he is a big enough fool you can get him to realise the character of the friends only while they are absent; their presence can be made to sweep away all criticism. If this succeeds, he can be induced to live, as I have known many humans live, for quite long periods, two parallel lives; he will not only appear to be, but will actually be, a different man in each of the circles he frequents. Failing this, there is a subtler and more entertaining method. He can be made to take a positive pleasure in the perception that the two sides of his life are inconsistent. This is done by exploiting his vanity. He can be taught to enjoy kneeling beside the grocer on Sunday just because he remembers that the grocer could not possibly understand the urbane and mocking world which he inhabited on Saturday evening; and contrariwise, to enjoy the bawdy and blasphemy over the coffee with these admirable friends all the more because he is aware of a "deeper," "spiritual" world within him which they cannot understand. You see the idea—the worldly friends touch him on one side and the grocer on the other, and he is the complete, balanced, complex man who sees round them all. Thus, while being permanently treacherous to at least two sets of people, he will feel, instead of shame, a continual undercurrent of self-satisfaction. Finally, if all else fails, you can persuade him, in defiance of conscience, to continue the new acquaintance on the ground that he is, in some unspecified way, doing these people "good" by the mere fact of drinking their cocktails and laughing at their jokes, and that to cease to do so would be "priggish," "intolerant," and (of course) "Puritanical."

Meanwhile you will of course take the obvious precaution of seeing that this new development induces him to spend more than he can afford and to neglect his work and his mother. Her jealousy and alarm, and his increasing evasiveness or rudeness, will be invaluable for the aggravation of the domestic tension.

Your affectionate uncle,
SCREWTAPE

Chapter XX

MY DEAR WORMWOOD,

I note with great displeasure that the Enemy has, for the time being, put a forcible end to your direct attacks on the patient's chastity. You ought to have known that He always does in the end, and you ought to have stopped before you reached that stage. For as things are, your man has now discovered the dangerous truth that these attacks don't last forever; consequently you cannot use again what is, after all, our best weapon—the belief of ignorant humans that there is no hope of getting rid of us except by yielding. I suppose you've tried persuading him that chastity is unhealthy?

I haven't yet got a report from you on young women in the neighbourhood. I should like it at once, for if we can't use his sexuality to make him unchaste we must try to use it for the promotion of a desirable marriage. In the meantime I should like to give you some hint about the type of woman—I mean the physical type—which he should be encouraged to fall in love with if "falling in love" is the best we can manage.

In a rough-and-ready way, of course, this question is decided for us by spirits far deeper down in the Lowerarchy than you and I. It is the business of these great masters to produce in every age a general misdirection of what may be called sexual "taste." This they do by working through the small circle of popular artists, dressmakers, actresses, and advertisers who determine the fashionable type. The aim is to guide each sex away from those members of the other with whom spiritually helpful, happy, and fertile marriages are most likely. Thus we have now for many centuries triumphed over nature to the extent of making certain secondary characteristics of the male (such as the beard) disagreeable to nearly all the females—and there is more in that than you might suppose. As regards the male taste we have varied a good deal. At one time we have directed it to the statuesque and aristocratic type of beauty, mixing men's vanity with their desires and encouraging the race to breed chiefly from the most arrogant and prodigal women. At another, we have selected an exaggeratedly feminine type, faint and languishing, so that folly and cowardice, and all the general falseness and littleness of mind which go with them, shall be at a premium. At present we are on the opposite tack. The age of jazz has succeeded the age of the waltz, and we now teach men to like women whose bodies are scarcely distinguishable from those of boys. Since this is a kind of beauty even more transitory than most, we thus aggravate the female's chronic horror of growing old (with many excellent results) and render her less willing and less able to bear children. And that is not all. We have engineered a great increase in the license which society allows to the representation of the apparent nude (not the real nude) in art, and its exhibition on the stage or the bathing beach. It is all a fake, of course; the figures in the popular art are falsely drawn; the real women in bathing suits or tights are actually pinched in and propped up to make them appear firmer and more slender and more boyish than nature allows a full-grown woman to be. Yet at the same time, the modern world is taught to believe that it is being "frank" and "healthy" and getting back to nature. As a result we are more and more directing the desires of men to something which does not exist making the role of the eye in sexuality more and more important and at the same time making its demands more and more impossible. What follows you can easily forecast!

That is the general strategy of the moment. But inside that framework you will still find it possible to encourage your patient's desires in one of two directions. You will find, if you look carefully into any human's heart, that he is haunted by at least two imaginary women—a terrestrial and an infernal Venus, and that his desire differs qualitatively according to its object. There is one type for which his desire is such as to be naturally amenable to the Enemy—readily mixed with charity, readily obedient to marriage, coloured all through with that golden light of reverence and naturalness which we detest; there is another type which he desires brutally, and desires to desire brutally, a type best used to draw him away from marriage altogether but which, even within marriage, he would tend to treat as a slave, an idol, or an accomplice. His love for the first might involve what the Enemy calls evil, but only accidentally; the man would wish that she was not someone else's wife and be sorry that he could not love her lawfully. But in the second type, the felt evil is what he wants; it is that "tang" in the flavour which he is after. In the face, it is the visible animality, or sulkiness or craft or cruelty, which he likes, and in the body, something quite different from what he ordinarily calls Beauty, something he may even, in a sane hour, describe as ugliness, but which, by our art, can be made to play on the raw nerve of his private obsession.

The real use of the infernal Venus is, no doubt, as prostitute or mistress. But if your man is a Christian, and if he has been well trained in nonsense about irresistible and all-excusing "Love," he can often be induced to marry her. And that is very well worth bringing about. You will have failed as regards fornication and solitary vice; but there are other, and more indirect, methods of using a man's sexuality to his undoing. And, by the way, they are not only efficient, but delightful; the unhappiness produced is of a very lasting and exquisite kind.

Your affectionate uncle
SCREWTAPE

Chapter XXI

MY DEAR WORMWOOD,

Yes. A period of sexual temptation is an excellent time for working in a subordinate attack on the patient's peevishness. It may even be the main attack, as long as he thinks it the subordinate one. But here, as in everything else, the way must be prepared for your moral assault by darkening his intellect.

Men are not angered by mere misfortune but by misfortune conceived as injury. And the sense of injury depends on the feeling that a legitimate claim has been denied. The more claims on life, therefore, that your patient can be induced to make, the more often he will feel injured and, as a result, ill-tempered. Now you will have noticed that nothing throws him into a passion so easily as to find a tract of time which he reckoned on having at his own disposal unexpectedly taken from him. It is the unexpected visitor (when he looked forward to a quiet evening), or the friend's talkative wife (turning up when he looked forward to a tete-a-tete with the friend), that throws him out of gear. Now he is not yet so uncharitable or slothful that these small demands on his courtesy are in themselves too much for it. They anger him because he regards his time as his own and feels that it is being stolen. You must therefore zealously guard in his mind the curious assumption "My time is my own." Let him have the feeling that he starts each day as the lawful possessor of twenty-four hours. Let him feel as a grievous tax that portion of this property which he has to make over to his employers, and as a generous donation that further portion which he allows to religious duties. But what he must never be permitted to doubt is that the total from which these deductions have been made was, in some mysterious sense, his own personal birthright.

You have here a delicate task. The assumption which you want him to go on making is so absurd that, if once it is questioned, even we cannot find a shred of argument in its defence. The man can neither make, nor retain, one moment of time; it all comes to him by pure gift; he might as well regard the sun and moon as his chattels. He is also, in theory, committed to a total service of the Enemy; and if the Enemy appeared to him in bodily form and demanded that total service for even one day, he would not refuse. He would be greatly relieved if that one day involved nothing harder than listening to the conversation of a foolish woman; and he would be relieved almost to the pitch of disappointment if for one half-hour in that day the Enemy said, "Now you may go and amuse yourself." Now, if he thinks about his assumption for a moment, even he is bound to realise that he is actually in this situation every day. When I speak of preserving this assumption in his mind, therefore, the last thing I mean you to do is to furnish him with arguments in its defence. There aren't any. Your task is purely negative. Don't let his thoughts come anywhere near it. Wrap a darkness about it, and in the centre of that darkness let his sense of ownership-in-Time lie silent, uninspected, and operative.

The sense of ownership in general is always to be encouraged. The humans are always putting up claims to ownership which sound equally funny in Heaven and in Hell, and we must keep them doing so. Much of the modern resistance to chastity comes from men's belief that they "own" their bodies-those vast and perilous estates, pulsating with the energy that made the worlds, in which they find themselves without their consent and from which they are ejected at the pleasure of Another. It is as if a royal child whom his father has placed, for love's sake, in titular command of some great province, under the real rule of wise counsellors, should come to fancy he really owns the cities, the forests, and the corn, in the same way as he owns the bricks on the nursery floor.

We produce this sense of ownership not only by pride but by confusion. We teach them not to notice the different senses of the possessive pronoun—the finely graded differences that run from "my boots" through "my dog," "my servant," "my wife," "my father," "my master," and "my country," to "my God." They can be taught to reduce all these senses to that of "my boots," the "my" of ownership. Even in the nursery a child can be taught to mean by "my Teddy bear," not the old imagined recipient of affection to whom it stands in a special relation (for that is what the Enemy will teach them to mean if we are not careful), but "the bear I can pull to pieces if I like." And at the other end of the scale, we have taught men to say "my God" in a sense not really very different from "my boots," meaning "the God on whom I have a claim for my distinguished services and whom I exploit from the pulpit the God I have done a comer in."

And all the time the joke is that the word "mine" in its fully possessive sense cannot be uttered by a human being about anything. In the long run either Our Father or the Enemy will say "mine" of each thing that exists, and specially of each man. They will find out in the end, never fear, to whom their time, their souls, and their bodies really belong—certainly not to them, whatever happens. At present the Enemy says "mine" of everything on the pedantic, legalistic ground that He made it. Our Father hopes in the end to say "mine" of all things on the more realistic and dynamic ground of conquest.

Your affectionate uncle

SCREWTAPE

Chapter XXV

MY DEAR WORMWOOD,

The real trouble about the set your patient is living in is that it is merely Christian. They all have individual interests, of course, but the bond remains mere Christianity. What we want, if men become Christians at all, is to keep them in the state of mind I call "Christianity And." You know Christianity and the Crisis, Christianity and the New Psychology, Christianity and the New Order, Christianity and Faith Healing, Christianity and Psychical Research, Christianity and Vegetarianism, Christianity and Spelling Reform. If they must be Christians, let them at least be Christians with a difference. Substitute for the faith itself some Fashion with a Christian colouring. Work on their horror of the Same Old Thing.

The horror of the Same Old Thing is one of the most valuable passions we have produced in the human heart—an endless source of heresies in religion, folly in counsel, infidelity in marriage, and inconstancy in friendship. The humans live in time, and experience reality successively. To experience much of it, therefore, they must experience many different things; in other words, they must experience change. And since they need change, the Enemy (being a hedonist at heart) has made change pleasurable to them, just as He has made eating pleasurable. But since He does not wish them to make change, any more than eating, an end in itself, He has balanced the love of change in them by a love of permanence. He has contrived to gratify both tastes together in the very world He has made, by that union of change and permanence which we call Rhythm. He gives them the seasons, each season different yet every year the same, so that spring is always felt as a novelty yet always as the recurrence of an immemorial theme. He gives them in His Church a spiritual year; they change from a fast to a feast, but it is the same feast as before.

Now, just as we pick out and exaggerate the pleasure of eating to produce gluttony, so we pick out this natural pleasantness of change and twist it into a demand for absolute novelty. This demand is entirely our workmanship. If we neglect our duty, men will be not only contented but transported by the mixed novelty and familiarity of snowdrops this January, sunrise this morning, plum pudding this Christmas. Children, until we have taught them better, will be perfectly happy with a seasonal round of games in which conkers succeed hopscotch as regularly as autumn follows summer. Only by our incessant efforts is the demand for infinite, or unrhythmical, change kept up.

This demand is valuable in various ways. In the first place it diminishes pleasure while increasing desire. The pleasure of novelty is by its very nature more subject than any other to the law of diminishing returns. And continued novelty costs money, so that the desire for it spells avarice or unhappiness or both. And again, the more rapacious this desire, the sooner it must eat up all the innocent sources of pleasure and pass on to those the Enemy forbids. Thus by inflaming the horror of the Same Old Thing, we have recently made the Arts, for example, less dangerous to us than, perhaps, they have ever been, "lowbrow" and "highbrow" artists alike being now daily drawn into fresh, and still fresh, excesses of lasciviousness, unreason, cruelty, and pride. Finally, the desire for novelty is indispensable if we are to produce Fashions or Vogues.

The use of Fashions in thought is to distract the attention of men from their real dangers. We direct the fashionable outcry of each generation against those vices of which it is least in danger and fix its approval on the virtue nearest to that vice which we are trying to make endemic. The game is to have them all running about with fire extinguishers whenever there is a flood, and all crowding to that aide of the boat which is already nearly gunwale. Thus we make it fashionable to expose the dangers of enthusiasm at the very moment when they are already becoming worldly and lukewarm; a century later, when we are really making them all Byronic and drunk with emotion, the fashionable outcry is directed against the dangers of the mere "understanding." Cruel ages are put on their guard against Sentimentality, feckless and idle ones against Respectability, lecherous ones against Puritanism; and whenever all men are really hastening to be slaves or tyrants we make Liberalism the prime bogey.

But the greatest triumph of all is to elevate this horror of the Same Old Thing into a philosophy so that nonsense in the intellect may reinforce corruption in the will. It is then that the general Evolutionary or Historical character of modern European thought (partly our work) comes in so usefully. The Enemy loves platitudes. Of a proposed course of action He wants men, so far as I can see, to ask very simple questions: Is it righteous? Is it prudent? Is it possible? Now, if we can keep men asking: "Is it in accordance with the general movement of our time? Is it progressive or reactionary? Is this the way that History is going?" they will neglect the relevant questions. And the questions they do ask are, of course, unanswerable; for they do not know the future, and what the future will be depends very largely on just those choices which they now invoke the future to help them to make. As a result, while their minds are buzzing in this vacuum, we have the better chance to slip in and bend them to the action we have decided on. And great work has already been done. Once they knew that some changes were for the better, and others for the worse, and others again indifferent. We have largely removed this knowledge. For the descriptive adjective "unchanged" we have substituted the emotional adjective "stagnant." We have trained them to think of the future as a promised land which favoured heroes attain—not as something which everyone reaches at the rate of sixty minutes an hour, whatever he does, whoever he is.

Your affectionate uncle
SCREWTAPE

Fill in each of the following blanks with the correct explanation or answer.

3.67   In Chapter 10, Wormwood's patient makes the acquaintance of some unbelievers. What does Screwtape tell Wormwood to persuade his patient to postpone?

_____

3.68   What does Screwtape notice about the content of modern Christian writings?

_____

3.69   Who does Screwtape credit with the negative connotation associated with the term *Puritanism*?

_____

3.70   On what other grounds does Screwtape encourage Wormwood to persuade the patient to maintain his new acquaintances?

_____

3.71   In Chapter 20, Screwtape attributes the creation of fashionable sex types to demons. What is the purpose behind this cultural endeavor?

_____

3.72   What is the result of the public exposure and misrepresentation of women's bodies in popular culture?

_____

3.73   Why does Screwtape encourage Wormwood to persuade his patient to marry a Venus-type woman?

_____

3.74   In Chapter 21, Screwtape encourages Wormwood to persuade his patient that he has many claims on life. What does he hope this will accomplish?

_____

3.75   What can result from the modern belief that we "own" our bodies?

_____

3.76   How does Screwtape want Wormwood's patient to understand the pronoun *my*?

_____

3.77   Why have demons taught men to use the terminology *my God*?

_____

3.78   According to Chapter 25, in what state of mind do demons want to keep Christians?

_____

3.79   Why does Screwtape tell Wormwood to work on the horror of the Same Old Thing?

_____

3.80   What pleasure is more subject than any other to the law of diminishing returns?

_____

3.81   Why do demons use fashions in thought?

_____

3.82   What is the greatest triumph concerning the use of the horror of the Same Old Thing?

_____

Before you take this last Self Test, you might want to do one or more of the following self checks.

1. _____ Read the objectives. Determine if you can do them.

2. _____ Restudy the material related to any objectives that you cannot do.

3. _____ Use the **SQ3R** study procedure to review the material:

     a. **S**can the sections.
     b. **Q**uestion yourself again (review the questions you wrote initially).
     c. **R**ead to answer your questions.
     d. **R**ecite the answers to yourself.
     e. **R**eview areas you didn't understand.

4. _____ Review all vocabulary, activities, and Self Tests, writing a correct answer for each answer that you got wrong.

SELF TEST 3

Fill in each of the blanks using items from the following word list (each answer, 2 points).

~~Virginia Woolf~~	~~Christian~~	~~socialism~~
~~"Sailing to Byzantium"~~	~~progressive~~	~~C.S. Lewis~~
~~Irish~~	~~victory~~	~~"Adam's Curse"~~
~~The Love Song of J.~~	~~stream of consciousness~~	~~Oxford~~
~~Alfred Prufrock~~		

3.01   Virginia Woolf and her siblings started the Bloomsbury Group to discuss _progressive_ ideas about art, literature, politics, and religion.

3.02   In her books and essays in support of the women's suffrage movement, _Virginia Woolf_ articulated her belief that a society dominated by males will always lead to the oppression of women.

3.03   Woolf's "new" style incorporated the _stream of consciousness_ technique.

3.04   The two great apologists for orthodox religion in the twentieth century were G. K. Chesterton and _C.S. Lewis_.

3.05   Lewis taught English at _Oxford_ for twenty-nine years.

3.06   At the outbreak of World War II, Lewis was asked to give a series of radio lectures on basic _Christian_ beliefs.

3.07   W. B. Yeats's first poems convey an interest in _Irish_ folklore.

3.08   George Bernard Shaw's main purpose in writing plays was to make _socialism_ seem more appealing.

3.09   According to Yeats's poem titled "_Adam's Curse_", the modern world thinks that creating poetry is worthless work.

3.010   In "_Sailing to Byzantium_", the narrator sails to Byzantium to escape the degradation of old age.

3.011   The narrator's view of modern relationships in "_the love song of J. Alfred prufrock_" is that they are empty and meaningless.

3.012   In his speech to the House of Commons on May 13, 1940, Churchill said that the aim of his administration was _victory_.

Answer _true_ or _false_ for each of the following statements (each answer, 2 points).

3.013   _____   In Virginia Woolf's story _The Duchess and the Jeweller_, Oliver Bacon is a middle-class merchant who seeks the society of the upper class.

3.014   _____   The voice of Oliver's mother in his head almost makes him stop writing the check for the Duchess.

3.015   _____   Oliver has flashbacks to when he was a boy selling stolen dogs to fashionable women because his dealings with the duchess are very similar.

3.016   _____   The Duchess sells Oliver real pearls.

3.017   _____   In light of Matthew 13:45–46, Oliver is dissatisfied with his dealings with the Duchess because he has spent his life and his fortune trying to win the favor of upper-class society but has only remained at best a middle-class merchant.

3.018   _____   In James Joyce's _Araby_, the boy goes to the bazaar because he wants to buy a gift for a girl with whom he is infatuated.

3.019   _____   The boy describes the silence of the bazaar as if it were a tomb.

3.020   _____   The odd thing about the young people surrounding the stall in the bazaar is that they all speak with Irish accents.

3.021   _____   The boy doesn't buy anything at the bazaar because he doesn't have enough money.

3.022   _____   The boy eventually sees himself as a "creature driven and derided by vanity" because his effort to buy something for the girl resulted only in frustration and anger.

3.023 _True_ The First World War caused people to doubt the goodness of God and the goodness of technology.

3.024 _true_ Britain refuses to grant Ireland total independence because many Protestants living in Northern Ireland wish to remain under British rule.

3.025 _____ In Shaw's play *Pygmalion*, Professor Higgins behaves like a middle-class gentleman to Eliza Doolittle.

3.026 _____ Alfred Doolittle comes to Higgins to demand the return of his daughter, Eliza.

Circle the letter of the line that best answers each of the following questions (each answer, 2 points).

3.027 According to Huxley's *Brave New World*, why does the World Controller describe old books such as the Bible, *The Imitation of Christ,* and *The Varieties of Religious Experience* as "pornographic?"

a. They provoke feelings in people. c. They make people nervous.

b. They make people numb. d. They cause people to love one another.

3.028 Why does Mustapha Mond think that modern society can be independent of God?

a. Because modern society has removed all forms of suffering.

b. Because modern society loves to suffer.

c. Because morality is relative.

d. Because truth does not create a stable society.

3.029 According to Mustapha Mond, how does God manifest Himself to modern men?

a. In the Scriptures

b. In miracles

c. In relationships

d. As an absence

3.030 What does the Savage think makes man noble and heroic?

a. The absence of God

b. Immoral behavior and desires

c. Belief in the existence of God

d. Romantic feelings

3.031 What kinds of things which modern society has kept from mankind does the Savage want to experience and feel?

a. Technology, science, and entertainment

b. Distractions and pleasures

c. Suffering, freedom, nobility, passion, sin, goodness, and disease

d. Pleasure, stability, community, ease, and comfort.

3.032 In Chapter 10 of *The Screwtape Letters*, on what grounds does Screwtape encourage Wormwood to persuade the patient to maintain his new acquaintances?

a. That he might enjoy the pleasures of the world

b. That he might learn the ways of the world

c. That he is being a witness to them, and not to associate with them would be "Puritanical"

d. That he might live in accordance to the Enemy's wishes

3.033   In Chapter 20, Screwtape attributes the creation of fashionable sex types to demons. What is the purpose behind this cultural endeavor?

   a. To wreck any chances of people having healthy marriages

   b. To perpetuate the existence of lust

   c. To distract people from praying for a mate

   d. To cause divorces to multiply

3.034   What is one of the results of the public exposure and misrepresentation of women's bodies in popular culture?

   a. A woman's spiritual maturity is the most important aspect of her attractiveness.

   b. A woman's appearance is the most important aspect of her attractiveness.

   c. A woman's body is praised as the work of a beauty-loving Creator.

   d. Women's bodies are treated with respect.

3.035   In Chapter 21, Screwtape encourages Wormwood to persuade his patient that he has many claims on life. What can result from the modern belief that we "own" our bodies?

   a. A sincere effort to behave morally

   b. The belief in God's sovereignty

   c. The belief that our bodies are the Lord's

   d. A resistance to moral behavior

3.036   According to Chapter 25, in what state of mind do demons want to keep Christians?

   a. "Christianity And"

   b. "Open Sinfulness"

   c. "Practical Atheism"

   d. "Humbleness"

3.037   Why does Screwtape tell Wormwood to work on the horror of the Same Old Thing?

   a. It is an endless source of pleasure and happiness.

   b. It is an endless source of heresy, unfaithfulness, and foolishness.

   c. It produces in men a fear of God that makes them not want to pray.

   d. It produces in woman a desire for faithfulness.

3.038   According to Hardy's poem "The Respectable Burgher," why do the "Reverend Doctors" think that the stories that include supernatural events are included in the Bible if they don't believe that they are true?

   a. The stories contain historical details that are not found anywhere else.

   b. The stories add a romantic air to religion.

   c. The stories are truthful.

   d. The stories were inspired by the Holy Spirit.

3.039   In *Heart of Darkness*, what are Kurtz's last words?

   a. "The horror. The horror."

   b. "My love. My love."

   c. "Save me from this hell."

   d. "The jungle is a dark, dark place."

3.040　According G. K. Chesterton's book *Orthodoxy,* what is the "natural fountain of revolution and reform?"

    a.　A skepticism of traditional moral and beliefs

    b.　Liberal theology

    c.　Atheism

    (d.)　Old orthodoxy

Underline the correct answer in each of the following statements (each answer, 3 points).

3.041　Joyce rebelled against the (Protestant, <u>Roman Catholic</u>, Muslim) beliefs of middle-class society.

3.042　In 1914, Joyce published (*A Portrait of the Artist as a Young Man*, <u>*Ulysses*</u>, ~~*Dubliners*~~), a collection of short stories containing symbolic meanings of the modern world.

3.043　Published in Paris in 1922, (*A Portrait of the Artist as a Young Man*, *Ulysses*, <u>*Dubliners*</u>) uses the stream of consciousness technique to reveal the inner life of various characters on a given day in Dublin in 1904.

3.044　Aldous Huxley was the grandson of Thomas Huxley, the champion of (Protestantism, <u>Darwinism</u>, mysticism).

3.045　(*Crome Yellow*, <u>*Brave New World*</u>, *Point Counter Point*) is a "satirical fantasy" set in seventh century A.F. (After [Henry] Ford) where humans are conditioned from conception to take their place in a caste system based on scientifically graded intelligence.

3.046　Later in life, Huxley turned to (<u>mysticism</u>, Christianity, philosophy) for the answers to the cold materialistic world.

3.047　During the First World War, (<u>G. K. Chesterton</u>, C. S. Lewis, T. S. Eliot) was asked to write pamphlets in support of England's efforts to stave off German aggression.

3.048　Winston Churchill's writing style can be characterized as (modern, grand, <u>colloquial</u>).

For Thought and Discussion:

Explain to a teacher/parent the premise of *The Screwtape Letters.* Be sure to explain who Screwtape is and his relationship to Wormwood. Discuss the implications of Screwtape's advice to Wormwood. If "the road to Hell is a gradual one," then why do you think that Screwtape encourages the use of "small" sins over "big" sins? Why is it important to compare our everyday motives and actions with Scripture (cf. 2 Corinthians 13:5; 1 John 2: 15–17)?

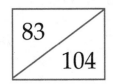

Score   _____

Adult Check   _____

            Initial   Date

Before taking the LIFEPAC Test, you might want to do one or more of the following self checks.

    1. _____　Read the objectives. Check to see if you can do them.

    2. _____　Restudy the material related to any objectives that you cannot do.

    3. _____　Use the **SQ3R** study procedure to review the material.

    4. _____　Review activities, Self Tests, and LIFEPAC vocabulary words.

    5. _____　Restudy areas of weakness that were indicated by the last Self Test.